Psychology, Religion, and Spirituality

Psychology, Religion, and Spirituality provides readers with a critical overview of what psychology tells us about religion and spirituality. It is concise without being simplistic, and the first such broad overview to be published for some years. Fraser Watts recognizes that "religion" is complex and multi-faceted, taking different forms in different people and contexts. The book presents a broad view of psychology; whatever kind of psychology you are interested in, you will find it covered here, from biological to social, and from experimental to psychoanalytic. It focuses particularly on the varied concepts that psychologists have employed to make sense of religion and subjects them to critical examination. The book is also concerned with practical applications so the book will help those engaged in religious ministry. It will be of interest to undergraduates and general readers, as well as specialists in religious studies, psychology, and philosophy of religion.

Fraser Watts has combined a distinguished career as a psychologist with a distinguished record in theology and religious studies. For almost twenty years at Cambridge, he led one of the largest research groups in psychology and religion. He received the APA William Bier Award and founded the Cambridge Institute for Applied Psychology and Religion.

Cambridge Studies in Religion, Philosophy, and Society

Series Editors

PAUL MOSER, *Loyola University Chicago*
CHAD MEISTER, *Bethel College*

This is a series of interdisciplinary texts devoted to major-level courses in religion, philosophy, and related fields. It includes original, current, and wide-spanning contributions by leading scholars from various disciplines that (a) focus on the central academic topics in religion and philosophy; (b) are seminal and up to date regarding recent developments in scholarship on the various key topics; and (c) incorporate, with needed precision and depth, the major differing perspectives and backgrounds – the central voices on the major religions and the religious, philosophical, and sociological viewpoints that cover the intellectual landscape today. Cambridge Studies in Religion, Philosophy, and Society is a direct response to this recent and widespread interest and need.

Recent Books in the Series
Roger Trigg *Religious Diversity: Philosophical and Political Dimensions*
John Cottingham *Philosophy of Religion: Towards a More Humane Approach*
William J. Wainwright *Reason, Revelation, and Devotion: Inference and Argument in Religion*
Harry J. Gensler *Ethics and Religion*

Psychology, Religion, and Spirituality

Concepts and Applications

FRASER WATTS

CAMBRIDGE
UNIVERSITY PRESS

CAMBRIDGE
UNIVERSITY PRESS

University Printing House, Cambridge CB2 8BS, United Kingdom

One Liberty Plaza, 20th Floor, New York, NY 10006, USA

477 Williamstown Road, Port Melbourne, VIC 3207, Australia

4843/24, 2nd Floor, Ansari Road, Daryaganj, Delhi – 110002, India

79 Anson Road, #06–04/06, Singapore 079906

Cambridge University Press is part of the University of Cambridge.

It furthers the University's mission by disseminating knowledge in the pursuit of education, learning, and research at the highest international levels of excellence.

www.cambridge.org
Information on this title: www.cambridge.org/9781107044449
10.1017/9781107360549

© Fraser Watts 2017

First published 2017

Printed in the United Kingdom by Clays, St Ives plc

A catalog record for this publication is available from the British Library.

ISBN 978-1-107-04444-9 Hardback
ISBN 978-1-107-63056-7 Paperback

To
Léon Turner and Sara Savage
Friends and colleagues from the
Psychology and Religion Research Group at Cambridge

Contents

Preface

I hope that this book does what any survey of the psychology of religion and spirituality needs to do, and gives an overview of what psychology can tell us about them. I believe it does that in a reliable and up-to-date way, and does it concisely and fairly comprehensively. I have tried to write in a way that assumes no background in psychology and will be accessible to theologians, philosophers, sociologists, church leaders, and the general public.

I have not tried to give a reference to scientific research for every factual claim made here; that would have turned it into a different kind of book. However, I hope that every factual claim made here is one that could be substantiated in that way; there are always references to good secondary sources that go into particular research studies in more detail than is possible here. Where I have speculated, I have tried to make clear that is what I am doing, and I have only offered speculations in which I have a reasonable amount of confidence.

"Religion" and "spirituality" are related and overlapping topics, and I welcome and endorse the recent trend to extend the psychology of religion to include the psychology of spirituality as well. So far, there is less psychological research on spirituality than on religion, but that is rapidly changing. Though I have tried to summarize what psychology can tell us about religion and spirituality, I have tried to do more than that. To be specific, I have tried to do three additional things.

First, I have tried to offer a critical appraisal of current psychology of religion, and to indicate what current lines of enquiry seem to me to be most promising to pursue in the coming period. I believe that several potentially important topics are not currently receiving the attention they deserve. I have tried, to some extent, to stand outside the current preoccupations of people working in the field, and to ask what would most interest people not working in the field.

Second, I have tried to attend to conceptual issues. These are hugely important in every academic discipline but are often ignored. They are certainly important in the psychology of religion. My intention here is to move to-and-fro between conceptual and empirical material, showing how there can be fruitful interplay between the two. I subscribe to the view of philosophy that sees it as a second-order discipline that does its best work not when it is going it alone, but when it is attending to the conceptual issues in other disciplines, such as the psychology of religion. Much can be learned about religion from attending to conceptual issues and distinctions.

Third, I have also tried to keep in mind what religious people them-selves ("insiders") think about their experiences, beliefs, and practices, and to bring that into dialogue with what psychology has to say from the perspective of "outsiders." I believe there can be mutual enrichment between those two perspectives. Psychologists can learn from the perspec-tive of religious people, even though they will not regard it as the last word and will want to make their own investigations. In the other direction, religious people can benefit from a psychological perspective on religion. I suggest that is, for the most part, perfectly compatible with a participant's perspective and provides a complementary viewpoint. It broadens the psychology *of* religion to become "psychology *and* reli-gion." I admit to a Christian bias in the way I have approached the psychology of religion, but that reflects the bias of most of the available research, and the fact that most psychology of religion is carried out in predominantly Christian countries.

My broad assessment from taking stock of the work on the interface of psychology and religion, as I have done in writing this book, is that the field is good heart. It has been gathering strength and momentum in recent decades and is now going through one of its stronger periods. I have enjoyed writing this overview of where the field has gotten to, and I hope that readers enjoy it too.

I benefited enormously in writing this book from almost twenty years of teaching and research on psychology and religion at the University of Cambridge, and I have dedicated this book to two of my close colleagues from the Psychology and Religion Research Group (PRRG), Léon Turner and Sara Savage. I owe a lot to them and to many others including Nick Gibson, Alastair Lockhart, Ryan Williams, Liz Gulliford, and Miguel

Farias. Some of the work we did together is now being continued through the Cambridge Institute for Applied Psychology and Religion. I am also grateful to successive year-groups of very bright undergraduates at Cambridge to whom I tried to teach psychology and religion and who were a constant challenge to clarify my own thinking.

Concepts and Approaches

Any book on psychology and religion needs to begin by considering what is meant by "religion" and by "psychology." As it is intended that this book should give more attention than most comparable books to conceptual issues, it is especially important to consider these two key terms. Neither is straightforward. Having done that, we will need to consider ways of bringing them into relation with each other.

What Is Religion?

The concept of "religion" has changed massively over the centuries, and it is really only since the latter part of the nineteenth century that having a religion has come to refer to the extent to which someone adheres to a faith tradition, and to be contrasted with non-religion. Before that, someone's religion (*religio*) might have been his or her pattern or rule of life. "Religion" is used in this book as a shorthand for "religiosity" or "religiousness" and is contrasted with non-religion.

"Religion" has had slightly different meanings in different cultures and historical periods. In most countries, Christianity is an elective religion, that is, people opt in or out of it. The same is probably true of Western Buddhism. However, most other religions are closely intertwined with cultural identity (rather in the way that being Protestant or Catholic in Ireland is intertwined with cultural identity). To be Jewish, for example, is as much a matter of cultural or racial identity as of what is now thought of as "religion."

"Religion" also has different connotations in a culture in which everyone is religious, from one in which religion is contrasted with non-religion. The psychological study of religion has largely been carried on in the latter kind of culture, and so the psychology of religion is largely concerned with different aspects of religiousness or "religiosity."

Though there are many religious traditions around the world, religion has been most extensively studied from a psychological point of view in the United States and in Europe, where Christianity predominates. It has to be admitted that, so far, the so-called psychology of religion is largely the study of American and European Christianity, and mainly Protestant Christianity. There is no reason in principle why it should be limited in that way. In fact, it would greatly enrich the psychology of religion if it included more cross-cultural psychology of religion, and there are promising trends in that direction.

One of the main problems facing the psychology of religion is that religion is multi-faceted. Adherence to a religion is now generally recognized to be complex, in that a person can be religious in one way but not in another. For example, someone might be a believer but not a religious practitioner. Of course, empirically, there tend to be correlations between different aspects of religion, but it is nevertheless true that different people are religious in different ways. Psychology has perhaps been too ready to assume that religiousness is unitary. It is part of a general problem of psychology being over-impressed with the explanatory power of traits. We constantly need to be reminded of just how different people can be in different situations. It is also important to remember just how different religious people can be from one another. Under some circumstances, the different aspects of religion can become unusually dissociated, as may happen, for example, in some patients with neurological disorders.

So, how does religion subdivide? The most important distinctions are probably between experience (or feeling), practice (or behavior), and belief (or thinking). As a general framework for understanding how humans function, it is not specific to religion and goes back to Aristotle. Some such threefold categorization arises in many areas of psychology; it applies equally to morality, for example.

This threefold distinction has been made in varying terminologies and is the most commonly used framework in books on the psychology of religion (e.g., Loewenthal, 2000). It features in what is probably the most widely used such scheme, developed by Glock and Stark (1965), which distinguishes (among other things) between what they called the ritualistic dimension (i.e., religious practices), the ideological adherence (i.e., adherence to religious beliefs), and the experiential dimension (i.e., religious feelings and experiences). Chapters 5–7 of this book will consider, in turn, religious experience, practices, and beliefs.

I think this conceptual framework is more helpful than one that is currently fashionable in the sociology of religion, between "believing, belonging, and behaving" (sometimes "becoming" is added too). The main deficiency is that this scheme leaves out religious experience; any conceptual framework that has no place for that is clearly inadequate. (I am not saying that experience is especially important, just that it ought to be included.) There is also a problem in distinguishing between belonging and behaving, as belonging is largely manifest through behavior.

An important recent issue has been whether and in what sense "spirituality" extends beyond religion, and what the relationship is between spirituality and religion. Spirituality is notoriously difficult to define and, despite considerable effort, there is a lack of agreement about what spirituality is and how psychology should study it. One problem is that spirituality, like religion, is multi-faceted.

Some circles tend to regard one of these aspects of religion as foundational, and the others as derivative. William James, in his *Varieties of Religious Experience* (James, 2012/1902), regarded experience as primary, and the organizational and doctrinal aspects of religion as secondary. It is a view for which he has been much criticized, because it is over-individualistic and neglects influences in the other direction, that is, social and doctrinal influences on experience. In contrast, some sociological thought regards society, language, and culture as primary. Yet again, the current atheist critique of religion tends to focus on religious belief as the root of the religious problem, and to regard that as primary.

All of these views are, in different ways, "foundationalist" in that they take one aspect of religion as foundational. I suggest that no single aspect of religion should be regarded as foundational to the others, and that there are mutual influences between all three of these facets of religion – each one influences the others in a systemic pattern of interrelationships. Psychology can make a contribution to understanding each of them.

The relative importance of different aspects of religion can change over time. The psychology of religion has a long tradition of distinguishing between different "conversion types." People can have different entry points into religion; experience, practice, and belief can all, in principle, be the point of entry to religion. In principle, intellectual conversions can arise from extensive exploration, though it is generally agreed that these are relatively rare. Mystical conversions can arise from a sudden, powerful religious experience, but they are also probably not very common. What might be called "affectional" conversions can arise from the experience of being loved by members of a religious community.

The most common point of entry to religion is probably "belonging," that is, becoming part of a religious community, though there can be exceptions. Whichever aspect of religion is the initial draw and point of entry, there will be a tendency for other aspects of religion to be added. For example, those whose first contact with religion is through social contacts and public religious practices are likely to develop religious beliefs and private religious practices too.

Another important distinction is between relatively social and relatively individual aspects of religion. It seems that religion often starts social, though again there can be exceptions. It sometimes seems that the sociology and psychology of religion are locked in an ideological clash about the relative importance of society and the individual. I suggest that is unhelpful. Social and individual aspects of religion influence each other. They are both interesting and important, and psychology studies both. It is worth dispelling the idea that psychology only studies the individual. Psychology includes social psychology and can focus on social processes. The distinction between social and individual aspects of religion is perhaps clearest for religious practices, and it is something to which we will return in Chapter 6.

Some facets of religion occur more frequently than others, and I suggest that distinction between frequent and infrequent aspects of religion may also be quite important. There seems to be a tendency for the more common aspects of religion to be rather general, and for the less frequently occurring forms of religion to be more specific. That is seen most clearly with religious belief. The most common form of religious belief is to "believe in God" or, even more generally, to think that at least there is "something more" than the natural world. Fewer people hold religious beliefs that are defined in more specific terms, such as belief in the virgin birth of Jesus.

A significant development in the psychology of religion has been the study of non-religion. From the point of view of those who see non-religion as the obvious, rational default position, there may not be much need to study it psychologically. However, the psychological study of religion and non-religion makes no presuppositions about the truth of either. Both religion and non-religion are worthy of psychological study, regardless of assumptions about their validity.

What Is Psychology?

Let us now turn to psychology. There has long been interest in matters that we would now call "psychological," mainly under the auspices of either philosophy or religion. However, psychology only emerged as an independent discipline in the late nineteenth century. It has generally endeavored to be "scientific," though that term has been understood in different ways at different times.

The psychology of religion has had a fluctuating position within this new discipline of psychology. (For a good overview of the history of psychology of religion, see Paloutzian, 1996). It was an important part of psychological theory and research in the early decades of the discipline, and William James's *Varieties of Religious Experience* is the classic of that period. By c. 1925, psychology generally was moving into a more behaviorist period, with much less interest in the psychological study of religion (though psychoanalytic approaches to religion continued to be influential with the general public in the middle of the twentieth century, even if they had little impact in academic psychology).

By c. 1970, interest in the psychological study of religion had revived, and an impressive volume of research has accumulated in recent decades that sheds interesting light on almost every aspect of religion. However, this revived psychology of religion has had its limitations. It has never regained a position of importance within psychology as a whole. It has also tended to be rather atheoretical, and to concentrate on collecting detailed information rather than answering big questions.

Psychology is, in part, a human science seeking reasons and interpretations, but it is also a natural science seeking causal explanations. This raises the fundamental issue of how best to understand people; that question arises whether the focus is on their religion or anything else. Experimental psychology has aspired to be a natural science and has tried to apply to people the same scientific approach as would be used with anything else, looking for the "laws" or universal processes that will enable us to understand why humans function in the way they do.

An alternative approach (e.g., Harré and Secord, 1972), albeit a minority one, has suggested that a different explanatory style is needed for people than is appropriate in the natural sciences. The claim is that people have intentions that govern their actions, and indeed that how we describe actions often implicitly includes assumptions about intentions. The task in understanding the actions of people is to understand their reasons for their actions, rather than the causes of their observable behavior. It takes a first-person rather than a third-person approach to understanding people. People's accounts of why they acted as they did are highly relevant, if not the last word.

This debate has sometimes been very fierce, but my approach to it is peaceable. I see value in both approaches and do not want to discard either, but I also see limitations in both approaches. Each can be enriched by taking the other into account, and each benefits from checking its claims against those of the other. Applying this to religion, I suggest that what religious people have to say about their religious life (i.e., why they do what they do, and how they experience it) is far too rich and interesting to be ignored. However, given the limitations of human awareness, and given the extraordinary human capacity for self-deception, augmenting it with the more rigorous, albeit restricted, approach of the natural sciences has great benefits, as far as that is possible. A psychology of religion that takes this binocular approach will have more to offer than a monocular approach based solely on either the natural or human sciences.

It is important to distinguish two very different enterprises in the psychology of religion. One is concerned with why humans in general tend to be religious, with what makes humans the religious primate. The other is concerned with differences between people, with why some people are religious and others are not, and with why religion takes different forms in different people.

The question of why humans tend to be religious has probably had particular urgency and fascination for psychologists who are not themselves religious, and who find religion deeply puzzling. Why should so many people be engaged in something that seems to them to be so manifestly false? Answers to that question fall into three groups. First is a sociological answer, which falls outside the scope of this book. For Durkheim, for example, religion provided society with the symbolic language by which society could understand itself. A second set of answers has focused on what religion does for the individual. Freud, for example, in *The Future of an Illusion* (Freud, 1961/1927) argued that religion assuages the sense of helplessness that people would otherwise feel by providing them with belief in an all-loving and all-powerful God. We will return to that in the next chapter. Both of those explanations have focused on the social or personal benefits that religion may confirm, despite religion being presumed to be false.

The third approach to explaining why humans are religious has taken a different tack and has suggested that religion is an inevitable by-product of how humans have evolved. The idea is basically that we are religious because our brains are "hardwired" in such a way that religion comes naturally to us. As we will see, a minority position holds that religion has evolved because it has adaptive value, but most people think that it is a by-product of other evolutionary developments. We will return to that in Chapter 3.

It is important to emphasize that psychology is a multi-faceted discipline that holds together various perspectives and methodologies. It is really a family of disciplines, each with its own subject matter, questions, and methodology. In principle, almost every subdiscipline of psychology can be used to study religion from its own distinctive perspective, though some of these psychologies of religion are much better developed than others. Many are covered in this book, and it will be helpful now to introduce briefly some of these subdisciplines.

Psychoanalysis is rather on the fringe of psychology and is in fact largely ignored in academic departments of psychology. That is largely because there is widespread doubt about whether psychoanalysis is sufficiently scientific to be admitted to mainstream psychology. On the skeptical view, there is so much speculation in psychoanalysis, mixed in with whatever empirical element there may be, that it is thought to be wholly unreliable. Another complication when psychoanalysis is applied to religion is Freud's own personal hostility to religion, though it has become increasingly clear that psychoanalysis does not need to share Freud's own negative view of religion. Though the psychoanalysis of religion needs to be handled with care and can never be accepted uncritically, it has a depth and range that are not easily matched by other approaches to the psychology of religion and, in my view, should not be ignored.

The biological wing of psychology has come into prominence in recent decades, and both evolutionary psychology and neuropsychology have made significant contributions to understanding religion. Relating psychological functioning to brain processes has proved enormously fruitful in many areas of psychology, especially in understanding cognitive processes such as memory. It has also proved useful in the study of religion, though it has sometimes been associated with the simplistic idea that once you know which areas of the brain are involved in particular aspects of religion, you have explained religion away completely.

It has undoubtedly proved useful to place religion in an evolutionary context, and to try to understand how and why humans became religious. The problem with evolutionary psychology, as we will see in Chapter 3, is that it has limited evolutionary data to work with. That leaves the way open for rather speculative evolutionary theories to be presented in an over-dogmatic way, and for what are really only presuppositions to be presented as research findings. One thing that the three areas of psychology we have considered so far (psychoanalysis, evolutionary psychology, and neuropsychology) have in common is that, when applied to religion, they have tried to answer the most general question – why are humans religious?

The question of why humanity is religious is intriguing and currently the focus of much controversy, but it is also a frustratingly general question. It glosses over important details in significant ways. First, it neglects differences between people. People differ in how religious they are, and those who are religious differ massively in what form that religiousness takes. The psychology of religion tries to understand how those differences between people arise.

Psychology is partly concerned with the psychological processes that normal, healthy humans have in common, but it is also concerned with how people differ and with why some people do one thing and some another. A well-established approach to psychology, and one that has been extensively applied to religion, is concerned with "individual differences." It is an approach to psychology that has made extensive use of the psychological questionnaire as a research tool, and a huge number of such questionnaires are now available in the psychology of religion. Some provide general, overall measures of religiousness; others focus down on particular aspects of religion. I will suggest in Chapter 9 that it has proved more fruitful to look at why different kinds of people are religious in different ways than to look at why some people are religious and others not.

Another important strand in psychology has been to focus on developmental processes, with how people change over time. It has certainly been fruitful to chart how children change in their religiousness as they grow up. In some areas of religion, particularly the ability to understand religious ideas, that seems to follow a standard path, and to reflect maturational development. Other aspects of religion change in a less predictable way through childhood, and the same is true of changes of religiousness in adults. It is less clear that such changes should be regarded as "development" in a strict sense of the term. Another strand in developmental psychology has tried to use aspects of people's childhood to predict how they function as adults. Some fruitful research of that kind has occurred recently, using childhood patterns of attachment to predict what form religion will take in adulthood (Granqvist and Kirkpatrick, 2008).

A prominent strand of psychology has been concerned with problems or abnormalities and their treatment. The main focus has been on mental and physical health, but a wide range of personal and behavioral abnormalities can also be considered. Psychological factors have been found to play an important role in many personal problems and disorders, and an interesting strand of the psychology of religion is concerned with the role of religion, for example, with how religion helps people cope with problems.

This is not an exhaustive list of the range of subdisciplines within psychology, but it covers the main ones and gives an indication of the scope of psychology.

Relating Psychology and Religion

The final issue to be considered in this chapter is how psychology in general and the psychology of religion in particular relate to religious life and commitment. This can be seen as a special case of the more general question of the relationship between science and religion, about which there is much controversy.

It is best to begin with the question of whether psychology explains religion so completely that it explains it away and leaves no room for any other kind of explanation in terms of God or the spiritual world. Note first that it is only some aspects of the psychology of religion that are offering sufficiently general explanations of religion that they could possibly be seen as explaining it away; those are the areas of psychology to be considered in the next three chapters, psychoanalysis, evolutionary psychology, and neuropsychology and the cognitive science of religion.

I will argue that none of these can be assumed to offer *complete* explanations of religion. That can only be asserted if it can be shown that no other explanatory factors could possibly be relevant. In fact, of course, that is never the case, and it is hard to see how it could possibly be proved. What can sometimes be claimed is that the psychology of religion provides a sufficient explanation of religious life, so that it is unnecessary to invoke other factors to make sense of it. However, that leaves open whether non-psychological factors are relevant. In the nature of things, it is not something that psychology can settle. I see no basis for claiming that psychology can explain religion completely, or explain it away, in a fashion that leaves no room for any distinctively religious factors.

Another argument is sometimes advanced here, based on the assumption that simple explanations are always to be preferred. If psychology provides an adequate explanation of religion, it is argued that it is simplest and therefore best to accept that, and not to invoke any other explanatory factors to do with God. I would suggest, in response, that whether simple explanations are to be preferred depends on context. In physics, the search for simple and elegant explanations seems a guide to the truth. However, most things to do with humans seem to have multiple causes (e.g., both biological and social ones), so I see no general case for claiming that simple, mono-causal explanations, such as psychological explanations of religion, are always to be preferred.

However, that leaves many questions about how to bring psychological explanations of religion into relationship with the accounts given of religion by religious adherents. If we are willing to consider both kinds of accounts, what is the relationship between them? In most books on the psychology of religion, "religion" is treated just as a phenomenon to be studied. However, it also itself offers an interpretative perspective, that is, a religious perspective on religious phenomena can be brought into dialogue with the perspective of psychology.

Psychology offers an explanation of religion from an outsider's perspective, but it can also contribute to religious interpretation from the inside, interpreting the psychological significance of the scriptural texts and doctrinal beliefs. This interpretative role has been relatively neglected. This book will also give more attention than usual to the to-and-fro between the outsider's perspective of the psychologist and the insider's perspective of the faith community.

Some might say that though psychology cannot rule religious accounts out, psychological and religious accounts are answering such completely different questions that no useful engagement between them is possible. That would be the counterpart of the position, argued more generally for science by Stephen Jay Gould, that science and religion are "non-overlapping magisteria" (Gould, 2002).

Against that view, I want to maintain that there can be fruitful contact between psychology and the perspective of religious people themselves. I claimed earlier in this chapter that it is helpful to consider both the kind of external causal explanations that the natural sciences try to offer and the first-person accounts in terms of reasons and intentions that participants offer. In the case of religion, first-person accounts will normally come from people who are themselves religious and who see things in religious terms. Psychology is normally offering an outsider's perspective, whereas religious people are offering an insider's perspective. I suggest that these are best seen as complementary perspectives, not as mutually exclusive.

Most books on the psychology of religion make no mention of the insider's perspective of religious people themselves, though their perspective cannot be entirely excluded from the study of religious experience. I shall refer to how religious people see things, where that is relevant and of interest. My general stance is that, on occasions, cross-talk between the two perspectives can be useful.

I don't think that psychology can rule a religious perspective in or out, but I do think it can influence how an insider's perspective can most plausibly be framed. For example, when considering glossolalia (speaking in tongues), I will suggest that psychology makes it very unlikely that people are miraculously speaking languages with which they have had no previous acquaintance. However, it does leave open the possibility that this is spiritually inspired utterance, serving spiritual purposes.

Science generally has more influence on the religious viewpoint than vice versa. However, with psychology, I think there can be constructive mutual influence in both directions. That arises from the fact that religion has a long history of reflective and practical engagement with what are, in effect, psychological phenomena. Though psychology has advanced our understanding in many ways, I shall suggest that there are points at which religion can offer psychology some broader perspective and conceptual enrichment out of its rich tradition, for example, in its understanding of forgiveness.

Finally, there is the question of the practical application of the psychology of religion. Psychologists generally study religion just to understand it, not with any practical objectives in mind. However, I will suggest that the psychology of religion actually has considerable practical application. It makes no difference to that whether or not the psychologists concerned are themselves religious. Another way in which this book departs from many introductions to the psychology of religion is that it will include more emphasis on the practical application of the psychology of religion, focusing mainly on the Christian church.

Plan of the Book

The chapters of this book fall into four main groups. First are chapters on those areas of psychology (psychoanalysis, evolutionary psychology, neuroscience, and cognitive science) that at least sometimes offer general explanations of why humans are religious. Next are chapters on what I have suggested are the three main facets of religion: experience, practice, and belief, and then a further chapter on "spirituality." That will be followed by a group of chapters dealing with how people differ, including religious development, different ways of being religious, and how religion relates to health and adjustment. The last few chapters will deal with practical and theological applications of psychology to religion, particularly from a Christian point of view.

Summary

- Religion has various components, including religious experience, practices, and beliefs. People can be more religious in one of these ways than in the others. No one component of religion should be seen as the primary one, from which others are derived. Different facets of religion may have a different causal basis, and cultural assumptions about their relative importance can change.
- Psychology is a complex discipline, with various subdisciplines, such as developmental psychology, each of which can focus on religion in its own distinct way. Though the primary focus of psychology is on the individual, it is also both a biological and a social science.
- Psychology has generally tried to study religion with objectivity. It can discover much of interest about religion, including the effects of religion, but it has no basis for reaching conclusions about the truth or falsehood of religious beliefs. There is value in bringing the outsider's perspective of psychology into dialogue with the insider's perspective of religious people themselves.

2

Psychoanalysis

This chapter will focus on psychoanalytic approaches to religion. It will be important to consider not only Freud himself but also some post-Freudians, some of whom take a much more positive view of religion than Freud himself did. For convenience, I will include Jung in this chapter too, though strictly speaking, Jung's approach is termed "analytical psychology" rather than "psychoanalysis."

Freud

Psychoanalysis operates with a general concept of religion, and, as we have already noted, psychoanalysis is one of the psychological perspectives that try to explain why people are religious at all, rather than just attending to particular religious phenomena. Most psychoanalytic thinking about religion fails to consider that different forms of religion may have psychological appeal for quite different reasons. It also fails to consider that some forms of religion may be pathological and others not. For Freud, it is all just "religion."

Another problem that we need to note at the outset is that Freud has no single psychology of religion. It is a subject to which he returns frequently, which suggests that it had a certain fascination for him (for an overview, see Meissner, 1984). Each time he develops a somewhat different position, though these are not necessarily incompatible with one another. Two of his books on religion, *Totem and Taboo* and *Moses and Monotheism*, are based on such dated and unreliable anthropology that I will not say much about them here, though it is intriguing that he was interested enough in Moses to present his own unorthodox quasi-rabbinic interpretation of the Moses story.

Let us focus first on one of the key ideas in Freud's psychology of religion, God as projection. Freud suggests that God is a projection of the human mind, an idea that is to be found in a more general form in Feuerbach (2008/1841), though Freud developed it considerably by fleshing out the psychological mechanisms by which he thinks the projection arises. It is an idea that he treats most in his essay on Leonardo (Freud, 1965).

Freud seems to be unaware of a fundamental problem in his treatment of God as projection. It is one thing to argue that people's concepts of God are shaped to some extent by psychological processes that can be understood as projection. That is almost certainly true. However, it is going far beyond that to suggest, as Freud seems to do, that God is nothing but a projection of the human mind. Our concepts of other people, Freud assumes, are shaped by projections, but that does not imply that other people are nothing but projections, or that they are, in effect, just figments of the human imagination. To suggest that God is nothing but a projection is a philosophical point, for which he provides no argument, and which goes beyond what can possibly be substantiated on the basis of psychology alone.

Again, Freud overgeneralizes. Some people's ideas about God may be shaped by projections more than those of others, a point that is actually quite helpful from a religious point of view, as Paul Homans has argued (Homans, 1970). Indeed, it is quite close to the apophatic tradition to suggest that psychological processes can distort the human understanding of God. Freud can be taken, as Homans does, as giving an account of the projective mechanisms by which these inadequate and misleading concepts of God arise. However, again, that does not lead to the conclusion that God is nothing but a projection.

I will not enter here into discussion of Freud's ideas about the role of the Oedipus complex in shaping ideas about God, though it is worth saying something in more general terms about God as an exalted father figure. Two lines of evidence support the view that concepts of God are shaped by concepts of the human father. One comes from the admirably careful and detailed reports by Ana-Maria Rizzuto (1979) of psychoanalytic work with patients with religious issues. She presents tables that set out such remarkable similarities between what a particular client says about his or her human father and about God that it is hard to resist the conclusion that the latter are shaped by the former.

The other relevant line of evidence comes from questionnaire studies, especially those of Vergote and Tamayo (1981). When people rate the qualities they associate with God and with human parents, there is a statistical correlation between the two, though not a strong one. Freud assumed that God was seen as a father figure, but the evidence suggests that God is actually seen as combining the best qualities of father and mother. There are also indications that God is seen as an ideal parent, and not just a replica of actual parents.

Of Freud's works on religion, *The Future of an Illusion* (Freud, 1961/ 1927) is probably of most enduring interest. What is "illusion"? For Freud, it is a technical term that means "wish fulfillment." At one point, he is careful to distinguish between "illusion" and "delusion." A delusion is, by definition, an error, but that is not necessarily true of illusion. Freud's point is that the unpredictability of human life engenders a sense of helplessness. To assuage that, humans wish to believe in a God who is all-loving and all-powerful. In that sense, for Freud, religion is wish fulfillment, that is, illusion.

It is implicit here that Freud is operating with the philosophical assumptions of a naive realist. For Freud, reality is a hard fact; we are either right or wrong about it. Freud is also moralistic about facing up to things as they actually are; that is a virtue. It is what people with a strong ego do; they face facts as they are and accept reality as it is. The weak ego, in contrast, takes comfort in illusions because it cannot face reality.

As we will see, Freud's view of religion has not been universally accepted on this point, even within psychoanalysis. However, let us first tackle the general question of the status and authority of psychoanalysis. Need we believe what Freud says? On this, there has been much debate, with a tendency for opinions to become polarized. Freud tends to be either accepted too uncritically or dismissed as being totally unscientific and completely unreliable.

It seems to me important not to overgeneralize about Freud. Some of his works are more careful than others. Some parts have stood the test of time better than others. In some core parts of his theory, he proceeds in a fairly careful, empirical way. His theory is always somewhat speculative, but on some topics you can see him revising his theory in the light of new clinical data. He may not always be right, but at least he is responding to evidence. It was new clinical data that led him, for example, to add the superego and the death instinct to his theory.

But on cultural topics such as religion, his methodology is largely unconstrained by data. He is not usually studying religion in an empirical way. Rather, he is using psychoanalysis to provide a perspective on religion. It is one that he presumably hopes will be interesting and plausible, but even he does not claim that it necessarily needs to be accepted. In a revealing remark in a letter to his Lutheran friend Oskar Pfister, Freud made clear that the views he expressed in *The Future of an Illusion* were his personal views, and not part of psychoanalytic theory. He added, "if I drew on analysis for certain arguments, that need deter no one from using the nonpartisan method of analysis for arguing the opposite view" (Meng and Freud, 1963, p. 117).

Freud's remark to Pfister is a massive concession about the status of his psychology of religion. He would never have conceded as much about core areas of psychoanalysis, such as his theory of psychosexual development. With religion, in contrast, apart from a couple of case studies, he is not doing psychoanalytic research but is applying psychoanalytic theory to a phenomenon he had scarcely studied, and in a way that he conceded was speculative. That robs Freud's view of religion of any scientific authority it might be thought to have. He did not derive his view of religion from psychoanalytic data but just used psychoanalysis as a theoretical framework with which to elaborate this view.

What then led Freud to adopt such a negative view of religion? I suggest that it was a combination of personal experience and background philosophical assumptions. Freud used psychoanalysis to explain why people were religious; but the tables can be turned, and psychoanalysis can be used to try to explain why Freud himself was antireligious, as Rizzuto (1998), among others, has done. It seems likely that his experience of a harsh Christian nanny was a key factor. Though Freud talks generally about religion, it seems that it is his nanny's Christianity, rather than his own Jewish tradition, that he has in mind. Freud is in some ways a deeply Jewish thinker, as David Bakan and others have shown (Bakan, 1958).

Freud's negative view of religion also seems to have been shaped by the atheistic culture developing in the Vienna of his day, a culture that spawned logical positivism. Several elements come together in Freud's outlook: (i) a rather simplistic philosophical realism about the external world; (ii) a scientistic assumption that science offers the only rational way to study that world; and (iii) a disparaging view of religion as a world of childish illusion that will be swept away by the onward march of science. The latter half of *The Future of an Illusion* becomes a manifesto for science. Freud was saying there many of the same things in 1927 as Richard Dawkins (2006) and other New Atheists are saying now.

Post-Freudians

It is an intriguing feature of the psychoanalysis of religion that different theorists have developed such different views of religion. Some, such as that of Freud himself, are negative about religion; others are much more positive about the psychological value of religion. This may seem puzzling, but it falls into place once we realize that none of these views is actually derived from psychoanalysis; each is using psychoanalysis to elaborate a different view of religion.

Freud's Lutheran friend Oskar Pfister wrote a response to *The Future of an Illusion* almost immediately. It was wittily called *The Illusion of a Future* (Pfister, 1993). Freud's view of the future as one in which religion would be swept away by science has indeed proved to be just wish fulfillment (illusion). A psychoanalytic view of religion rather similar but more detailed than that of Pfister was set out by R. S. Lee in *Freud and Christianity* (Lee, 1948). Lee is now a rather neglected figure, though he wrote several good books on psychoanalysis and religion.

Both Pfister and Lee take issue with Freud's assumption that religion is the refuge of people with a weak ego, that is, people who, to adapt a phrase of T. S. Eliot, "cannot bear very much reality." They point out that on Freud's own assumption, ego strength shows itself in a capacity for love and work, and that religious leaders such as Jesus, on that criterion, show exceptionally strong ego functioning. Freud seems to have assumed that religion would be associated with poor mental health. The empirical evidence that has accumulated subsequently is complex, as we will see in Chapter 11. However, for the most part, religion has proved to be associated with good mental health.

It is sometimes suggested that the development of a positive psychoanalytic view of religion depended on the development of object relations theory, as Donald Winnicott (1971) in particular exemplified. I dissent from that view. Certainly psychoanalytic views of religion were massively influenced by Winnicott's work on object relations theory. However, a positive psychoanalytic view of religion was already in place before object relations theory, which involves a fundamental shift from Freud's focus on psychic energy to a focus on human relationships. Though a positive psychoanalytic view of religion began to develop before object relations theory, it is clear that it contributed to a significant transition in the development of a positive psychoanalytic view of religion. Several of the key figures in object relations, notably Ronald Fairbairn, Harry Guntrip, and Winnicott, were sympathetic to religion. Guntrip, who emerged as the main historian and philosopher of the movement, had previously been a minister of religion.

These psychoanalytic theorists were influenced by the relational philosophy developed by John Macmurray (1961) and others. Both psychoanalysis and theological anthropology took a relational turn at the same time, under the same influences, which facilitated a rapprochement between the two. In addition, the new focus on relationship rather than psychic energy gave psychoanalysis a less reductionist tone than previously.

No one was more influential in developing a positive view of the relationship between psychoanalysis and religion than Winnicott. That is partly due to his exceptional warmth and humanity, and his accessible style. Though he was capable of writing highly technical papers, he was a gifted communicator with the general public, through radio broadcasts and in other ways. However, Winnicott's important role in the psychoanalysis of religion was also due to his theoretical ideas, especially his key idea of "transitional" objects and, more generally, of transitional space.

Winnicott was a pediatrician who became intrigued by the special role that an object such as a piece of blanket came to have in an infant's life. Though in one sense it remained an external object, it also had so much significance that, in another sense, it was part of the infant's inner world. It was in a transitional space between the two, "inside, outside, at the border" (Winnicott, 1971, p. 2). Winnicott thought that transitional objects helped the infant adjust to the external world, bridging the gulf between subject and object. It was his book *Playing and Reality* (Winnicott, 1971) that transformed the relationship between psychoanalysis and religion.

He then extrapolated this to adults and suggested that they also have a transitional world that stands between inner and outer, and which also enables them to broker a good adjustment between the two. He identified art and religion as being especially important in adult transitional space. Note, however, that this is a somewhat speculative extrapolation, as Flew and others have complained (Flew, 1978). Some parts of Winnicott's ideas arise from empirical observation of infants. However, there is no comparable body of observational research on art and religion as transitional objects. As with Freud, when Winnicott comes to apply his ideas to religion, he is applying ideas developed elsewhere, not doing research on religion itself.

Note also that Winnicott is only suggesting that religion is good for adjustment. He is not commenting on whether or not religious beliefs are true. That is implicit in the way he links art and religion. Art may be "true" in some personal, relativistic sense, but it is not generally thought to have the kind of transpersonal, metaphysical truth that religion claims to have.

Winnicott's ideas have opened up a new wave of thinking in the psychoanalysis of religion that is much more open to the value of religion. Paul Pruyser developed somewhat similar ideas, though with the different terminology of the "illusionistic" rather than the "transitional" world (Pruyser, 1991). Pruyser distinguished three worlds: an inner autistic or self-contained world, an external world, and an in-between illusionistic world. Pruyser's concept of the illusionistic world is indebted to Winnicott, though not identical with it. One interesting feature of Pruyser's approach is that he retains Freud's concept of religion as illusion but redefines it to mean something more positive. There is thus an appearance of staying faithful to Freud's authority, rather as a religious person might stay faithful to scripture, while reinterpreting it.

The distinction between the autistic and illusionistic worlds is philosophically important and is somewhat parallel to the distinction Coleridge made long ago between fancy and imagination (see Barfield, 1972). It takes us a long way from Freud, who has no such distinction, and from the naive realism that runs through *The Future of an Illusion*. Pruyser's approach reflects the shift from modernity to postmodernity.

Jung

Jung was a protégé of Freud, and his analytical psychology grew out of psychoanalysis. Their divergence was as much over religion as anything else, though there may have also been personal reasons for their difficulties in working together. Freud had once seen Jung as his most promising pupil. Jung did not intend to discard what he had learned from Freud, but just to broaden and develop it in a way that recognized the religious function of humanity. However, Freud, with his reductionist attitude and personal hostility to religion, found that intolerable.

Though Jung thought that religion was an important human function, it should not be imagined that he was enthusiastic about the church as he found it. His father had been a Protestant pastor, and Jung found his father's religion lifeless and of no practical value. Indeed, he believed that the church in general had lost contact with the psychic significance of the symbols with which it was dealing, like a cathedral built over long-forgotten secret vaults.

Jung's psychology evolved considerably over the years, and his psychology of religion evolved with it. Heisig (1979) has provided a helpful map of its development. In the first phase, Jung was still quite close to Freud, and religion was understood as relating to large-scale or unexplained movements of psychic energy. In the second phase, represented by his Terry Lectures on psychology and religion given in the United States (Jung, 1938), Jung was much influenced by Rudolf Otto's concept of the "numinous" (Otto, 1950), and religion was virtually equated with whatever was numinous (experience that carried the presence or power of divinity). In the third phase, Jung focused more on particular religious ideas, doctrines, and practices.

He divided his attention about equally between Eastern religion and Christianity and showed no particular allegiance or preference among the religions he discussed. Indeed, it is not even clear that he gives any priority to religion at all as it would normally be understood. He was as interested in alchemy as he was in religion, and he seemed to see them both as rather comparable bodies of symbolic thought that mapped onto, and indeed were equivalent to, deep psychic processes.

It might be thought that Jung reduced religion to psychology, but I do not think that is quite correct. For Jung, an equivalence or parallelism existed between the clinical material he encountered in his analytical work and the symbolic systems he encountered in religion and alchemy. Each could be used to help understand the other. If there is reductionism, it is at least a two-way reductionism in which clinical and religious material each helped elucidate the other.

To probe Jung's approach to religion in more detail, we will have to see how he extended psychoanalysis and how that gave him the theoretical resources to approach religion in the way that he did. The key move was to add the collective unconscious to Freud's concept of the personal unconscious. Jung's concept of the collective unconscious evolved a good deal. At first, he saw it as grounded in the physical brain. It was rather like a universal capacity for language in all humans, but one that took different forms in different cultures.

Jung framed the content of the collective unconscious in terms of archetypes. Some of these archetypes were common to all people. So, for example, everyone has a "persona" (an outer mask) and a "shadow" (a hidden dark side). Similarly everyone had an ego (a center of conscious life) and a Self (the whole, complete personality that people have the potential to become). Other archetypes, such as the *Senex*, the *Wise Mother*, and the *Puer Aeternus* (eternal youth), though collective, are not necessarily universal. They are more evident in some people than others, and Jungians sometimes frame psychological problems in terms of "over-identification" with one of these archetypes. Some archetypes are specific to particular cultures, such as the ancient German God *Wotan*, with whom Jung thought that Nazi Germany became over-identified.

Though Jung initially saw the collective unconscious as arising from universal symbolic schemas, he increasingly reified the archetypes. They become not just symbols that were common to many people but take on a transpersonal life of their own, so that human thought and behavior can be explained in terms of what the archetypes were doing. You almost get the impression that Jung thought that even if humanity were exterminated, the archetypes would continue to exist.

One way of pressing the question about the ontological status of archetypes is to ask whether Jung is just *describing* human events at the level of archetypes or whether he is offering archetypes as a causal *explanation*. It seems to me that, for example, when he explains Nazi Germany in terms of the archetype *Wotan* awakening from his slumbers, he is doing the latter.

Another way of pressing the question is to ask what is changing when he talks about a particular archetype changing, as he talks about God changing in his late book *Answer to Job* (Jung, 1984/1952). Most Jungians probably assume that he is just talking about changes in the human conceptualization of archetypes. However, it seems to me that when Jung talks about the need for God to incarnate to facilitate God's own individuation, he is implicitly assuming a God who exists beyond the human psyche.

Archetypes are important for Jung's psychology of religion. As he says, they "can be shown empirically to be the equivalents of religious dogmas." The Self archetype is especially important for his understanding of religion. As we have said, the Self is the whole and complete personality. It is the end point of that process of integration that Jung calls "individuation," by which opposites such as persona and shadow are unified. However, it also seems to have a role in inviting and facilitating the process of individuation. The Self can announce itself to the ego, leading to the establishment of the kind of healthy access between ego and Self that in turn enables progress to be made toward individuation.

It is especially important for the psychology of religion that Jung saw the Self as the image of God in the psyche. Did Jung believe in God? When John Freeman asked him that question on TV toward the end of his life, he replied, "I don't need to believe, I know." This interview can be seen at

https://cosmolearning.org/documentaries/bbc-face-to-face-carl-gustav-jung/.
Much discussion followed about what he meant by that. I suggest that he
was saying that the image of God in the psyche was not a matter of belief
but of knowledge. He found evidence of the image of God everyday in his
clinical work.

Did he think there was a God beyond the psyche? It is apparent that
God subscribed to a Kantian epistemology, as J. J. Clarke (1992) has
pointed out. For Kant, the world we know is constructed, and we cannot
have direct knowledge of things-in-themselves that may exist beyond that
constructed world. Similarly, for Jung, there was no way of having knowledge of what he called a "metaphysical" God, beyond the image of God in
the psyche. In addition to these background epistemological assumptions,
Jung was also making a professional point. He was saying that he was
a psychologist, and that all he could speak about in his professional
capacity was the image of God in the psyche. As a psychologist, he
could not speak about a metaphysical God.

A parallel issue arises about the reality of evil. We might have expected
Jung to handle it in an exactly parallel way, but he does not. He might
have said that he saw the image of evil in the psyche, but that he could have
no opinion about whether there was a metaphysical evil beyond the psyche.
In fact, however, he bangs on about the reality of evil more trenchantly than
almost anyone else in the twentieth century. It is surprising that it should be
a psychologist who does so.

Jung makes the heterodox proposal that the Trinity should be
expanded into a quaternity to incorporate evil. However, this proposal
seems to make an illegitimate extrapolation from psychology to metaphy-
sics, as David Burrell (1974) has pointed out. It is exactly the kind of move
that Jung is unwilling to make when it comes to God. It is also worth
noting that a Jungian approach to religion does not actually require this
move.

Jung was preoccupied with the fourfold structure of the mandala as
a symbol of wholeness, which was another reason why he preferred
a fourfold to a threefold God. However, Edward Edinger, who has
made extensive use of Jungian psychology in interpreting Christianity
(Edinger, 1972), rejects this move and claims that in his own clinical
work, threefold structures can serve equally well as symbols of wholeness.

At several points, we find clear parallels between Jung's psychology and
religious thought. The Self is the image of God. Jung would add that in
Christendom, Christ is a powerful symbol of the Self. As the collective
unconscious became increasingly reified as Jung developed his theoretical

position, it became analogous to the spiritual world but was peopled with archetypes rather than saints and angels. The journey toward wholeness that Jung calls individuation is analogous to the journey toward holiness in the religious life.

How do these parallels arise? I think Jung would say he discovered them rather than contrived them. He would claim that the structure of symbolic life that he discovered in the psyche proved to be remarkably parallel to religious symbol systems, and that it is precisely because of this parallelism that the two are so helpful in elucidating each other.

Evaluation

Jung was obviously more sympathetic to religion than Freud. However, what Jung means by "religion" is so broad, and sometimes so unorthodox, that some religious people have thought that they might be better off with an enemy like Freud than a maverick friend like Jung.

The matter is complicated by the fact that, as we have seen, the Freudian tradition, in the hands of some of Freud's successors, has proved more sympathetic to religion than might have been expected. Equally, the Christian church has been more receptive of Freudian thinking than might have been expected on the basis of Freud's personal views. Paul Tillich, by any standards one of the great theologians of the twentieth century, made rich use of Freudian thinking (Cooper, 2001). In the nineteenth century, Aubrey Moore remarked of Darwin that though he had appeared in the guise of a foe, he had actually done the work of a friend (Moore, 1889). The same might be said of Freud. I suggest that religion is stronger for assimilating Freud's critique of it.

Jung's contribution to religion is different. The rich parallelism between Jung's psychology and religious thought provides a way of translating much of what religion is trying to say into terms that, for some people, have less baggage and are more accessible. He also provides rich resources for understanding what is at stake, at a human level, in the apparently abstract concepts of theology. Few people have had as vivid a sense as Jung of the personal resonance and significance of religious symbols. His view of religion is ambivalent. He saw it as potentially of great importance, but he was also despairing of religion in its current state. He believed that religious practitioners had lost all sense of the psychic power of what they were dealing with, but he tried to recover some of that.

Summary

- The dependability of psychoanalytic theory is questionable, and that is especially true of Freud's work on cultural phenomena such as religion, where he is applying psychoanalysis in a speculative way. His most enduring ideas about religion are that God is a projection, and that religion is wish fulfillment (illusion). Both may be true, at least for some religious people, but it does not follow that religion is delusion (i.e., error), or that there is no God.
- More recent psychoanalytic work on religion, which has been associated with the relational turn in psychoanalysis, has taken a more positive view of religion and its contribution to adjustment. Winnicott's concept of the transitional has played an important role in such post-Freudian theorizing about religion.
- Jung's psychology has developed a particularly rich engagement with religion, partly through his concept of the collective unconscious. Jung sees a close link between archetypes and religious dogmas and in particular sees the Self as the image of God in the psyche. This enables Jungian psychology to provide a rich interpretative framework for religious thinking. I claim that this is not as reductionist as it might appear, and that it does not have to be as heterodox as Jung himself is.

3

Genetics and Evolution

In this chapter, I turn to the related questions of how and why religion has evolved, and what genetic influence there has been on religion. They have both been lively areas in the study of religion in recent years. I begin with genetics, as it is the more empirical of the two topics, and what you conclude about the genetic basis of religion influences where you stand on some of the debates about the evolutionary basis of religion.

Genetics of Religion

The investigation of the genetic basis of religion is an interesting and complex matter. It is still somewhat inconclusive, despite recent progress. To anticipate my conclusions, it seems likely that some genetic influences are relevant to religion. However, it is doubtful whether there is any genetic basis for religiousness as such, as a unitary package. There is probably more genetic influence on some aspects of religion than others. Also, the most significant genetic influences relevant to religion probably influence a broader range of things, not just religion.

The most widely publicized claim for the genetic basis of religion was made in Dean Hamer's book, *The God Gene: How Faith Is Hardwired Into Our Genes* (Hamer, 2004). Even if genes influence religiosity, the title is thoroughly misleading. First, genetic influence usually arises from multiple sites in the DNA, not from a single gene. No satisfactory evidence exists for a single "God gene," and it is highly improbable that there would be one. Second, to talk of faith being "hardwired" implies a simplistic genetic determinism in which genes alone are supposed to control faith. Debate continues about how strong genetic influence on religion might be, but religion is certainly not *controlled* by our genes. At best, there is genetic influence on religion, not determination.

In discussing this, we also have to take into account radical developments in genetics that have occurred (e.g., Noble, 2006) that have made it problematic to engage in the old project of trying to gauge the relative influence of "nature" and "nurture." It is now assumed that the interaction between the two is so rich and complex that the distinction between nature and nurture no longer makes any sense. The widespread acceptance of "epigenetic" factors (i.e., factors other than the underlying DNA that influence gene expression) shows how contextual factors such as climate change can influence the gene expression by switching genes on or off. Causal effects seem to run in both directions. It is not just that genes affect "phenotype" (the living organism); the phenotype can also influence how the genes operate. It now seems that everything arises from interaction between the two.

Linked to that is a related question of how exactly genes exert whatever influence they might have. In many cases, the pathways of influence are unknown, but they are likely to be complex, and much of the influence is likely to be indirect. The standard methodology relied on the study of twins and assumed that identical twins had more genetic similarity than nonidentical twins, who in turn had more genetic similarity than other siblings. The problem is that patterns of upbringing may also differ in a similar way.

Identical twins may be brought up in ways that are more similar than those for nonidentical twins, who in turn are brought up more similarly than non-twin siblings. So, if we find the most religious "concordance" (similarity in religiousness) for identical twins, and least for non-twin siblings, we cannot be sure how far that is due to genetic similarity and how much it is due to similarity in upbringing. There are other problems too. The old approach to calculating the relative influence of genetics and environment made assumptions about the amount of variation between environments, but that is more difficult to calculate mathematically than genetic variation.

So, with all those caveats, what is the state of the relevant evidence? Chapter 1 emphasized that religion is multi-faceted. Thus, genes may be more relevant to some aspects of religiosity than others, and that does indeed seem to be the case. One of the largest studies was the Virginia study of 14,781 twin pairs (D'Onofrio et al., 1999), which found different patterns of genetic influence for different aspects of religion. Bradshaw and Ellison (2008) reached similar conclusions, so we can have reasonable confidence about the claim that genes have differential effects on different aspects of religion. An important distinction emerged between religious affiliation (i.e., which faith or denomination people adhere to) and religious attendance. Genes have little influence on religious affiliation; that seems to depend on family and culture rather than genetics. Modest heritability was reported for church attendance, and somewhat greater heritability for conservative religious attitudes.

Consensus is growing that religious affiliation is the aspect of religion least likely to be influenced by genes. On the other hand, more internal aspects of religion, or "self-transcendence," may be more influenced by genes (Eaves et al., 2008; Rose and Exline, 2012). For example, Koenig and Bouchard (2006) claim that inner aspects of religion, such as prayerfulness, have a stronger genetic basis than external aspects. It is now highly desirable that further research on the heritability of religion should be more careful over the choice of measures of religion, and focus selectively on those aspects of religion that seem most likely to be influenced by genetics.

Also, some puzzling findings that relate to how genetic influences vary with age deserve further examination. Most studies have been conducted with adults. However, some have studied adolescents (Eaves et al., 2008). The puzzle is that studies of adults generally report heritability for religion, but that appears not to be the case for adolescents. It seems that in adolescence any supposed effect of genes is swamped by family and environmental factors, leaving no demonstrable effect of inheritance. That is problematic for claims of the heritability of religion. If there is indeed heritability for religion, it should be demonstrable at any age, including adolescence. The fact that it seems not to be found in adolescence casts doubt on whether there is genuine heritability of religion. Bearing in mind how hard it is to separate out the effects of similar genes and similar environments, some of the variance in religiousness that has been attributed to genes in adults may be more properly attributed to environment. This needs further exploration.

In looking for genetic influences on religion, it may actually be best to look beyond religion itself. So, it may be fruitful to look at personality traits whose influence extends beyond religion, but which can have considerable impact on the form that religion takes. For example, evidence is growing for a general trait of conservative (vs. liberal) attitudes that seems to have some genetic basis and shows itself in the "moral values triad" or authoritarianism, conservatism, and religiousness (Koenig and Bouchard, 2006). That has been explored so far more in political psychology than in the psychology of religion. However, quite a strong association exists between conservatism in religion and in wider social-political attitudes.

Conservative religion, such as biblical literalism, is one of the aspects of religion where genetic influence seems strongest (Bradshaw and Ellison, 2008; Hibbing et al., 2014). The genetic basis for being "born again" seems to be high, far stronger than for mere church attendance. The genes that influence conservative religion also influence conservative attitudes to other matters such as sexuality, so it seems that what is inherited is a predisposition to conservative attitudes that affects both religion and other moral, social, and political issues.

It may also be the case that there is genetic influence on internal aspects of religion such as spirituality. That actually seems very likely. One way of conceptualizing and measuring the relevant personality trait would be in terms of absorption, the tendency to become engrossed in inner life, a trait that seems important in spirituality and has a moderate genetic basis (Finkel and McGue, 1997). That is discussed more fully in Chapter 5. As noted there, the fact that similar rates of occurrence of spiritual experience, broadly defined, seem to be found in cultures where religious attendance is markedly different is consistent with a greater genetic influence on spiritual experience than religious attendance. It also seems likely that transliminality, the tendency to be open to an unusually wide range of psychological experience (Thalbourne and Delin, 1999), like conservatism, may have a range of influences that go beyond religion.

To sum up, it seems reasonably clear that religion is influenced by genetic factors, though this is not a simple, direct effect. Some aspects of religion are more influenced by genetics than others. Also, it seems a plausible hypothesis that the genetic influences that are most relevant to religion, conservatism, and spirituality (or transliminality) do not influence religion solely and specifically but impinge on other areas as well as religion. Their mode of influence on religion will no doubt be complex and subtle and is not yet well understood.

Religions as Evolutionary Adaptation

Let us now turn from genetics to the evolution of religion. To begin with basics, I assume that there is sufficient evidence, from the fossil record and other sources, that evolution of species has occurred, and that natural selection has played a key part in it (though I am not committed to the view that random mutation and natural selection are the only processes at work in evolution).

I also accept the general view that a crucial period, the Upper Paleolithic, began about 200,000 years ago, when primates who were recognizably human first made their appearance. That period is often characterized by a "cultural explosion" in which a wide range of cultural practices developed almost simultaneously, including burial practices that seem to be recognizably religious. The question is why and how these early forms of religion evolved.

A key general assumption of evolutionary theories of religion is that religion is a universal human phenomenon. That is actually a more complex claim than at first appears. It involves creating a general category of "religion" that transcends rather conspicuous differences, and applying the modern concept of religion to cultural phenomena that would not have been seen in that way at the time. There is also the obvious fact that not every human is religious, though it may be the case that all humans with normal functioning have a capacity for religion.

Why did religion evolve? The range of views on the evolution of religion is quite broad (see Bulbulia et al., 2008), but there are currently two main views. One says that religion evolved because it was adaptive and had advantages in terms of natural selection. Though a variety of adaptive advantages have been claimed for religion, the majority view is that religion is good for social cooperation, and that cooperation is good for survival. The alternative view is that religion was a by-product of other evolutionary developments. Lee Kirkpatrick (2005) has been a trenchant opponent of explaining the evolution of religion in terms of adaptation. By-product theory is currently the majority view, though the debate is not yet settled, and it seems difficult to get closure on it. That is partly there is evidence that is consistent with the adaptation view, but not evidence that skeptics find compelling. Some have argued for the adaptive value of religion solely at the level of advantages for the individual, but others have argued for multilevel selection at both individual and group levels.

Also, it increasingly seems to be a mistake to pit the two views against each other as stark alternatives. If you assume that religion has evolved as a result of natural selection acting on genetic mutations, thereby conferring adaptive advantage, it is necessary to assume that religion has a genetic basis. By-product theory does not need to assume that, but adaptation theory does. However, as we have just seen, though evidence suggests that genetics is relevant to some aspects of religion, that evidence is too patchy to sustain the view that "religion" as a coherent package evolved because it was adaptive.

There is often a regrettable tendency in the scientific study of religion to treat it as a unitary construct, when differentiation and subdivision are needed. It seems that what we now call "religion" probably evolved in stages, and it started with practice rather than belief. Bellah (2011) distinguishes three phases, drawing on a theoretical framework advanced by Merlin Donald (1991). First is a mimetic culture, with bodily practices that reach new levels of complexity. Then, drawing on language, mythic culture includes the development of narratives that we would now call religious. Third is the more abstract thought of a theoretic culture in which religious thinking takes a more doctrinal form. Dunbar (2014) has developed a similar view and sees shamanic religion as evolving a good deal earlier than doctrinal religion.

Different aspects of religion contributed to social cohesiveness in different ways. Dunbar claims that the synchronized rhythmic movement of trance dancing contributed significantly to social bonding and enabled humans to reach larger group sizes than previous species. The communal release of endorphins in trance dancing probably played a significant role in building communities. Doctrinal religion, in contrast, may have been useful in social regulation and enabled a community to sanction free riders. David Sloan Wilson in *Darwin's Cathedral* (Wilson, 2002) examines the regulative functions served by many religions and concludes that they help define the boundaries of a group, promote coordinated behavior within it, and prohibit cheating. Religious practices can help define group membership by requiring costly, or at least difficult-to-fake, signals of group loyalty (Rappaport, 1999). Religion can enforce cooperation by providing supernatural sanctions for noncooperation, coupled with omniscient surveillance of noncooperation. Religious communities do indeed seem to be more stable and enduring than comparable secular utopian communities (Sosis and Bressler, 2003).

However, establishing that religion is adaptive is not sufficient on its own to prove that religion evolved *because* it was adaptive. That causal hypothesis is more difficult to establish. The importance of cooperation in evolution has probably been underestimated, as Novak and Coakley (2013) have argued. There could well have been a mutually reinforcing interconnection between the evolution of cooperation and the evolution of religion in which social cooperation was one of the factors that led to the evolution of religion, but also religion, once it had evolved, further reinforced social cooperation.

One problematic feature of the debate between adaptation and by-product theorists is that it assumes a sharp demarcation between religion and non-religion. It presses the question of whether religion evolved because of the evolutionary advantages of religion itself or of some other nonreligious trait or activity. That very distinction between religion and non-religion is a modern one that goes back not much further than the late nineteenth century. It is misleading to project that distinction back on to emerging humanity for whom the distinction between religion and non-religion would have been much more blurred.

I argued earlier in this chapter that genetic influences on religion may be carried not so much by genes for religion as by other traits that are intertwined with religion and have a stronger genetic basis. Rather than focusing entirely on how religion itself is adaptive, it may be better to broaden out to consider the adaptive advantage of traits that impinge on religion.

If my tentative suggestion is correct that transliminality is a trait with a strong genetic basis that is relevant to religion, the question arises of what adaptive value it might have. One answer that has been suggested is that it evolved because people with high transliminality benefited more from shamanic healing rituals, thus conferring survival advantage (McClenon, 2006). In a similar vein, it would be plausible to suggest that conservatism evolved because it had adaptive advantage in terms of social regulation and authority, and that conservatism then impinged on a range of religious, moral, and social aspects of human life.

Cognitive Science of Religion

I turn now to another prominent view of the evolution of religion, and the one that currently commands the most widespread acceptance, namely the evolutionary application of the cognitive science of religion (CSR). The core assumption is that religion arises naturally, almost automatically, from the normal functioning of the human cognitive system, and that there is no need to invoke assumptions about the adaptive value of religion to explain its evolution. Tremlin (2006) has provided an accessible, mainstream account of CSR.

The development of CSR has been a significant intellectual achievement, but I ought to admit here that I am somewhat skeptical about it. No evidence shows that it is wrong, or that any other theory is better. However, any theory deserves some healthy competition, and CSR has so far had too little competition. I will suggest that general considerations render CSR less plausible than it might at first sight seem, even if they do not actually show it to be wrong (Watts and Turner, 2014).

It is important not to assume that religion emerged at a single point in the evolutionary process; it must have come together only very gradually. The aspect of religion on which CSR has focused more consistently has been the interpretation of the world in terms of supernatural agents. In that sense, it has assumed that religious or supernatural thinking is foundational in religion. It has been less interested in other aspects of religion such as the evolution of religious practices, which probably evolved earlier, or with the evolution of religious doctrines and social structures, which probably evolved later, when humans came to live in settled agrarian communities.

Let us recall that religion evolved as part of the cultural explosion. CSR ignores that. It focuses on just one particular aspect of the cultural explosion – religion – and explains that alone. It seems to me much more likely that there was a common explanation for the cultural explosion that applies to religion among other things. I suggest that it is more sensible and parsimonious to look for what caused the cultural explosion as a whole, not just for why religion evolved.

The obvious cognitive explanation for the cultural explosion is in terms of the evolution of the general cognitive capacities that made humans different from other primates. Why doesn't CSR take that obvious route? The answer seems to be that most CSR theorists are committed, more or less strongly, to the view that the mind is made up of specific modules. There undoubtedly are specific modules; I do not dispute that. However, I do not see any good reason to press modularity to the point of ruling out general capacities, and rejecting evolutionary explanations couched in terms of them.

Even among those who are happy with the project of explaining the evolution of religion in cognitive terms, CSR seems unnecessarily constrained in its assumptions and approach. Most CSR theorists are committed to a modular view of mind and assume that religious thinking arises from specific cognitive devices or modules, such as a hyperactive agency detection device. Watts (2014) has argued that CSR, by its overstrong commitment to a modular view of mind, unnecessarily eliminates alternatives to its own approach, such as theories of the evolution of general cognitive capacities.

Despite broad similarities in approach, the CSR theory of the evolution of religion has been developed in different ways by different people. Let us consider first Pascal Boyer's version of CSR (Boyer, 1994, 2001). It makes use of the concept of intuitive knowledge, proposing a near-universal intuitive knowledge of three domains: an intuitive physics, an intuitive biology, and an intuitive psychology. This lays out the three basic categories of intuitive knowledge, and it also proposes that there are intuitive distinctions between these three categories. Boyer then makes a proposal about why religious ideas spread in such a contagious way. He suggests that religious ideas violated these intuitive categories, albeit only in a minimal way. That "minimal counter-intuitiveness" makes religious ideas more memorable than ideas that are either not counterintuitive at all or radically counterintuitive.

It is an ingenious and intriguing theory. Certainly it fits with a lot of evidence that material that sits uneasily in a schema is better remembered than material that fits neatly in it or is unrelated to the schema at all. The weakness of the theory is its reliance on intuition, and overconfidence about what would have been intuitively obvious to emerging humanity. The evidence that CSR has amassed in support of its assumptions (e.g., Tremlin, 2006) has largely come from studies of children. There is often an analogy between individual and evolutionary development, but it is not secure and cannot be assumed.

It seems entirely possible that CSR is mistaken in its assumptions about what was intuitively obvious to emerging humanity. If distinctions between categories were intuitively obvious to emerging humanity, why were they violated so frequently? CSR focuses on a proposal about why violations, if they occurred, should have been memorable and contagious. It seems to me more likely that distinctions between categories were acquired gradually. If so, ideas that transgressed boundaries would have occurred precisely because the boundaries between categories were not yet clearly established. As the categories became better established, violations would have become less likely.

Justin Barrett has formulated CSR theory in terms of a hyperactive agency detection device (Barrett, 2004). In some ways that is a helpful move. Barrett is right to focus in on agency detection as the key point where boundaries between categories become blurred, and right to assume a degree of anthropomorphism in emerging humanity who interpreted the natural world in terms of a supernatural agent. That can seem to us a quaint mistake that calls for explanation.

However, we cannot simply assume, without argument, that seeing agency behind nature is a mistake. An alternative view that at least deserves consideration is that emerging humanity had a more transliminal mode of consciousness, which led to the intuition that nature and spirit were a unity. They might actually have been correct in that intuition. Most CSR theorists (though not Barrett himself) hold a naturalistic interpretation of the world, in which it is assumed that the natural world is merely natural, and not connected to any supernatural agents. That naturalistic view seems intuitively correct to them, and they perhaps assume too readily that it must have been intuitively correct for emerging humanity as well.

To explain excessive agency detection, Barrett invokes a hyperactive agency detection device. It is characteristic of the modular "tool kit" theory of mind assumed by most CSR theorists that a specific "device" explains agency detection. However, it is not clear whether that actually explains anything, rather than just re-labeling it. It could constitute an explanation, but, for that to be the case, the concept of an agency detection device would have to be embedded in a network of well-substantiated claims that gave it construct validity. That does not so far seem to be the case.

Though supernatural agents are at the core of CSR, it has developed theories of various other aspects of religious cognition (Whitehouse, 2000) and been ready to invoke specific cognitive propensities in each case. Belief in an afterlife, for example, has been traced to the inability to terminate mental states. Similarly, creationism has been traced to a natural preference for teleological interpretations.

A recurrent complaint about the CSR approach to evolution of religion has been that through placing such a strong emphasis on the cognitive basis of the evolution of religion, CSR has neglected the contribution of sociocultural. Recognition has been growing of the importance of the social embeddedness of cognition, but CSR seems to be operating with a view of cognition that takes it out of the sociocultural context.

Evolving Cognitive Architecture

I will now turn to a different kind of cognitive theory that looks for an explanation of the evolution of religion in terms of how the general cognitive architecture evolved, rather than in terms of specific cognitive devices. Such theories can more readily place the evolution of religion in the context of the broader cultural explosion that took place in the Upper Paleolithic period.

One prominent theorist who looks for a single explanation of the whole cultural explosion is Steven Mithen, who set out his views in *The Prehistory of Mind* (Mithen, 1996). Mithen is sometimes regarded as a CSR theorist, but it seems to me that his approach is radically different from the standard CSR theory. He seeks to explain the development of the whole range of distinctively human capacities included in the cultural explosion in terms of evolutionary developments in the general structure of mind.

Mithen's proposal is that mental capacities started specific and modular. He mentions three specific ones, a technical intelligence, needed for the creation and use of tools; a social intelligence, needed for rudimentary social cooperation; and a natural history intelligence, needed for effective hunting. He assumes that in Neanderthals, intelligence was entirely modular, with these specific intelligences operating separately. He suggests that fluid processing capacity arose from collapsing the boundaries between specific modular intelligences, and that it was the resulting integration of specific modular capacities that made art and religion possible.

The components needed for art were all present in these modular intelligences. The technical intelligence provided for a mental conception of an image, the social intelligence made intentional communication possible, and the natural history intelligence made it possible to attribute meaning. However, for art to develop it was necessary for these three to work together in a new way. Mithen sees religion, similarly, as also requiring the integration of separate intelligences. That, for him, is what leads to the concept of supernatural beings that (following Boyer) partly conform to, but also partly violate, intuitive assumptions about agents.

This seems that is a more helpful theory than CSR in two ways. It is looking to explain the whole cultural explosion, not just religion. It is also proposing an explanation in terms of a restructuring, as humanity emerged, of the entire cognitive architecture. However, I am not persuaded that it is the right formulation of that restructuring. Elsewhere (Watts, 2014), I have proposed an alternative model, making use of the cognitive architecture developed by Philip Barnard, known as Interacting Cognitive Subsystems, which he has applied to cognitive evolution. I will say more about that model in the next chapter but will just say here what is needed to set out how his theory of cognitive evolution provides an alternative to Mithen.

Barnard (Barnard et al., 2007) proposes a model of the human cognitive architecture with nine distinct subsystems. He traces how the evolving capacities of primates were made possible, as a series of stages, by the gradual addition of extra subsystems. On his theory, the crucial step, which led to Homo sapiens, and the cultural explosion, was when the single central subsystem of our primate ancestors differentiated into two distinct central subsystems. For Barnard, what is distinctive about humans is that they have two distinct central subsystems. That gives humans a new cognitive versatility because they have two different modes of central cognition at their disposal; it also allows the central engine of cognition to have significantly enhanced integrative capacity. For Barnard, it is the addition of an extra central subsystem that makes it possible for humans to do art, religion, and so on.

Mithen is suggesting that what made human intelligence possible was the collapse of the boundaries between different specific intelligences. Barnard, in contrast, is suggesting that cognitive evolution is a process of gradually adding extra subsystems, with the crucial addition in humans of an extra central subsystem. It is difficult to settle this kind of debate conclusively, but at least two general considerations lead me to side with Barnard rather than Mithen. First, I think it is hard to give a convincing account of the cognitive capacities of prehuman primates without any central processing capacities. Second, I suggest that it is more plausible, on general grounds, that cognitive evolution proceeds by differentiation rather than by amalgamation.

However, these two positions may not be as much opposed as appears at first sight. As the cognitive architecture develops, it is likely that processes of differentiation and integration proceed in parallel (Watts, 2014). They are certainly not incompatible. Interestingly, at one point Mithen seems open to either possibility. He uses the metaphor of modular intelligences being like chapels and suggests that windows were opened between them to form a kind of cathedral. However, he says that this "final major re-design of the human mind" took place "when doors and windows were inserted in the chapel walls, or perhaps when a new 'super-chapel' was constructed" (Mithen, 1996, p. 174). In that terminology, Barnard's theory proposes a new superchapel rather than just doors and windows, the superchapel being the new central subsystem.

Mithen also comes close to Barnard's position when discussing the development of language, which he sees as arising from the demands of social interaction. For example, it provided a quicker and more economical way of maintaining social relations than grooming, making larger social units possible. Mithen envisages language as initially being developed out of social intelligence. That seems entirely plausible. There was probably a coevolution of the cognitive architecture with observable behavior and function, and it was probably the demands of social interaction that drove the development of language.

Actually, the new specific intelligence needed for language is close to the new central subsystem that Barnard proposes, which, for the first time, is able to propositionalize meanings. Even if language arose first in conjunction with social intelligence, it seems likely that subsequently it would be deployed in conjunction with other specific intelligences such as the technical and natural history ones. I suggest that linguistic intelligence (which is almost another name for Barnard's new central subsystem) was the superchapel of which Mithen speaks, which integrated specific intelligences for the first time, and made art and religion possible. If language functions as a new kind of central, integrative intelligence, there is no need to invoke the additional step of knocking direct doors and windows between the separate chapels of modular intelligence.

Most CSR theorists would not want to follow this kind of attempt to explain the emergence of religion and art in terms of the evolution of the cognitive architecture. They would want to focus on the evolution of religion alone and would handle it entirely in terms of specific modules, with no role for central evolving cognitive capacities. It seems to me that there are good reasons to be cautious about the currently popular CSR approach, and that the alternative approach in terms of evolution of the cognitive architecture deserves serious consideration.

The questions of how and why religion evolved are by no means settled. However, I put the main emphasis on religion being the result of general changes in cognitive capacities. However, that does not rule out the possibility of some aspects of religion having adaptive value, which would have facilitated and shaped its further development.

Summary

- Evidence is growing for a genetic predisposition to at least some aspects of religion. I suggest that there is a particular genetic predisposition to (i) conservatism, including conservative religion, and (ii) spirituality and absorption in inner life. Both are relevant to religion but extend beyond it.
- Debate has been vigorous about whether religion evolved because it was adaptive or because it was a by-product of other adaptive developments. The debate is hard to resolve, partly because it presupposes too sharp a distinction between religion and non-religion.
- The most high-profile recent approach to the evolution of religion has made use of the cognitive science of religion. Though in many ways this represents a significant achievement, I claim that it is also open to criticism for (i) being unnecessarily constrained in its mode of cognitive theorizing, (ii) taking religion out of the context of the cultural explosion of which it was part, and (iii) largely ignoring social context.

- An alternative cognitive approach to evolution of religion sees it as arising from developments in central processing capacities that are an important part of human distinctiveness. Two such theories are discussed, focusing (i) on the integration of capacities that were initially distinct or (ii) the development of an additional central cognitive system.

4

Brain and Cognition

We will now turn to studies of religion from the perspectives of neuroscience and cognitive psychology. It is a relatively new area in the psychology of religion and one that has recently aroused much interest.

Neural Reductionism

First, let us dispose of the bogey of neural reductionism. It is an issue raised by William James (2012/1902), who devoted the first chapter of his classic *Varieties of Religious Experience* to this issue, which he called "medical materialism." The book is based on James's Gifford Lectures given at the University of Edinburgh in 1901 and 1902, and it has become the classic text of the early days of psychology of religion. James had propounded a rather materialist theory of emotions (see Dixon, 2006), but clearly he wanted to be less materialist about religion. He made an important distinction between two kinds of judgments, existential judgments concerned with how something originates and spiritual judgments concerned with its value. It is a version of the well-known distinction between fact and value. James's point is that one cannot be reduced to the other, and that knowing how religious experience arises does not settle questions of its value and significance. He is surely right in his general point that admitting that spiritual experience has an organic basis does not invalidate it as spiritual experience, a point of much contemporary relevance. He is also scathing about the then fashionable survival theory of religion (which has echoes in current evolutionary theory of religion). James's chapter still repays careful study, but then he is the most distinguished philosopher ever to have worked on the psychology of religion.

There is no justification for using research about the role of the physical brain in religion to reach reductionist conclusions about religion. Equally, it is worth emphasizing that religious believers have no reason to be disconcerted by research on the role of the physical brain in religion. From a theological point of view, the brain is part of God's creation. If there is a God, and he wishes to reveal himself to humanity through religion, no theological argument suggests that God would want somehow to bypass the physical brain. It is often assumed in these debates that religious people are committed to a dualistic view of the human person. However, as we will see in Chapter 13, that is really not the case, even though Christianity went through a period of alliance with dualism after Descartes.

Whether there is any tension over reductionism between the religious assumptions and those of the brain sciences depends on what is meant by "reductionism." Everyone agrees that there is no problem about methodological reductionism, which is the project of trying to explain one thing in terms of another as far as you can, with no prior assumptions about how successful that will be. Beyond that, terminology has become rather confused, as different people use key terms in different ways, so I will try to handle this in a transparent and nontechnical way. No one objects to trying to explain human functioning in terms of brain processes as far as possible, provided there are no strong prior claims about how far that is going to go, and what the consequences will be if success is complete. Clearly, what is going on in the brain is going to be a key part of an adequate account of religious functioning, but problems stem from two sources.

First is a tendency to take the brain out of context, and to ignore more general bodily and social context. However, a strong movement has recently begun to recognize the contextual nature of human cognition, which is welcome from a religious point of view as it sits better with the holistic view of human nature found in the Hebrew Bible. However, much simplistic neuropsychological reductionism has not caught up with this important scientific development.

The other problem comes with the notion of a "complete" explanation, an idea that plays a pivotal role in the reductionist project. It is important to recognize that we generally do not get to a complete explanation. It is an objective that recedes as you chase after it, like gold at the end of a rainbow. Most interesting human phenomena, like religion, are too complex and multi-faceted to lend themselves to complete explanation. There is also the epistemological problem that even if you reached a complete explanation, it would be hard to prove that you had, as it would depend on showing that no other factors were relevant.

But the real problem, from a religious point of view, is with what is supposed to follow from getting a complete explanation. Sadly, reductionists often do not wait until they actually have a complete explanation; they often just assume that they will get there and make their next move "on account." That next move is usually to claim that once you have a complete explanation for something, it has been "explained away" and is not what it appears. So, for example, it is suggested that if we have a complete explanation of religious experience, or the human soul, in terms of brain processes, it will show that they are not what they seem. It is then suggested that they really ought to be redescribed in terms of brain processes rather than in terms of God, consciousness, or religion. My point is that even if we got the hoped-for complete explanation, it would not follow that things had been explained away, and that religion was not what it seemed.

It is interesting that Andrew Newberg has drawn a different conclusion from scanning studies of the religious experiences people obtain in meditation (Newberg, 2010) from the usual reductionist one. From demonstrating that there are neural correlates of these experiences, he thinks he has shown that those experiences are biologically "real." Of course, religious experiences are indeed real, but it is not clear what credible theory is being disproved by that claim. It only shows that reports of religious experience are not being faked. However, it would be quite illegitimate to go from a demonstration that religious experience is real to the conclusion that God is real.

Empirical Studies

We will now turn to empirical research on the role of the brain in religion. One of the main sources of data available about the role of the physical brain in religion comes from fMRI (functional magnetic resonance imaging) studies, which provide data about blood flow in different parts of the brain when people are engaged in particular activities. For good recent overviews, see Beauregard (2012) or McNamara and Butler (2013).

Though scanning studies represent a major advance, they also have significant limitations. There are problems that beset all scanning studies, not just studies of religion. The research is so expensive that numbers tend to be small. That problem is exacerbated by the fact that people show different patterns of brain activity when doing what is supposed to be the same thing. Further, to interpret scanning studies, you need a good theory linking areas of the brain with particular functions. Without such a theory, it is hard to know how to interpret the fact that one part of the brain is more active than another when people are performing a particular activity.

However, the most serious problem with scanning studies of religion is probably the significant restrictions on what religious activities can be performed in a scanner. Some studies have looked at religious practices such as meditation. For example, you can study individual religious practices, but you cannot easily study collective ones. You can study deliberate practices such as meditation, but you cannot study sponta- neously occurring religious experiences. Moreover, conditions in a scanner are so abnormal and distracting that only highly experienced and disciplined practitioners are likely to be able to demonstrate good- quality religious activity, though that does not apply to the same extent to studies using the older technology of single-photon emission computed tomography (SPECT) scanning.

Studies of meditation have generated some really interesting results, though it needs to be recognized that meditation is a highly specific religious activity, and also that relatively few religious people practice it with the seriousness of those who have taken part in scanning studies. One of the best known of such studies was Andrew Newberg's research on nuns who were meditating (Newberg et al., 2003), showing reduced activity in areas of the brain concerned with fear and with orientation in time and space, and increased activity in areas concerned with focused concentration. The research of Richard J. Davidson on mindfulness med- itation has also been important scientifically in confirming the neural effects of meditation (e.g., Lutz et al., 2008).

Though meditation has clear effects on brain activity, the results are not easy to summarize. One problem is that different kinds of meditation produce different patterns of brain activation. For example, meditating on an external object produces different effects from meditating on a mantra. Long-term meditators have different patterns of brain activa- tion than novice (e.g., eight-week) meditators. However, in very broad terms, meditation tends to lead to increased frontal activity in the brain (the area that is involved in self-regulation) and reduced activity farther back, for example, in the parietal-occipital area, which is involved with sensory input.

An important distinction needs to be made between the brain activity of meditators while they are actually meditating from their brain activity at other times. A change in the latter would be much more significant; it is far more striking if meditation affects people's brain activity even when they are not actually meditating. It seems likely that such differences exist, though they have not proved easy to demonstrate. However, provisional indications of such long-term effects come from Richard Davidson's research group (Lutz et al., 2008). For example, it seems that in experienced meditators there may be less amygdala response to emotional stimuli and possibly also differences in electrical rhythms in sleep. Such long-term effects remain the most important scientific question, and we still need some well-replicated research findings.

Though meditation probably results in long-term changes to brain activity, no evidence indicates that it produces any structural changes to the brain. For example, no part of the brain gets bigger as a result of meditation, in the way that taxi drivers have been shown to have enlarged spatial areas in the brain.

Some studies have asked people questions about their religious belief or experience and looked at the pattern of brain activation that occurs when they answer. The broad conclusion is that nothing very specific about brain activity is associated with answering questions about religion. Brain activation is much the same as when they are answering questions about other things.

One such study is that of Sam Harris (Harris et al., 2008), who found no differences in brain activation between when people were answering verifiable questions about mathematics and when they were answering unverifiable questions about religion. There was a difference in brain activation when people were saying "Yes" to questions and when they were saying "No," but that was not specific to religion. Harris also found no differences between believers and nonbelievers in the areas of the brain involved in processing religious statements, a finding that suggests that the study was not getting at any fundamental aspect of religion.

Another somewhat similar study by Dimitrios Kapogiannis (Kapogiannis et al., 2009) focused on three religious questions, which an earlier phase of their research had suggested were the key ones. They asked questions first about people's sense of God's involvement with them, and second about God's feelings toward them. The pattern of brain activation associated with answering those questions was the same as if the questions had been asked about other people. That suggests that the sense of relationship with God makes use of the same parts of the brain as are involved in social cognition generally. Third, and perhaps more interestingly, Kapogiannis et al. also looked at differences between questions about religious beliefs in doctrinal or experiential form and found that different areas of the brain were involved in processing the two. That suggests an important distinction between official and personal belief, or between "head" and "heart," to which we will return.

Another way in which the effects of the brain on religion can be studied is through looking at what effect neurological disorders have on religion. Such disorders provide a naturally occurring experiment in which we can examine whether changes in the brain lead to changes in religion. It seems (Coles, 2008) that most neurological disorders have no dramatic effects on religion. However, in some cases, a blunting of religious engagement occurs, which may affect private religion more than public. As with other medical conditions, some neurological patients may turn to religion to help them cope.

Much the most dramatic religious change in a neurological disorder occurs with temporal lobe epilepsy. Such patients often experience ecstatic religious experiences, of the kind that have been brilliantly described by Dostoevsky. In many ways, they are like religious experiences that arise in other ways, though it is important to note that seizures in the context of epilepsy are only interpreted in religious terms by people who have a religious background. Even when they are interpreted religiously, the sense of the presence of God is often lacking (Fingelkurts, 2009). It seems that these experiences are religious in an experiential sense but often not in an interpretative sense. There also does not seem to be reliable evidence that temporal lobe epilepsy affects any other aspect of religion; earlier claims that such patients became more religious in a general sense seem not to be dependable. So, religion fractionates in temporal lobe epilepsy; the temporal lobes are involved in ecstatic religious experiences, but other areas of the brain are involved in other aspects of religion.

The special role of the temporal lobes in religious experience has been the basis of the research program of Michael Persinger, who has developed a special helmet to give electrical stimulation to the temporal lobes to generate religious experiences (Persinger, 1983). It is a program of research that has not been found convincing by much of the scientific community. Nevertheless, it seems likely that in at least some people, electrical stimulation of the temporal lobes can induce something akin to a religious experience. The key questions are how many people show that effect, and how close the similarity is to a religious experience. At best, it represents only one component of religion and does not establish that there is a "God spot" in the temporal lobes.

Beyond the God Spot

Despite much popular interest in finding a God spot in the brain, there are good reasons why it is implausible that religion should be localized in the brain in this way. One is that religious practice is too complex and multi-faceted for such localization to be plausible. The other is that the brain operates systemically, not in a series of isolated areas. Another is that religion, which developed late in evolution, is likely to make use of structures that had already developed for other purposes rather than giving rise to brand new brain structures.

Indeed, one of the most interesting and important findings to emerge from brain-scanning studies of religion is precisely that no area of the brain is dedicated exclusively to religion. All religious activity seems to make use of pathways that seem to have developed initially for other purposes. For religious believers, that will be consistent with assumptions about a God who reveals himself in the ordinary things of life.

It has also proved interesting how different parts of the brain are associated with different aspects or modes of religion. Brain scientists have sometimes explored opponent processes in the brain, and the basic distinctions between front-back and left-right will enable us at least to illustrate how different parts of the brain are involved in different religiosity activities.

It will help to approach the different roles of the frontal lobes and the more posterior temporal lobes via the kind of two-factor theory of religious experience suggested by Wayne Proudfoot (1987), which will be discussed more fully in the next chapter. It seems that two sets of factors may contribute to religious experience, one set yielding the sense of something powerful and transcendent, and the other contributing an interpretative framework. If we accept that some such two-factor theory of religious experience is roughly correct, we can ask which areas of the brain are involved in each of them. It is plausible to suggest that the temporal lobes are more heavily involved in religious *experience*, and that the frontal lobes are more heavily involved in religious *belief*. Wildman and Brothers (1999) have proposed a somewhat similar position.

Turning to the role of left and right brain in religion, it needs to be acknowledged that much simplistic popular psychology in this area has made many brain scientists wary of the whole topic. However, handled carefully, I suggest that lateralization theory provides a helpful neuropsychological approach to religion. The general theory of lateralization on which I am leaning here is McGilchrist's magisterial review of the scientific evidence (McGilchrist, 2009). Let us acknowledge that in talking about left and right brain we are, for simplicity, talking only about the 70 percent of the population whose language ability is served by the left brain. We also need to move beyond the idea that one-half of the brain does one set of things and the other half a different set of things. Both halves of the brain can do almost anything, though they do them in different ways.

It is worth noting two important anatomical facts about left and right brain in humans. First, they are less interconnected than in other species, so that they do provide humans to some extent with two alternative brains, something that I suggest provides humans with greater cognitive versatility than any other species. Second, the right (less linguistic) brain is much more strongly connected with the rest of the body and represents a highly embodied mode of cognition, whereas the left (more linguistic) brain is more densely interconnected within itself, but less well connected with the rest of the body.

McGilchrist (2009) has provided a helpful summary of the cognitive styles of the two sides of the brain. The left brain focuses on what is already known; it deals with information in a more discrete, linear, abstract, propositional way. The right brain is more open to the unknown and deals with information in a more holistic, intuitive, concrete, contextual way. Both hemispheres can deal with any kind of material, but each does so in way that reflects its own predominant cognitive style.

It is not difficult to extrapolate from this to the kinds of religion that the two hemispheres would be expected to give rise to. Sara Savage (2013) suggests that fundamentalism is exactly the kind of religion that, on this theory, would be expected of the left brain. The rise of fundamentalism at the present time fits with McGilchrist's general theory that we live in a culture that prioritizes left brain cognition, and that even areas such as art and religion that might have been expected to provide some counterbalance to that trend have shown increasing left brain influence.

As Savage points out, radicalized religion is often associated with a sense of stress. She suggests that stress not only tends to prioritize the tightly interconnected thinking of the left brain but also impairs frontal lobe functioning, leading to more emphasis on the more emotional, less conceptual processes associated with the anterior and lower areas of the brain.

I hope that this discussion, cast in terms of the role of different lobes and hemispheres, will be sufficient to illustrate the point that much of the brain can be involved in religion in one way or another. The brain works systemically, but different parts of the brain are associated with different aspects of religion and have different emphases.

Cognitive Architecture: Interacting Cognitive Subsystems

I now propose to set out a parallel argument, not focusing on the physical brain but on the "cognitive architecture." By that I mean the structure of cognitive systems that we can infer from data about how people function. Some would argue that the best scientific strategy is to proceed first at this functional level, and only after you have identified functional systems to consider how they are instantiated in the physical brain. My own view is that it is helpful to proceed with the two approaches in parallel, looking for points of convergence.

Agreement is widespread about the need to distinguish between at least two cognitive systems. From different starting points, people have arrived at similar, albeit not identical, conclusions. From a psychoanalytic standpoint, Wilma Bucci has distinguished between symbolic and sub-symbolic cognitive systems (Bucci, 1997). From the standpoint of social cognition, Seymour Epstein has distinguished rational and experiential systems (Epstein, 1991). Within his comprehensive model of the cognitive architecture, Interacting Cognitive Subsystems (ICS), Philip Barnard has distinguished two central systems concerned with meaning, the propositional and implicational (or intuitive) subsystems (Barnard, 2007; Teasdale and Barnard, 1993).

Harvey Whitehouse, coming from an anthropological perspective, has proposed a somewhat similar distinction between the imagistic and doctrinal aspects of religion (Whitehouse, 2000). Imagistic religion arises from religious practices that are highly arousing and may be traumatic, but occur infrequently. Doctrinal religion, in contrast, arises from the repetition of less arousing experiences. There are other differences too. With imagistic religious practices, meanings are internally generated and are communicated in a multimodal way. With doctrinal religion, meanings are learned and are communicated through narrative or logical integration.

To illustrate this general approach, I will take ICS as an example and show how Barnard's two central subsystems are involved in religion in different but interrelated ways (Watts, 2013a). Some of the important differences between the central subsystems follow from their different interconnections. The implicational subsystem is connected to body state, whereas the propositional subsystem is not. This gives a more emotional tone to implicational meanings. They are more psychosomatic, being both influenced by bodily states and in turn finding physical expression. The propositional subsystem has no comparable links with body state.

In contrast, the meanings of the propositional subsystem can feed directly into articulation, whereas the implicational subsystem has no direct route to articulation, except through the propositional subsystem. The implicational subsystem is intuitive but inarticulate. The two subsystems map onto what has traditionally been meant by "head" and "heart." If the propositional subsystem is the head, the implicational subsystem is the heart. The meanings of the implicational subsystem are similar to what Eugene Gendlin refers to as "felt meanings" (Gendlin, 1962).

Many mystics have commented that what they experience in mystical states is "ineffable." They claim that in those states they have knowledge; in William James's terms they are "noetic," but they cannot put that knowledge into words. It makes sense of that feature of mystical experience to suggest that mystical understanding arises in the inarticulate implicational subsystem. In fact, many mystics do write extensively about their experiences. However, to do that they clearly have to translate them into a different form from that in which they were originally experienced, one that they believe fails to fully recapture the original experience.

The two subsystems also differ in the kinds of meanings they generate. They talk a different kind of language or, as Barnard puts it, have a different code. Implicational meanings are "schematic." They are richer, thicker, often concerned with broad patterns of meaning that span very different circumstances. Religious meanings often seem to be of this type. In Christian thinking, for example, the "death to resurrection" scheme crops up in many places, for example, in the crucifixion of Jesus, in the symbolism of baptism, in finding a way through personal adversity, and in many other circumstances. For example, when the cathedral in Coventry was bombed in World War II, it was immediately interpreted in terms of this schema, that is, that the cathedral had died with Christ and would rise again with him. The meanings of the propositional subsystem seem, in contrast, to be more focal and specific, but less evocative.

Many religious practices seem designed to reduce the activity of the propositional subsystem, so as to give the implicational subsystem a clearer run. As we will see later, many forms of meditation seem designed to do that. But equally, we will see that speaking in tongues, a practice found in many Charismatic and Pentecostal churches, seems designed to do the same thing. Even when words are used in religious practices, they seem to be used in an unusual way, less referentially but more evocatively.

Various patterns of relationship between the two subsystems can develop. Teasdale and Barnard (1993) have explored how that develops in depression. Essentially, a negative mood develops at the implicational level that gives rise to negative thoughts at the propositional level, which in turn reinforce the negative mood, setting up a vicious circle. Something similar probably develops with strong religious faith. There is presumably a basic sense of relationship to God, and religious commitment at the implicational level, that leads to prayer and other forms of religious articulation at the propositional level. Those religious thoughts in turn strengthen this basic religious commitment and sense of relationship to God. For this to work, it is essential that the religious thoughts that people express really do articulate their basic religious felt meanings. Otherwise a disconnection would develop between the two subsystems in which there was no effective interrelationship between them.

Though most religions seem to be primarily implicational, that sometimes switches round. In fundamentalist religion, for example, the essence of religion is held to be what is explicitly affirmed at the propositional level. The focal, often literal, meanings of the propositional subsystem are then emphasized, rather than the more schematic meanings of the implicational subsystem.

The Mystical Mind

Any comprehensive cognitive-neuropsychological theory of religion would necessarily be very speculative. The most thorough attempt at such a theory so far is that of d'Aquili and Newberg (1999) in *The Mystical Mind*. One strength is that it sees religion as arising from normal cognitive and neural processes; most people would agree that is the right assumption to make. Consistent with that, it builds on a theory of religious cognition that is framed in terms of general-purpose "cognitive operators." Again, that seems the right kind of move. The problem is that this model of the mind in terms of cognitive operators has not been applied to anything else apart from religion and has not won any widespread acceptance in cognitive psychology. In that it differs from ICS, which has been applied to a range of psychological phenomena and won a measure of general acceptance in the scientific community.

Of the range of operators that d'Aquili and Newberg propose, they think that two are important in religion. Both are also involved in everyday cognition. One is the holistic operator that, in everyday mode, integrates perceptual experience but can also go into overdrive and produce a sense of absolute unity. Also relevant to religion is the causal operator that, in everyday mode, generates causal interpretations of events but which, in religious mode, can give rise to a sense of divine action.

D'Aquili and Newberg are especially interested in the neuropsychological basis of mystical experience and suggest that the autonomic nervous system plays an important role in that. The autonomic nervous system has two distinct components, both of which can lead to mystical experience by different routes. The trophotropic system can lead to mystical experience via meditation; equally, the ergotrophic system can lead to mystical experience through arousing activities such as chanting or dancing. D'Aquili and Newberg make the interesting point that though these two systems normally inhibit each other, in exceptional conditions one can "spill over" into the other, resulting in both being activated at the same time, leading to mystical experiences of unusual intensity.

D'Aquili and Newberg have put forward an interesting neurological theory about how religious practices that are ostensibly different, some involving unusually high arousal, others unusually low arousal, can result in somewhat similar religious experiences. The initial route may be different, but their suggestion is that religious practices that are overtly different may converge on a common neurological pathway. They offer quite detailed proposals about the neural basis of these various processes and recognize how different areas of the brain can be involved in different ways in giving rise to mystical experience. Their theory is much more sophisticated than a simple proposal that there is a God spot in the brain. It may be somewhat premature as a theoretical synthesis, but it is a bold attempt at sketching out the right kind of theory.

Summary

- The exploration of neural mechanisms involved in religion has repeatedly led to the reductionist idea that religion is nothing more than a spin-off of neural activity. However, scientific research on the neural basis of religion has no means of confirming or denying that.
- In recent years, a series of brain-scanning studies has looked at which parts of the brain are involved in various religious activities or tasks. However, for various reasons, these have not yielded any strong

conclusions. Studies have also looked at religious functioning in neuro-logical patients, in which the most striking phenomenon is that patients with temporal lobe epilepsy often have ecstatic quasi-religious experi-ences, though such patients are not particularly religious in a more general sense.

- There has been interest in finding a single God spot in the brain. However, no single area of the brain is involved in religion. Religion is itself so broad and varied that various areas of the brain will inevi-tably make different contributions. For example, the left and right hemispheres are involved in different ways, as are the frontal and temporal lobes.

- There is a parallel exploration of how different aspects of the cognitive architecture are involved in religion. Many theorists distinguish between two central systems. Though terminology varies, one is more intuitive and experiential; the other is more analytical and articulate. Both are involved in religion in different ways.

5

Religious Experience

So far we have been considering religion in very general terms. Now we will redress the balance and get down to looking at the different facets of religion, one by one. A series of scholars have set out slightly different lists of the various facets of religion, but I will work here with the fairly simple one set out in Chapter 1. So, the next three chapters will look in turn at religious experience, practices, and beliefs, starting in this chapter with religious experience.

William James

We will start this chapter historically, looking once again at William James's *Varieties of Religious Experience* (James, 2012/1902). It has undoubtedly been a successful book, probably both James's most widely read book, and the most widely read book in the psychology of religion. Despite that, it has always been controversial and much criticized.

James had an ambivalent attitude to religion, being generally sympathetic to it and certainly respectful of it, but he was not a regular church-attender or able to make full creedal assent. His book is, on the face of it, a scientific *study* of religion, but James perhaps hoped that it would also be a scientific *defense* of religion. He remarked that writing the book was in itself a religious act.

The first chapter, as we have already seen, is a rebuttal of materialism and "nothing but" reductionism. In the next chapter, "Circumscription of the Topic," James sets out his program. It is notable that he proposes to focus on religious experience, apparently regarding it as foundational to all other aspects of religion (sociocultural, cognitive-credal, etc.). It is a later flowering of the new turn in theology initiated by Schleiermacher (1958/1799), which focused on the feeling of absolute dependence and grounded other aspects of religion in experience. In emphasizing experience, James is probably focusing on the aspect of religion most congenial to him. It also enables him to emphasize religious universalism, which was also clearly attractive to him.

The emphasis on experience is given an extra twist by James's individualism, which, he says, is founded on feeling. That emphasis on individualism is reflected in his definition of religion as "the feelings, acts, and experiences of individual men in their solitude, so far as they apprehend themselves to stand in relation to whatever they may consider the divine" (p. 31). Some critics, such as Nicholas Lash, seem to want to invert this individualism and make society primary (Lash, 1988), but I see no need to invoke primacy at all. There is probably more interplay between individual and society than James (or, in a different way, Lash) recognizes.

James's respectful attitude to religious experience is grounded in his proposal that it is "pure" (i.e., unmediated). That helps him claim that it should be accepted at face value, and that it is the universal core of all religions. However, it is doubtful whether any experience, religious or otherwise, can be quite as decontextualized as James suggests religious experience is. It is also a surprising view for James to take, given his general stance on psychological questions of cognition.

Note that James studiously avoids the word "God" with his phrase "whatever they may consider the divine." Unpacking that, he recognizes that it could lead to a broad definition of religious experience. However, he then backtracks and recognizes that such a broad definition would be "inconvenient," and he urges us to recall the usual associations of religion and suggests that there "must be something solemn, serious and tender" about the religious attitude.

The empirical part of *Varieties* largely draws on autobiographical accounts. The data is rich, but questions have been asked about how representative it is. James would not have claimed that it was representative, but he would have defended it as a set of "pure" examples of what he wanted to study. Though parts of *Varieties* can seem like a mere anthology, James is active in selecting, organizing, and commenting on the material.

Some parts of *Varieties* have stood the test of time better than others. One section of enduring interest is that on mystical experience, where he identifies four hallmarks: ineffability, noetic quality, transiency, and passivity. The first two are the most interesting, and there is a paradox that any experience could be both ineffable and noetic. Can we truly be said to have gained knowledge (*noetic*) if we cannot articulate what we know (*ineffable*)? James ducks the question of whether there is real knowledge, being content to claim only that it feels as though there is. He also ducks the question of the validity of mystical experience, accepting the authority of mystical experiences for those who have them (a very modest claim), but he does not think others are obliged to accept them.

James can be criticized on philosophical and theological grounds. The most trenchant and extended theological critique is from Nicholas Lash in *Easter in Ordinary* (Lash, 1988). Lash criticizes various aspects of James's individualism, including (i) his oversharp distinction between thinking and feeling and prioritization of the latter, (ii) his prioritization of experience in religion, (iii) his concept of "pure" experience, and (iv) his individualism and oversharp contrast between religious innovators and followers. It is an important question whether James's position could be phrased more carefully to withstand some of this critique. I suggest that it probably could.

Why is James's *Varieties* still so much discussed? It is partly because it is a fascinating and well-written book, and almost the only classic in the psychology of religion. It is also because James articulates a position that is close to the popular contemporary one of spirituality without religion, and he may have been one of the sources of that position. That helps explain why he both remains so popular and attracts so much fierce repudiation.

Conceptual Issues and Two-Factor Theory

The topic of religious experience is beset with conceptual problems. In this section, I want to address some sharp debates about what we mean, or ought to mean, by "religious experience." It is a debate that raises a lot of ideological issues. Indeed, the topic of religious experience can be a battleground for conflicting ideologies.

I propose to intertwine a discussion of these debates with a discussion of a two-factor theory of religious experience, which I suggest points the way to finding a place for different points of view, and integrating them in an overarching framework. Two-factor theory has long been a feature of psychological theories of emotion, as Wayne Proudfoot (1987) discusses.

Two-factor theory of religious experience emphasizes the distinction between its powerful and distinctive phenomenological quality and its distinctive religious framework. There can be sharp debate between those who think that religious experience is essentially characterized by its phenomenology and others who emphasize that the crucial requirement for an experience to be deemed to be religious is just that it is interpreted with reference to a framework of religious belief. If it helps to give labels to the two sides, we can call those who emphasize the quality of the experience, such as William James (2012/1902) and Robert Forman (1990), the perennialists, and those who emphasize the interpretative framework, such as Wayne Proudfoot (1987) and Steven Katz (1978), the constructivists.

Rather than taking one side or the other in this debate, I want to suggest, within the framework of two-factor theory, that both sides have a point. I suggest that the two sides in this debate about what should be regarded as a religious experience are both emphasizing just one facet of something that, by its very nature, has two facets. My conclusion is that core examples of religious experience meet both criteria; they should have both a distinctive experiential or phenomenological character and a religious interpretative framework, but that borderline cases meet one criterion but not the other.

The distinction between these two processes, one phenomenological and one interpretative, emerges, for example, in analyses of the Mysticism Scale developed by Ralph Hood and his colleagues (Hood at al., 2009, chap. 9). Some of the terms that are used to describe mystical experience are rather general; they focus, for example, on a general experience of unity (whether that is "introvertive," focusing on inner experience, or "extrovertive," looking outward at nature). Other ways of describing mystical experience implicitly make use of specific religious knowledge claims. The two sets of descriptors were found, empirically, to fall into different factors or clusters.

Some experiences have no special phenomenological characteristics but are interpreted in religious terms. A religious framework can be applied to any everyday experience, as is illustrated by ancient Celtic prayers from the Scottish Highlands about milking cows and lighting fires. Some experiences have the phenomenological characteristics of religious experience, such as the unity of all things, but lack an explicitly religious interpretive framework. Atheists can have a kind of religious experience of that kind.

This links into another debate, about whether or not religious experiences are the same across different traditions. Those who emphasize the interpretative framework, like Steven Katz (1978), naturally want to emphasize the differences between different traditions. Those like William James and Robert Forman, who emphasize phenomenological quality, naturally want to emphasize the commonalities. Again, I think both have a point, and that there are both similarities and differences. If you work with a two-factor theory, you will find more commonalities between religions concerning the phenomenological factor, and more differences between them concerning the interpretative factor.

Yet another debate is about whether religious experiences are fundamental in religion, as William James thought. That is a key reason why he focused on religious experience in his classic book on *Varieties of Religious Experience*. For James, religious systems of belief and church organizations were secondary to actual religious experience. Others have disagreed and have emphasized that everyone who has ever had a religious experience has been part of a cultural tradition that has shaped that experience. Jesus, for example, may have been a religious innovator whose experiences have shaped doctrines and religious organization for two millennia, but he was himself part of a Jewish cultural tradition. For example, he apparently used the Psalms to help him interpret key experiences (of baptism and crucifixion, etc.)

Again, I suggest that it depends partly on which factor you are mainly concerned with a two-factor theory of religious experience. But also, I suggest that it is important to recognize that there is a to-and-fro between culture and personal experience, in which each shapes the other, but neither is absolutely primary. I think that William James was wrong to imply that religious experiences came from nowhere, as Nicholas Lash and others have pointed out. But neither do I see any justification for going to the other extreme and implying that religious experiences are wholly determined by culture.

Yet another related question is whether religious experiences are pure, direct, and unmediated, as William James claimed. It is not entirely clear what James meant by this, though there have frequently been claims that in mystical experiences the veil of the senses is lifted, and people see things as they really are. For constructivists such as Wayne Proudfoot, this claim could not possibly be correct. He suggests that it is just a way of talking that people learn from the gurus who train them in spiritual practices. It does indeed run counter to most basic assumptions of cognitive psychology, and to postmodern philosophy, to suggest that there are any *pure* experiences.

Despite all this, I am reluctant to dismiss entirely the claim that religious experiences are direct experiences in some unusual way, though I do think it can only be entertained seriously in a soft or reduced form. It is conceivable that in certain kinds of religious experience, people can stand back to some extent from their usual patterns of construction and look at things with fresh eyes. If there is any possibility of doing that, it may not be unique to religion. Some artists may do something similar. It is also worth noting that within cognitive psychology, constructivist assumptions have not been universally accepted. The theories of James Gibson about direct recognition of features of the visual environment (Gibson, 1979) provide an alternative to constructivism and have continued to arouse interest over the past fifty years or more and are currently having yet another comeback in the context of the present wave of interest in the embodied nature of cognition.

An interesting piece of research by Arthur Deikman (1990) bears on this question of direct religious experience. He took the simple step of putting students in a bare room with just a blue vase. They were asked to avoid discursive thought and just focus on the vase "as it exists in itself." Such instructions are similar to those given to people learning to meditate. The participants in this study reported some striking experiences, such as the shape becoming unstable and the colors more intense, vivid, and luminous. People felt that sometimes they were merging with the vase or that the vase was radiating heat toward them. Time passed quickly. Many of the experiences were paradoxical, leading to difficulties in reporting them. For example, they might say that the vase did, but also did not, fill the visual field.

Deikman claimed that these experiences were similar to those reported in *The Cloud of Unknowing*, a classic, anonymous, mystical text of the late Middle Ages. That claim may be an exaggeration, but it is still striking that the combination of a simple visual environment and fairly basic instructions was sufficient to induce an unusual perceptual style that yielded experiences somewhat similar to those found in mystical experience.

Two-factor theory also makes sense of the "ineffability" that has often been said to characterize religious experience. As we have noted, people have experiences that they feel convey knowledge, but this knowledge remains ineffable. Ineffability is a mystical phenomenon that is readily interpreted in terms of the Interacting Cognitive Subsystems framework that we introduced in the last chapter. People have powerful mystical experiences that they claim they cannot articulate. These are presumably implicational-level experiences that are peculiarly difficult to translate into the different code of the propositional system, which would be necessary for articulation. Despite the claim of ineffability, mystical experiences often are articulated; mystics write lengthy books. So the re-encoding seems not to be absolutely impossible. However, there is often a strong sense that much of the original experience is lost in the process of translation into a code that makes articulation possible.

Survey Research

A number of surveys of spontaneously occurring religious experiences have been carried out. In the UK, the most important is that of David Hay (Hay, 1982). Clearly one key matter is how the lead question is framed about whether or not people have had a religious experience. Most researchers have, understandably, wanted to cast their net quite broadly. For example, David Hay asked people, "Have you ever been aware of, or influenced by, a presence or power, whether you call it God or not, which is different from your everyday self?" (p. 113). This is a broad definition. Hay found that 36 percent of people answered "Yes."

It is interesting that the percentage of people reporting religious experiences seems to be similar in studies carried out in the UK and the United States, despite the fact that the two countries have different levels of religious attendance. One typical U.S. question is the one that Andrew Greeley used in a survey of the National Opinion Research Center: "Have you ever had the feeling of being close to a powerful spiritual force that seemed to lift you out of yourself?" (Greeley, 1974). David Hay had administered the same question to a similar sample in the UK. Almost identical proportions of people answered "Yes" in the two cultures, 35 percent in the United States and 36 percent in the UK (Hay and Morisy, 1978). This supports the view that there is less cross-cultural variation in the frequency with which mystical or religious experience is reported than in other more external aspects of religion.

It would be interesting to extend such surveys to other cultures, such as the strikingly nonreligious countries of Scandinavia. However, from the data we have, it seems reasonable to suggest that the rate of spontaneous religious experience is relatively invariant across cultures, even with notable disparities in church attendance. Thus, some aspects of religion seem to show more cultural variation than others. Those that show little cultural variation seem likely to be more influenced by neural predisposition. Others that show more cultural variation will depend more on cultural influence. Once again, we seem to be brought back to some kind of two-factor theory.

In Hay's survey, many people (50 percent) were distressed at the time they had their religious experience, but the majority were at peace afterward. Though many of these experiences were very brief, they often had a dramatic effect on mood-state and well-being, and people remembered them for the rest of their lives. This rather sets them apart from the temporal lobe seizures discussed in the last chapter. Though there are similarities between the two kinds of experiences, temporal lobe experiences are more likely to be disturbing and are less memorable.

Another interesting fact is that people are often alone when they have religious experiences, though that is, of course, compatible with such experiences being strongly shaped by broad cultural background; 66 percent were completely alone when they had their religious experience (Hay and Morisy, 1978). It is also interesting that many never spoke to anyone about it, apparently feeling they would not be properly understood.

The proportion of people reporting religious experiences depends on various factors such as age, sex, education, social class, and so on. They show some relationship to religious belief, though it is striking that 24 percent of atheists and agnostics in Hay's survey say that they have had a religious experience. It seems not to be uncommon for atheists to have religious experience, and some have been left puzzled about how to interpret their experiences. The prominent atheist philosopher A. J. Ayer had a near-death experience that seems to have weakened his commitment to atheism and left him more open-minded about an afterlife (Ayer, 1988). However, it is notable that this did not lead him to embrace religion, or belief in a personal God.

Finding the spiritual side of life important is even more closely related than religious belief to having a religious experience; 74 percent of people who said the spiritual side of life was very important said they had had a religious experience, compared to only 11 percent of those who said it was unimportant. If we make a distinction between religious beliefs and a more general spiritual worldview, the latter seems to be significantly more closely related to the likelihood of having a religious experience.

Predisposition to Religious Experience

I want now to focus on predisposition to religious experience. It is a topic that seems to be of considerable importance in the psychology of religion, but which has not yet received the attention it deserves.

The basic idea I want to propose here can be simply stated, though it is in two parts. First, I suggest that there is a personality trait that makes people more likely to have certain kinds of religious experience (though the trait is probably of broader psychological significance and has implications that go beyond the confines of religion). Second, I suggest that certain religious practices develop this aspect of human personality, making religious experiences more likely.

That can lead to a positive feedback loop. Aspects of personality predispose people to religious experience. In turn, religious practices further strengthen that predisposition, so making religious experiences even more likely. If there is any truth in this theory, it is clearly of considerable importance for understanding the dynamics of religion. Interestingly, this dynamic may be a feature of rather different kinds of religion. To explore this further, we will look at relevant research, first on New Age religion, and then on evangelical Christianity.

One complication is that it is not yet clear how best to label, conceptualize, or measure this predisposing trait. Miguel Farias conducted a series of studies of New Age beliefs (see Farias and Granquist, 2007) and found that they were associated with magical thinking, schizotypal personality, and thin boundaries of the conscious mind. These have in turn been variously found to be associated with transliminality – relatively free access of ideas and emotions into consciousness (Thalbourne and Delin, 1999).

The fact that schizotypy is correlated with both psychosis and spirituality raises the interesting question of the relationship between the two (Clarke, 2010). Some see schizotypy as subclinical illness; others see it as a healthy personality trait that carries a higher than normal risk of psychosis. It may be that the same trait of schizotypy can lead in healthy form to spirituality, and in unhealthy form to psychosis. Some evidence indicates that spiritual practice can contribute to a healthy manifestation of schizotypy and can also lead people to regard mystical experience in a positive light (e.g., Hood et al., 2009, pp. 371–72).

In other studies (also reported by Farias and Granquist, 2007), New Age was found to be associated with "absorption," that is, the capacity to be totally focused on a single experience, whether within oneself or outside, and the capacity to exercise imagination, for example, to "see" things that are not physically present. It seems to be highly correlated with the other measures found to be associated with New Age, and also with traits such as hypnotizability and suggestibility.

Absorption was also the focus of Tania Luhrmann's research on evangelical Christians (Luhrmann, 2012). She found that absorption was not related to how much people engaged in prayer, but that it was related to prayer experience (a distinction that seems potentially important in the psychology of religion). High scores on the absorption questionnaire were related to people going to a "different place in their mind" when they prayed. It also related to whether they experienced God through their senses, and as a person, when they prayed. What makes that especially interesting is that almost nothing explicitly about religion appears in the absorption questionnaire. Luhrmann suggests that it reflects how people use their minds when they pray, something that some people are better able to do than others.

Absorption as a fixed personality trait is widely assumed, but Luhrmann makes the interesting suggestion that it can be trained, and she set up an experimental study involving spiritual exercises to test that. One key question that she asked participants was about "sensory over-ride" experiences, for example, whether they had heard an audible voice when no one was present. People who scored high on absorption were more likely to say they had. Moreover, the number of people reporting such experiences increased as a result of spiritual training. That seemed to be true for different kinds of spiritual training, both imaginative exercises involving Bible stories and a form of mediation involving focusing on a single word. It seems likely that both evangelical and New Age spiritual experiences work best in people who are naturally high on absorption, and that they both further enhance the likelihood that people will have powerful experiences that are interpreted in spiritual terms.

Another interesting thing about this personality trait (whether it is best called absorption, thin boundaries, transliminality, or whatever) is that there are indications that it has a clear neuropsychological basis and a genetic predisposition (see again Farias and Granquist, 2007), though further research is needed to clarify the details. As was suggested in Chapter 2, it may be more fruitful, rather than looking for the biological basis of religion in general, to look for the biological basis of aspects of personality traits that feed into different aspects of religion but have a broader reach.

Meditation vs. Spontaneous Experiences

There is no general category of "religious experience"; the events that pass under that label are actually quite varied. I particularly want to emphasize that religious experiences that occur spontaneously are very different from those that arise as a result of religious practices such as meditation. It often seems to be assumed that the two are essentially similar (or at least the distinction between them is not made as often as one might expect). In fact, the two kinds of experiences seem to be different in many ways.

For one thing, spontaneous experiences are less common, but more powerful.

Of course, the concept of "spontaneous" religious experience needs some comment. It is unlikely that such experiences occur randomly. Indeed David Hay's survey data shows that such experiences are most likely to occur when people are distressed. All that is really meant by saying they are spontaneous is that they are not sought, or induced, by any religious practice, and that they often take people by surprise. It seems quite likely that a series of background factors lead up to such experiences of which the person concerned is unaware.

Before emotion became a subject for scientific theory and research in the latter part of the nineteenth century, a distinction had been made between "passions" and "affections" (Dixon, 2006). Jonathan Edward's classic *Treatise on Religious Affections* (Edwards, 1959/1746) was the most significant contribution to this prescientific, religious understanding of such feelings. One notable point is that affections, unlike passions, are not contrasted with reason and intellect but are integrated with them. In terms of this distinction, spontaneous religious experience seems in some ways to be more like passions. The gentler religious states produced by religious practices seem more like affections.

There can be dissociation between ecstatic religious experiences and other gentler, more reflective religious experiences. For example, there is no reason to think that people with temporal lobe epilepsy who have ecstatic religious experiences will also necessarily have increased religious affections. These are clearly two different aspects of religious experience, and the neural basis of the two will be different. Ecstatic experiences seem to be associated with activity in a specific area of the temporal lobes. Religious affections, in contrast, seem likely to have a more diffuse neurological substrate.

Another important issue that arises from the distinction between religious experiences arising spontaneously and as a result of religious practices is that the former lend themselves more readily to interpretations in terms of social construction. Spontaneous experiences occur to a wide range of people, some of whom find them unexpected, and who are not part of a social community with an established pattern of interpreting such experiences. Of course, everyone is part of a culture that has a discourse about religious experiences. However, some people experiencing spontaneous religious experiences have little contact with that discourse and may explicitly reject it.

The situation is different with practices such as meditation that are designed to lead to religious experience. That usually involves considerable exposure to a trainer, who both gives instruction in the relevant religious practices and also talks extensively about what people can expect to experience. In that situation, the scope is broader for what people say about their religious experiences to reflect the instruction they have received. We will look at research on meditation in Chapter 8 on spirituality.

Summary

- William James's *Varieties of Religious Experience* is the leading classic text in the psychology of religion and has been influential. Nevertheless, most people have found his position unconvincing on key points. He exaggerates the extent to which religious experience is unmediated and overlooks the extent to which it is shaped by culture and tradition.
- Much controversy surrounds how religious experience should be defined, with some emphasizing its distinctive experiential quality and others emphasizing the religious interpretative framework. These different perspectives fall into place within a two-factor theory of religious experience, analogous to two-factor theory of emotion, with phenomenological and interpretative factors.
- Survey research indicates that about one-third of the population reports religious or spiritual experiences, defined in broad terms. The rate of occurrence seems not to reflect cultural differences in religious participation. Transliminality, a propensity to expanded boundaries of consciousness, may be a factor in predisposing people to religious experience. Spontaneous religious experiences differ in many ways from those arising from meditation.

6

Religious Practices

In this chapter, I turn from religious experience to religious practice. Some religious practices are collective and institutional; others are private. I will first examine that distinction and then look in detail at a sample of specific religious practices.

Public and Private Religious Practices

Most religious people engage in private religious practices such as individual prayer; they also attend public places of prayer or worship. The social science literature has often made this distinction between public and private religion. Grace Davie (2015) distinguished between religious "belonging" and "believing," with believing a more private matter than belonging to the structures of institutional religion.

Of course, some people practice religion just privately, and others just publicly. However, the norm is probably for people to do both, and for each to influence the other. A slight cultural shift may have taken place in recent decades toward private spiritual practices such as meditation, as well as a shift in the balance between public and private religion over the life-span. Impairments may affect some aspects of religion more than others. For example, if elderly people begin to suffer cognitive impairment, engagement in public religion might be sustained better than private spirituality.

I want to resist the idea that either public or private religion is foundational to the other, and take a systemic view. Certainly, private religion occurs in social, cultural, and linguistic contexts, as any sociologist would want to emphasize. However, I suggest the collective manifestations of religion are equally influenced by the personal religion of particular individuals, and that a systemic interrelationship normally occurs between public and private religion.

On the face of things, the distinction between public and private aspects of religious practices seems clear enough. However, the distinction may not actually be as clear-cut as at first appears. Much religious life is neither clearly in public institutions nor completely private. For example, it is an interesting feature of how religious life has developed in recent decades that many more small groups now meet in private houses for religious purposes. Some small groups meet for silent meditation rather than conversation or spoken prayer. Sometimes two religious people meet as prayer partners or soul friends. It is not clear whether such religious activities should be classified as public or private.

Also, some religious practices may be carried out entirely privately, but as a result of encouragement by a religious leader or community. People may say a particular prayer at a particular time because they are conscious that many others are saying the same prayer at that time. Much apparently private religious practice may in this sense be socially embedded. This fits well with the increasing recognition that human cognition is affected by humans being both embodied and social embedded, a perspective that is now being applied to religion (Watts, 2013b).

One of the most basic aspects of religious practice is attendance at church or other formal religious ceremonies. However, it is not the most interesting from a psychological point of view, and I will concentrate here on a sample of more specific religious practices of greater psychological interest: prayer, ritualistic worship, confession and forgiveness, speaking in tongues, spiritual healing, and serpent handling.

Prayer

The psychology or prayer can be taken either in a reductionist or a non-reductionist way. Some might see the benefits of prayer as entirely explicable in psychological terms. However, the psychological study of prayer does not have to make that assumption. It is also possible to assume that people are connecting in prayer with a God, and to see psychology as explicating, at a human level, how the God-given benefits of prayer are mediated. I suggest that the psychology of prayer is neutral on the issue of whether or not a transcendent God is involved.

I am considering prayer in this chapter as it is a religious practice. However, one can distinguish between the practice of prayer, experiences during prayer, and beliefs about prayer. These may have different psychological significance and correlates. The distinction between the practice and experience of prayer may be quite important, one belonging more to external religion (albeit done largely in private), and the other to internal religion.

"Prayer" is an umbrella term for a varied group of activities. Poloma and Gallup (1991), in their large-scale survey research, identified four types of prayer: meditative, ritualistic, petitionary, and colloquial. It seems a clear and helpful taxonomy. Some religious people engage in all four. However, complex cultural shifts are probably going on in the predominant mode of prayer. In evangelical religion, colloquial prayer probably still has priority, but those who are more spiritual than religious show a strong movement toward meditative prayer.

Another helpful approach to the classification of prayer comes from the work of Kevin Ladd (summarized by Spilka and Ladd, 2012, which also provides a helpful summary of much empirical research on prayer). Ladd has developed the distinction between upward, inward, and outward types of prayer and provided scales for measuring them. These three types of prayer seem to involve different psychological processes. Inward prayer involves a particular kind of self-exploration, whereas the other two involve reaching out. Outward prayer involves focusing attention on other people and is closely linked with the development of compassion. Upward prayer is another kind of relational prayer, the capacity for which is probably derived from reaching out to other people, but one that fosters wonder and reverence rather than compassion.

Another well-established classification of prayer in the religious literature distinguishes adoration, confession, thanksgiving, and supplication. Each of those aspects of prayer invites a different psychological explication (Watts, 2001a). For example, the psychological processes involved in thanksgiving can be considered from the perspective of the psychology of attributions, something to which we will return in the next chapter. Thanksgiving can also be seen as an exercise in fostering gratitude. Parallel exercises in developing gratitude can be developed in a secular context, without any specific religious framework and have been shown to have beneficial effects (Emmons and McCulloch, 2003).

Petition raises interesting issues about what to ask for (Watts, 2001a). People probably have a complex hierarchy of desires from which they can select. At one extreme, they ask for what they most want, regardless of any sense of the purposes of God. At the other, they can ask for what they believe they should ask for, even if there is little actual desire for it.

The psychological value of petition may lie partly in the transformation of desire; it may be analogous to the exploration of desires in psychotherapy. Petition can also be useful in focusing on change. Asking God for something also seems to require taking appropriate action oneself. Other forms of prayer have their main psychological value in combating egocentricity. Both intercession and worship can do that.

Most of these forms of prayer seem to contribute to coping, and to facilitate adjustment (see Hood et al., 2009, pp. 465–69). Each has a particular place in relation to the sequence of significant events. The one form of prayer that may not contribute much to coping is ritualistic prayer. However, that may depend on whether people use it as their sole form of prayer or in conjunction with other forms.

Psychology can illuminate how prayer benefits the person who prays. For example, much prayer involves reflection on the past. Any "working through" of stressful events can be beneficial and enables people to relate events to a broad framework of meaning. Ann and Barry Ulanov have developed an interesting theory of prayer as "primary speech" (Ulanov and Ulanov, 1982). They suggest that prayer involves an inner speech that is honest and unedited, in which people are just themselves. I am not sure how often prayer actually involves that kind of primary speech but, when it does so, it is a plausible hypothesis that it contributes to personal transformation.

One crucial thing about prayer is that it brings such primary speech into a broader context. Prayer can bring personal primary speech into dialogue with the explicit thought-world of theology, so that there can be a to-and-fro between them. In terms of the Interacting Cognitive Subsystems model developed in Chapter 4, it brings primary, "implicational" speech into dialogue with secondary, theological thought. It also does this in a relational context, or at least in the felt context of relationship with a loving but all-seeing God, with whom there is probably an attachment relationship (see Chapter 8). Attending to inner speech in the context of the helpful distancing that comes from a God's-eye perspective may have particular benefits, for example, in processing difficult experiences.

In psychotherapy, people engage in self-exploration in the context of a relationship with the therapist. Something similar can happen in prayer, where people review their lives, concerns, and feelings about themselves in the felt presence of God. It seems likely that where the relational context in which prayer is undertaken is real and immediate, the benefits of prayer will be greater. The felt relational context makes prayer more distinct from any other kind of personal reflection. Certainly, the analogy between prayer and psychotherapy seems worth pursuing.

Ritual and Worship

We now turn from the private world of prayer to the public world of religious ritual. Rituals do not occur exclusively in religious settings. Many other areas of life, such as courts of law, have their own rituals, but rituals seem to play a particularly important role in religion. Some Christian worship is more obviously ritualistic than others, though in a broad sense all forms of worship have their rituals.

Rituals involve an unusual and distinctive sense of time and space. A sacred space needs to be created in which the ritual can take place. Rituals also involve a sense of connecting with the timeless, or at least with long-established tradition. At best, the ritual becomes a "flow" experience, involving rapt concentration, and little awareness of the passage of time. Though rituals occur in a particular time and place, there is characteristically a sense of connecting with something that transcends that particularity or a sense that the divine is breaking into the ordinary time and space of the created order and human experience, and transforming it. That sense, which ritual fosters, helps explain why rituals are particularly important in religion.

Part of the value of religious rituals is that they foster personal transformation, and that is seen most clearly in pastoral rituals such as funeral services. Various religious resources are brought to bear in the process of transformation that can take place in a funeral. If grief is to be worked through, it is important that there should be a framework of meaning that is provided by a religious belief system. That enables the personal bereavement to be reconstrued within a transpersonal framework of meaning. It is also helpful if the funeral occurs in the felt presence of a loving and powerful God who transcends mortality, and in the supportive framework of a religious community.

To be psychologically effective, rituals need to be both engaging and transformative. Failures of the ritual process can occur at either stage. If they fail to engage, they can become empty and be what Erikson calls "ritual excess," where the ritual has no resonance and serves no function for people (Erikson, 1977). Ritual can also fail to contain the feelings aroused or to provide the resources for their transformation. To be psychologically effective, rituals should not be too transparent. They need to employ symbols that are not easily exhausted and have enough depth to be able to point beyond themselves. On the one hand, rituals that are too fixed may not engage people adequately and can become empty. On the other hand, if there is too little structure and resonance in the ritual, it may be too banal to have any powerful psychological impact.

Different areas of psychology can be brought to bear in understanding ritual. For example, there is a developmental perspective; Erik Erikson suggests that rituals originate in the earliest phase of infancy, when mother and baby gaze at each other. There is a neuropsychological perspective; for example, Eugene d'Aquili has considered how the rhythmic and repetitive aspects of rituals affect cortical arousal and contribute to altered states of consciousness (d'Aquili and Newberg, 1999). There is also a social perspective; for example, a funeral is a social process that marks the end of one pattern of relationships associated with the deceased and marks the beginning of a new pattern. The changes in relationships associated with rites of passage have been formulated in terms of the stages of separation, transition, and reincorporation.

Though the transformative power of rituals is most evident with pastoral ritual, I suggest that almost every religious ceremony has a similar scope for personal transformation. However, in regular church services that is usually less obvious, and less explicitly acknowledged, with the result that those leading church services often pay less attention to their transformative impact. Religious rituals often provide an opportunity for transformation of the sense of self, and in particular for resolution of conflicting positive and negative feelings about the self. For example, the Christian service of Holy Communion has multiple layers of symbolic significance. It can be experienced as taking the participant through a sequence of stages, from an initial sense of unworthiness to eventual union with Christ through the sacrament.

What may seem fairly minor changes in how the service is conducted can make a big difference to how it works at a psychological level. It makes a big difference whether the presiding priest faces the people or faces away from them. The former induces a sense of community in which all individuals can, to some extent, transcend the limitations of individuality as they feel themselves to be part of a community in which God is present. If the priest faces away from the people, there is a stronger sense of leading individual people in relating to a transcendent God. The psychological impact of changes in how rituals are conducted is often not considered as much as it might be.

Despite the potential value of ritual, various concerns have been advanced about it. From a psychological point of view, rituals can become an expression of human obsessionality; it was Freud who first drew attention to the analogy between religion and obsessional neurosis (Freud, 1959), even though he overstated his point. Though there is always a danger of religious rituals becoming over-obsessive, the analogy with obsessional neurosis is not close. For example, it causes great distress to a person with obsessional-compulsive neurosis if his or her ritual is disrupted. That may occasionally be the case with religious rituals, but it is not usually so. Freud seems not to have done any careful research on religious rituals before suggesting this analogy and seems to have been overgeneralizing.

An older anthropological critique of religious ritual is set out in James Frazer's *The Golden Bough* (1980/1890), that it is a survival of a primitive, magical worldview. However, it might be retorted that it is not necessary to accept the modernist rejection of everything that smacks of a prescientific worldview. The key issue is again how people engage in ritual, and whether this is done in a way that is self-aware and mature. A theological concern about ritual would be that the spiritual hunger of humanity is properly for God himself and is not one that ritual alone can satisfy. However, it might be retorted that God can work through human activity and experience. Whether or not that occurs depends, perhaps, on whether the ritual points beyond itself.

Confession and Forgiveness

Confession and forgiveness are religious practices of particular psychological significance. Confession plays an important role in the Christian tradition and occurs in almost every public act of worship, albeit in general form and with no articulation of personal detail. There is also opportunity for personal and private confession. Among those who choose to do that, some do so regularly, while others do so only occasionally and in special circumstances. Some churches, especially the Roman Catholic Church, have encouraged the practice of regular individual confession before a priest. Christians also have a practice of asking forgiveness of one another. Monastic communities, for example, often have a forum such as the "chapter of faults" in which ways in which one person has offended another are brought into the open so that forgiveness can be sought and given. At its best, sacramental confession is a place where guilt or shame can be transformed into an experience of liberation and reconciliation.

In principle, the experience of confession has two aspects. One is identifying and, at least in personal confession, articulating what has been done wrong. The other is being assured of God's forgiveness. Emotionally, these are contrasting experiences. One is likely to increase the sense of guilt; the other is likely to produce a sense of relief. Which of these predominates is likely to depend on the person concerned, and his or mood-state. Good evidence, mainly, though not entirely, from research on depression (e.g., Mayer et al., 1995), shows that people prioritize material that is consonant with their mood-state, and that is likely to apply here too. So, people who are already prone to guilt are more likely to have their sense of guilt exacerbated by making confession, while hearing that they are forgiven would make less impact.

Confession involves both sensitizing people to things that have been done wrong, but it also involves a process of re-framing those things. It is also helpful to make use here of the Freudian distinction between neurotic and realistic guilt. If confession sharpens the sense of realistic guilt, that may be helpful. However, confession does not seek to foster neurotic guilt. Indeed, confession, as its best, may help people make the distinction between neurotic and realistic guilt more clearly.

Identifying things that should be confessed can have a range of psychological consequences. On the positive side, it can provide a helpful context for self-examination and lead to greater self-awareness. Self-examination provides an opportunity for people to identify their causal responsibility, and that can predominate over their sense of self-blame (Watts and Williams, 1988). Religious confession can lead to a sense of guilt, and it might be hypothesized that the dangers of that would be greater with frequent confession. In one study, more spiritual growth occurred after religious confession in the form of a letter written to God than after a nonreligious confessional letter (see Pargament, 2007).

Little psychological research on forgiveness in explicitly religious contexts has been conducted, but much research has been carried out on forgiveness as a therapy that can be applied in secular contexts (e.g., Worthington, 2006). Though this research has mostly not been explicitly religious, it raises questions that are relevant to understanding religious forgiveness. It also illustrates the cross-migration of ideas and practices between religious and secular cultures.

Forgiveness has not proved easy to define, and it is easier to say what it is not than what it is. It can be distinguished from excusing, forgetting, pardoning, reconciliation, and so on. Also, it seems best to define it in terms of what is abandoned when forgiveness takes place, for example, resentment, negative feelings. In other words, unforgiveness is easier to define than forgiveness. Forgiveness is also multi-faceted and, like religion, has cognitive, affective, and behavioral components.

One important strand of psychological work on forgiveness sees it as "re-framing," an approach that is especially associated with the work of Robert Enright (Enright and Fitzgibbons, 2000). It follows in the tradition of Bishop Butler who advocated placing yourself "at a distance" and seeing the wrongdoing as "inadventure or mistake," rather arising from "malice or scorn" (Watts and Gulliford, 2004, pp. 60–62). Enright sees anger as the main obstacle to forgiveness. Enright's approach to forgiveness has several stages: "uncovering" or recognition of wrongdoing, a decision not to pursue retribution or retaliation, an unconditional decision to respond with mercy, and an intention to restore good relations. Though re-framing can be a valuable aspect of forgiveness, it can be seen as an overly intellectual approach that may not adequately reflect the richness of what happens in forgiveness.

Another strand of psychological work on forgiveness, associated with Everett Worthington, formulates what takes place in forgiveness in terms of a five-stage pyramid model (Worthington, 2006). He sees unforgiveness as arising from a process of conditioning, leading either to avoidance of a person who has hurt us or a desire to retaliate. The first stage is to imagine the offender in the context of a supportive environment to achieve de-conditioning. Next, clients are encouraged to empathize with the offender, both cognitively and emotionally. Third, clients are asked to work on humility, by reflecting on times when they have themselves been offenders. Next comes commitment to forgive. Finally, there are techniques for holding on to forgiveness when unforgiveness begins to reassert itself.

Some theologians such as Gregory Jones have been sharply critical of "therapeutic" forgiveness (Jones, 1995). Several issues are raised here, such as whether forgiveness can properly be taken out of religious context, whether the secular approach can wholly replace the religious one, and whether the secular approach presents forgiveness as being more cheap and easy than it really is. However, even if the psychological approach is currently somewhat limited, that may not be a necessary limitation of the approach, but something that could be rectified.

Though the traditional religious approach to forgiveness and recent work on psychological forgiveness have much in common, there are interesting differences of emphasis (Watts and Gulliford, 2004, chap. 4). The religious approach tends to emphasize the ethical context of forgiveness, whereas the psychological approaches tend to neglect it. In the religious world, forgiveness is seen primarily as a grace received and passed on, whereas psychology tends to emphasize that it is an initiative that is taken by the person concerned. That means that the religious approach is more likely to focus on receiving forgiveness, not just extending it to others. Views can also differ about whether forgiveness should be conditional or unconditional; divine forgiveness is sometimes assumed to be unconditional, but that may not be possible for human forgiveness.

Psychology has tended to focus on isolated individual acts of forgiveness. In contrast, the religious approach tends to see acts of forgiveness as resulting from the long-term cultivation of a capacity and disposition for forgiveness. For theologians such as Gregory Jones, forgiveness is more a craft or virtue than an isolated act. That raises issues about the personal capacity for forgiveness, a topic that has attracted surprisingly little attention, though psychodynamic psychology has a perspective on it in terms of object relations theory (Watts and Gulliford, 2004, chap. 8). It seems unlikely that people will be able to forgive until they can integrate positive and negative aspects of a situation. There are also different psychological and spiritual levels at which forgiveness can take place. From a religious perspective, the harder forgiveness is for the person concerned, the more spiritual benefits it will confer.

Glossolalia

Among charismatic phenomena, research has focused mainly on glossolalia (e.g., Huber and Huber, 2010). However, similar issues arise with other charismatic phenomena. One key question is whether speaking in tongues defies natural explanation, which is linked with the question of whether, in glossolalia, people are speaking languages that they do not know. The answer is that they are not, at least in the overwhelming majority of cases, though it is hard to completely rule out exceptions. There are several reasons for concluding that glossolalia is not language (Samarin, 1972). It is not normally possible to identify the language spoken. Further, glossolalic speech does not have the syntactical structure of language; it includes too much repetition of sounds, for example. There are also severe constraints on what you can say in glossolalic utterance that do not apply to language.

Research has enabled us to answer a number of other questions about glossolalia (see Maloney and Lovekin, 1985). Are people who speak in tongues unusual? Generally not, at least as far as intelligence, mental health, and suggestibility are concerned. However, personal stress, a life crisis, and ambivalence about relationships may be more relevant. The most important predictors of all are probably religious ones, a desire for a deeper spiritual life, and disillusion with other traditions.

Are people in an unusual state of consciousness when they speak in tongues? One idea is that it is like a trance state (Goodman, 1972), but research does not support that. However, it may be a "dissociated" state of consciousness of some other kind. Others (e.g., Griffith et al., 1980) have speculated that it may be a "regressive" state in which people become more open to unconscious processes. Attitudes to regressive phenomena are mixed; some see them as pathological, though it can also be claimed that the positive personality benefits of glossolalia may flow from its regressive aspects.

It seems likely that the cognitive architecture of the mind is being employed in an unusual way in glossolalia, though one that is not yet fully understood. One indication is that it is associated with increased activation of the right hemisphere of the brain, whereas reading aloud is associated with left brain activation (Philipchalk and Mueller, 2000). People who speak in tongues seem to know the gist of what they are saying (e.g., praising God), but that seems to feed through into an unusual kind of speech, without getting recoded into more definite semantic meanings on the way. In terms of Interacting Cognitive Subsystems, it seems that very general (implicational) meanings get through to speech. In that process, they would normally get propositionalized. However, in glossolalia, the propositional system seems to be virtually switched off. The nearest equivalent seems to be baby talk in which speech sounds lack lexical meanings even though the gist is clear. Experienced glossolalics seems to do that in a largely automatic way, though it takes novice glossolalics some time to learn to do so.

What effects does glossolalia have? Evidence indicates that it is associated with positive personality changes, being more open to feelings, more spontaneous, less depressed and anxious (Huber and Huber, 2010). It also results in less addictive behavior. However, these changes are not specific to glossolalia; they are similar, for example, to those produced by Transcendental Meditation.

Is speaking in tongues the result of social learning? A number of facts fit this idea, and a role theory of glossolalia has been advanced (e.g., Samarin, 1972). People who speak in tongues are often brought to a Pentecostal meeting by friends. There is often encouragement and suggestion about how to do it. People get better at it with practice. However, none of this necessarily implies that people are doing it in a contrived way; all the indications are that most practitioners believe it to be the gift of the Holy Spirit. Speaking in tongues also has social consequences, and it is especially relevant to people's status in a church. There are long-standing trends for people to use revivalist phenomena to enhance their power and standing in the church. St. Paul's first letter to Corinthians suggests that began in New Testament times.

This raises an important question about the relationship between approaches to glossolalia that put the emphasis on the state of the person and those that emphasize the social context. There is an interesting analogy with approaches to hypnotic behavior, which has also been seen both as a changed state of consciousness and in terms of playing a social role. Both explanations may be true, in different cases.

Glossolalia is not all the same, and research on it has been hampered by the lack of a dependable classification or typology. Pattison's distinction between playful and serious glossolalia is an example of the kind of distinction we need (Pattison, 1968). The two have more than only linguistic differences, with playful glossolalia being rhythmic, and having more repetition and laughter. The denominations in which it mainly occurs also differ (playful more in Pentecostal churches, serious more in mainline denominations), and in the types of people involved and how they approach glossolalia.

What are the implications of psychological research for the religious interpretation of glossolalia as the work of the Spirit? Though the research indicates that it is not language, it can still be seen as a kind of Spirit-inspired ecstatic utterance. Whether or not glossolalia is language may be less important theologically than is sometimes thought. If glossolalics were speaking languages that they did not know, it would require a supernaturalist explanation. However, the fact that their utterances cannot be recognized as languages still leaves open the possibility that they are, in some general sense, inspired by the Holy Spirit.

Spiritual Healing

Spiritual healing is another religious practice that raises many interesting issues. Relatively little empirical research from a psychological point of view has been carried out so far, though Watts (2011) has provided a psychological perspective. As with glossolalia, I suggest that looking at healing psychologically can nuance a religious understanding of it, but it does not necessarily lead to the reductionist assumption that healing is to be explained entirely in psychological terms.

The term "spiritual healing" itself raises issues and questions. What exactly is spiritual about it? The meaning of that term that makes the fewest assumptions is simply to take it to refer to healing that comes about through spiritual practice. We have already seen that meditation can have health benefits, and healing that comes about through such practices can be seen in one sense as spiritual healing.

A second meaning of the term would take it to be referring to healing in which spiritual aspects of the person are involved. That would make it comparable to psychosomatic healing, in which a person's psychological processes are thought to bring about healing. Christianity has a tradition of making not just a twofold distinction between body and mind (or soul) but a threefold distinction between body, mind (or soul), and spirit. Note that we are here talking only about a conceptual distinction between different facets of the person. It is not being suggested that these are separate or discrete substances or components. Among modern psychologists, James Hillman (1979) has revived the distinction between soul and spirit. For him, spirit tends to rise above problems, whereas soul tends to go deep. In terms of that distinction, both spirit and soul can contribute to healing, but in different ways.

Third, spiritual healing can be taken to refer to healing that comes about not just through the spiritual aspect of the human person, but through the action of a transcendent Spirit, in Christian terms, through the Holy Spirit, which is what most Christian practitioners of spiritual healing assume.

Healing is a practice that has migrated outside the religious domain and now probably takes place as much in secular settings as religious ones (with what would once have been called New Age healers, though that term is going out of fashion). The two have many similarities, both in how healing is practiced and in the assumptions made, though there are also differences (Bourne and Watts, 2011).

As far as practice is concerned, touch is used in both cases. That tends to be brief in religious healing but more prolonged in secular healing. Secular healers usually place their hands on the place that needs healing; religious healers may do that, but they may also just place hands on the person's head, regardless of where healing is needed. Religious healers would normally use audible words of prayer or invocation; secular healers would normally not speak but use silent "channeling," or music.

With regard to assumptions, most spiritual healers assume that a spiritual source of healing exists beyond themselves, though they conceptualize that differently. Healers in both settings often assume that there is a natural gift for healing, albeit one that can be developed, though in religious circles it is more common to assume that anyone can heal provided God is working through them. In both settings, healing is conceptualized holistically, not just in terms of relief of symptoms; it is often assumed that there needs to be spiritual and personal change for healing to occur.

Religious healers are also quite diverse among themselves. Some focus their healing effort very much on some specific target; others pray for healing in a more general way and leave it open (or to God) what form that healing might take. Some healers expect healing to take place and encourage that expectation in those they are working with; others deliberately refrain from that, while leaving open the possibility that a "miracle" might happen. It is probably the case that evangelical healers are more focused in their efforts and have stronger expectations of success. They would probably see that as reflecting confidence in the power of the Holy Spirit, but it could also be seen as maximizing the contribution of a placebo effect.

It is possible to identify some of the psychological and psychosomatic processes by which healing may be mediated, though, as I have said, that does not preclude transcendent spiritual sources of healing. The relationship between the healer and the person being healed may be important, and it is a reasonable, empirical hypothesis that trust in the healer and a good "therapeutic alliance" will be good predictors of healing benefit.

From a psychodynamic perspective, if the illness represents a hysterical conversion syndrome or a flight into illness, then spiritual healing may work, at least in part, in freeing people from psychologically based illness. The concept of "flight into health" is one that is especially relevant to spiritual healing and may offer at least a partial way of understanding it (Kinsey, 2011). It is significant that psychodynamic theory recognizes that the phenomenon exists at all, that is, that health can come about as a result of some kind of "flight." In terms of Hillman's distinction between soul and spirit, it is probably a spiritual process in the sense of rising above problems rather than going deeply into them. Flight into health has often been regarded with suspicion and has been suspected of being ephemeral, but some softening of that skeptical viewpoint has recently taken place. Maybe at least some examples of flight into health are durable and to be welcomed.

Psychobiological processes will also be involved in spiritual healing. One system that seems likely to be important in mediating healing of conditions such as cancer is the immunological system, as it is capable of regulating cell reproduction. It is also closely linked to mental and emotional states, and presumably to spiritual states too (Boivin and Webb, 2011). Its role in the mediation of spiritual healing deserves more careful exploration. It is also helpful to take an evolutionary perspective on the sense of connectedness that people may experience through spiritual healing, something that is especially mediated through touch, which is an almost universal feature of spiritual healing. The sense of connectedness that is induced by healing could be a powerful mediator of the benefits it confers (Gilbert and Gilbert, 2011).

This all raises the question of how to connect an emerging scientific understanding of spiritual healing with the perspective of religious practitioners. The tendency is to set up science and religion as incompatible alternatives, but that is by no means a necessary approach. As with glossolalia, religious practitioners often want to claim that healing is a miraculous event that defies natural explanation. However, even if the concept of miracle is retained, it does not have to be framed in that way. Richard Swinburne has defined a miracle as "an event of an extraordinary kind, brought about by God, and of religious significance" (Swinburne, 1970, p. 1). That does not rule out understanding the natural processes by which healing is mediated, which can in principle be understood in terms of psychological and scientific theory.

Science is constantly developing. That involves not just the addition of new factual knowledge but also revisions in the range of scientific explanations that are considered admissible. The general story of the development of science since the so-called scientific revolution in the seventeenth century has been one of allowing an ever-broadening range of explanations within what is recognized as science. Some of the more emancipated approaches to be found in radical science may allow us to develop scientific approaches to understanding at least some aspects of spiritual healing (Schlitz, 2011), alongside the contribution of a theological perspective.

Serpent Handling

Finally in this chapter, we will consider the religious practice of serpent handling, found in some conservative churches in the US South. Though the practice is not widespread, I include it here for two reasons. One is that it is intriguing why people should engage in something so dangerous;

understanding that better promises to provide important insights into the religious mind-set. The other is that serpent handling has been well researched (Hood and Williamson, 2008) and indeed is a good methodological example of using qualitative research to understand the religious mind.

Ralph Hood and his colleagues have done a remarkable job of getting inside the mind-set of serpent handlers through many years of close acquaintance with serpent-handling churches in which they have clearly won the confidence of handlers. However, they have allied that with thorough, rigorous analysis of the qualitative material they have obtained. It is research that potentially has implications for understanding a wider range of religious practices.

Following a predetermined schema, they have analyzed both sermons on serpent handling by pastors and material gained through interviews with handlers themselves. From this they identified the key beliefs held by the handlers, including the belief that there is a biblical mandate for handling serpents. The handlers also believed that handling serpents is a mark of power bestowed by God, that handling dangerous serpents without coming to harm is a sign of God's protection, and that it represents confirmation of his blessing.

Serpent handling seems to be an intense religious experience. It begins with a struggle about whether or not to do it, a struggle between obedience to what is believed to be the command of God and fear of the snakes. Framed in that way, it is predictable that obedience will win out, but not without a struggle. A key part of the ideology of handling is that it should only be done when you are obeying God's command to do it. It is that obedience that protects you, and it is thought to be dangerous to handle snakes other than in obedience to God. Many handlers have an intense experience of being anointed with the power of God to handle serpents. Doing something that could lead to death also requires a high level of obedience to what is perceived to be God's command.

Still, the fact remains that handling is dangerous and can lead to death. There seems to be no denial of the danger, and the real possibility of death is never far from the minds of the handlers. However, the possibility of death only serves to heighten the experience. It leads to a more intense concentration and engagement than what occurs with many religious practices. In a sense, the handlers believe that their obedience to God is enabling them to transcend the distinction between life and death, that is, whether they live or die they are being obedient to God and putting their lives in his hands. An intense religious joy seems to come from successful execution of this dangerous practice. Serpent handling offers an intense religious experience of an unusually embodied kind.

Serpent handling becomes, for those who practice it, the preeminent test of obedience to God. It illustrates a tendency in conservative churches to pick on one particular issue or biblical theme that to most people would seem fairly peripheral and to elevate it to being the key test of obedience to the faith. That leads to indirect benefits in the church community, in that handlers are marked as members of a kind of elect, in contrast to those who do not handle serpents. None of that is acknowledged in how serpent handling is presented. There is strict adherence to the official line about its being done solely in obedience to God, and in his power.

Another key question is how to interpret the sense of being anointed with the power of God that typically comes over handlers before they pick up serpents. It is clear that this is usually a powerful experience, and Hood and Williamson cite evidence from neuropsychological research to support that; the experience is not being faked. However, the question remains about whether it is a natural state, comparable to a trance, or whether it arises from supernatural grace. Hood and Williamson reject that dichotomy and see it as a religious state that is naturally induced, but nevertheless genuinely religious.

Theological and Psychological Perspectives

The psychological study of religious practices comes into dialogue with the perspective of religious practitioners. Religious doctrine has its own perspective on what is transacting in the various practices we have considered. I would claim, in each case, that psychology does not contradict this perspective. It can be taken *either* as offering an alternative nonreligious account of what is happening in religious practices *or* as supplementing the perspective of religious practitioners with a complementary psychological account of what is happening at a human level.

However, I would not go so far as to say that there is no cross-talk between the two accounts. Psychology can suggest some revision of the theological account, even if it cannot invalidate it. So, for example, I suggested that if speaking in tongues is being interpreted theologically, it sits better with the psychological perspective to see it as some kind of utterance that arises when people open themselves to a transcendent spirit than to see it as language.

Summary

- The distinction between public and private religious practices is an important one, with private practices more often reflecting strong personal commitment and transformative experience.

- Psychology can shed light on how different kinds of prayer affect the person who prays, though that does not imply that prayer is nothing more than a psychological process. Prayer, like therapy, provides an opportunity for self-reflection in the presence of an attachment relationship.

- Religious rituals also have transformative potential, something seen clearly with funerals. To be effective, they need to hold together emotional engagement with a religious structure and framework of meaning.

- Forgiveness, which has long been central to religion, has recently become a therapy and been the subject of a lively program of research. There are differences of emphasis in religious and psychological approaches, and scope for fruitful interchange between them.

- Glossolalia is the most investigated charismatic phenomenon. It seems not to be language but can still be regarded as having spiritual value. It usually arises in social contexts and reflects social learning. It seems to reflect an unusual cognitive mode of preparation for speech, though it is not a trance state.

- Spiritual healing need not be thought of as miraculous to be seen as of religious value and personal benefit. Various psychodynamic and psychobiological processes can be identified that contribute to its beneficial effects.

- Serpent handling represents an unusually embodied spiritual practice. It arises out of wrestling between danger and a sense of religious obedience. The danger of it contributes to highly focused attention that heightens its spiritual impact.

7

Religious Beliefs and Thinking

Having looked at religious experience and practice, we turn now to religious thinking and belief. It is not an area of the psychology of religion that has been explored systematically, so we will have to draw threads together from various sources.

Belief and Nonbelief

A long-standing tradition in philosophical theology provides rational arguments to support belief in God. The "five ways" set out by Aquinas provide a classic statement of that approach, though it is worth noting that they were intended to provide rational support for faith that people already held, not to provide a path to faith for nonbelievers.

These arguments took a new turn during the Enlightenment when they were brought into conjunction with empirical considerations and were used in a new way to argue for belief in God. That happened both through those such as William Paley who looked for evidence of design in nature and through those such as Friedrich Schleiermacher who looked for a foundation for faith in human feelings. It is not the role of psychology to evaluate the effectiveness of those arguments, though it is perhaps fair comment that they do not have a good track record of convincing those who do not already hold the conclusions to which they are intended to lead.

What is interesting about these arguments from a psychological point of view is that they challenge us to understand better the cognitive processes by which people actually arrive at belief. I suggest that this process is not as compelling as the kind of evidence-based or logical argument that would convince anyone. However, I also suggest that the path to faith is not wholly lacking in rationality, or lacking in an empirical basis. Religious belief is, after all, a matter of faith, but it is nevertheless rationally motivated. I suggest that cognitive psychology may, in principle, be able to tell us more about how the path to religious belief works than a philosophical approach that simply looks at whether the arguments are logically compelling.

There is nothing unique to religion about people holding views or beliefs with some rational basis, but no compelling argument. Indeed, the comment I would make from a psychological perspective is that this is the norm in human cognition, not the exception; it is not specific to religion. The broad conclusion to emerge from decades of research on human reasoning is that people do not run logical arguments through their heads. They operate by heuristics and short cuts that get them to the right conclusions most of the time. The ingenuity of the empirical study of human reasoning has been to use careful investigation of people's mistakes in reasoning to make inferences about what thought processes they are actually using.

It is now increasingly recognized that even scientific research does not use logic to reach conclusions. Over the past half century a new wave of post-positivist philosophy of science has paid closer attention to how scientists actually reason, and it has recognized that science does not make use of strict logic, any more than any other area of human life. This is true of religion too, but, in this, religion follows the general rule, rather than being an exception. Human rationality is pragmatic and embedded in everyday life and does not consist of the application of philosophical logic.

In the strident current debate about the rationality of belief, neither side seems to quite appreciate this point. Humans often do not hold beliefs for which there are compelling arguments. Rather, they operate on the basis of indications or heuristics that steer them one way or another but do not rule beliefs firmly in or out. Once this basic point has been grasped, I think it will be clear that cognitive psychology potentially has quite a lot to contribute to understanding how religious beliefs arise. That is a separate matter from whether they are rationally justified; psychology is concerned with how religious beliefs arise from the kind of thought processes that underpin most human rationality.

One of the positions about religious belief that is currently attracting most attention is atheism. Though it is a too complex a topic to treat fully here, a few basic points are worth noting. One is that atheism has arisen largely in countries that have historically been Christian. Many historians of atheism would argue that it is derived from arguments about God that arose within the Christian tradition (e.g., McGrath, 2004). It is also worth making a clear distinction between atheists and those who hold no religious affiliation ("Nones"). Surveys such as that conducted by the Pew Research Center in 2012 show that the majority of Nones are not atheists. Equally, within churches, there are people who espouse "religious naturalism," or a "non-realist" view of God, that is quite close to the position of atheists about God. Also, atheism is often strangely fundamentalist and quasi-religious about its own position about God.

There are also oddities about arguments for atheism. As many have observed, the God who is rejected by atheists is one that few religious believers would recognize. The standards of evidence that are expected for arguments for the existence of God are set higher than for many other things; it is also not clear that it is any easier to argue conclusively that there is no God than to argue that there is one. Religious phenomena can be explained by psychology without recourse to theism. Some have thought that provides an argument against atheism (e.g., Power, 2012), but at best it surely only shows that theism is unnecessary.

What psychology can contribute is an examination of how and why people reach the conclusion that there is no God. Relevant psychological factors incline people to atheism that can be studied by psychologists of religion, just as psychological factors incline people to believe in God. In neither case does such psychological study validate or invalidate the intellectual arguments. Some of the psychological literature on atheism consists of case studies of particular atheists such as Sigmund Freud (e.g., Rizzuto, 1998). However, there are also studies of atheists as a group. Research is at an early stage, but it seems that atheists may be motivated by a desire to avoid uncertainty and to achieve self-mastery (Farias, 2013).

General vs. Specific Beliefs

Surprisingly little psychological research has studied religious belief itself, in the sense of what religious views people hold. So, in this section, I will not so much try to summarize what we know about it, but to make some theoretical proposals about the structure of religious belief. As always, it helps to propose a theoretically significant distinction between different kinds of belief, and I suggest that it will be fruitful to distinguish between general and specific religious beliefs.

The most general form of religious belief is simply to believe in God. It is this most general belief that has the most adherents. As beliefs get more specific, they are held by fewer people. Fewer people believe in a "personal God" than simply believe in God. For example, the Pew Religious Landscape Survey of 2008 (published online by the Pew Research Center) found that 92 percent of Americans believed in God, but only 60 percent believed in a personal God. Fewer still would say that they believed in specific credal statements such as (in Christianity) the resurrection of Christ or the inerrancy of the Bible. It seems clear that the percentage of people holding religious beliefs decreases as they become more specific.

I suggest that this maps on to religious participation, and that specific religious beliefs are held mainly by those who actually participate in public religion on a regular basis, and who regard themselves as church members. In contrast, I suggest that a general belief in God is held quite widely by those who do not publicly participate in religion. Belief in God seems to be shared by religious insiders and outsiders, and also by people adhering to different faiths. If the question was phrased in an even more general way, rather like the survey question about religious experience used by David Hay (Hay, 1982), such as, "Do you believe in a presence or power, whether you call it God or not, which is different from your everyday self?" the number of people assenting would probably be even higher.

This connects with the well-known distinction drawn by Grace Davie (2015) between believing and belonging. She suggests that in our present society, believing is more common than belonging. I would want to nuance that by saying that it is general beliefs that are particularly common among those who do not "belong," while more specific religious beliefs are less commonly found among those who do not belong. Since the Second World War, the number of non-belongers who hold specific religious beliefs has shrunk and, if society becomes more secular, that trend will continue.

Further, I suggest that different causal factors are involved in general and specific beliefs. I suggest that specific religious beliefs are largely shaped by the religious communities to which people belong. Such beliefs are taught by those communities, and holding them is taken as a mark of membership. In contrast, I suggest that whether or not people believe in God is much more influenced by basic personality factors, and that such general beliefs are shaped more by psychological factors and less by social ones. Further, I suggest that genes will have some influence on whether people believe in God, but much less influence on whether people hold more specific religious beliefs. That would be parallel to the suggestion made in the last chapter, that inheritance influences private, internal aspects of religion more than public, external ones.

Conservative religious people are likely to be conservative in both their general and specific beliefs. Liberal religious people, in contrast, may show a hybrid pattern of being more conservative in their general belief in God than in more specific beliefs. That would be somewhat analogous to adherence to scientific claims, where a distinction can be made between an inner core of essential claims and an outer belt of negotiable claims. For liberal religious people, belief in God may function as a kind of core belief of the paradigm or "research program," while more specific beliefs are like an outer belt of claims that can be reinterpreted without calling the basic religious paradigm into question.

Attributions

In the remainder of this chapter, I will focus more on religious thinking than on belief. Understanding religious thought processes can show how belief arises and how it operates, whereas focusing on belief alone can give us little insight into the psychological processes that underlie it. Similarly, I will focus less on *what* religious people think than on *how* they think it.

A way into studying religious thinking that has proved quite fruitful is the pattern of attributions found in religion. It is well known from other areas of psychology that causal attributions have far-reaching implications. For example, an unusual pattern of attributions is found in depression. Whereas nondepressed people tend to attribute successes to themselves and failures to other causes, depressed people show the opposite pattern. In particular, they tend to attribute negative events to themselves, and in particular to see the personal qualities that have led to negative outcomes as being stable (unlikely to change) and global (pervasive in their effects).

Attribution theory was introduced to the psychology of religion by Proudfoot and Shaver (1975) and seemed to provide a helpful way of investigating religious thinking. On the face of things, religion seems to introduce a distinctive style of religious attributions. At the heart of religious attributions are attributions to God. However, I suggest that it is a limitation of much research on religious attributions to see them as consisting exclusively of attributions to God. They also include attributions to religious practices, to the religious community of which people are part, and so on.

Another tendency has been to assume that religious attributions replace other attributions, though I am doubtful whether that is the case. It is perhaps more likely that religious and nonreligious attributions coexist in a pattern of mutual influence. This is basically an empirical question, though one that it would take subtle methods to investigate. If you ask people for just one attribution, they will tend to give the predominant one, but they may have another attribution in the background that could come to the surface in different circumstances. There are theological reasons for thinking that might be so. For theologians such as Aquinas, God is seen as a different kind of cause, a "primary" cause, and not in competition with other "secondary" causes. Empirical evidence shows that religious and naturalistic attributions often coexist (Lupfer and Layman, 1996).

Another weakness in research on religious attributions is that most of it has been concerned with how people would attribute hypothetical events, not with how people attribute events that are actually occurring in their lives. The former may be a poor guide to the latter. A recent study of religious attributions of real-life events made use of a massive archive of people who had applied for healing to the Panacea Society in Bedford, England, mainly between 1925 and 1950 (Williams and Watts, 2014). The healing used a particular kind of healing water that it was believed would bring healing from most ailments. Applicants entered into correspondence with the society about its use of the water, and it was possible to see from their letters how they attributed whether or not they were improving. They tended to attribute improvements to the water, or the society, but lack of improvement to a variety of extraneous nonreligious factors. The basic pattern was not too surprising, but it emerges more clearly from this study of attributions of real personal issues than of hypothetical situations.

Some aspects of prayer seem to involve a kind of attributional retraining, though the effects of prayer on attributions have not been much investigated empirically. Thanksgiving, in particular, seems to involve a way of learning to attribute things to God. Thanksgiving is the form of prayer that most clearly assumes that attributions to God are appropriate, and the range of things for which people can potentially thank God is wide. It is well established in psychology that it makes a big psychological difference whether events are attributed internally or externally. However, attributions to God may not fit neatly into that distinction. How an attribution to God functions may depend on a particular person's sense of relationship to God. It is important to note again that God is not an ordinary kind of cause, nor an alternative to other causes. So, attributions to God are likely to supplement other attributions but not replace them.

One of the interesting questions that arises here concerns the range of things to which thanksgiving is applicable. It is one thing to attribute good outcomes to God, as the Panacea Society water users did. However, a strand in religious thinking suggests that everything good or bad should be attributed to God. In the end, that would lead to a reclassification of events, such as that used by Ignatius of Loyola in his Spiritual Exercises, in which the key question is whether events give people a sense of being closer to God or further away from him. That takes priority over the distinction between good and bad outcomes.

Figurative Thinking

Another important topic in religious thinking is the kind of concepts people use. It has often been commented that people think metaphorically (or analogically) about God (Watts and Williams, 1988, chap. 9). Theologically, the reason for this is that God defies exact description by humans. God cannot be described literally, so he can only be spoken about analogically. So, God is often thought of as "light," Jesus as a "shepherd," and so on. Metaphors are pervasive in our language and are to be found even in science. However, religious metaphors are different from scientific ones. They do not just contribute to understanding; they also express feelings and evoke a response (Barbour, 1974).

To understand why people use metaphorical concepts so much in religion, it may help to pay particular attention to what function they might serve. It has been suggested that one of the functions of metaphor is to convey interconnections (Olds, 1992). Religion is often concerned to do that; it places the particular in the context of the whole. The metaphorical strand in religious thinking seems to be good at engendering a sense of interconnection.

Actually, I think it is debatable whether "metaphor" is exactly the right term here. It depends on assumptions about how metaphors arise. Metaphors are often thought to arise from people taking terms with a literal meaning and extending them so they take on a metaphorical meaning. I am skeptical about whether that is the right account of how metaphors arise. As Owen Barfield (1973) has pointed out, if you trace the meanings of words, you generally find that they get more metaphorical, not less, as you go back in time. He suggests that language may have started by being metaphorical, or perhaps "figurative" would be a better term. Language seems to have started with double-aspect terms that referred to both observable and to psycho-spiritual realities, and then to have thinned out to form more "literal" meanings.

Our present culture is so wedded to naturalistic assumptions that it is easy to assume that naturalism must be correct. It is assumed that language must have started as a description of the natural world, and then been extended to capture religious and spiritual meanings. It seems to me equally possible that language started with double-aspect terms because they reflected the reality that people were then experiencing. It adds credence to this view that the social psychologist Solomon Asch (1958) has found that historically independent languages show the same double-aspect concepts. That invites the conclusion that those linkages occurred because they reflected how the world was experienced.

So, when religious people think, for example, of God as light, they are perhaps not devising a metaphor, but returning to a more ancient, double-aspect way of understanding reality. It could be a kind of regression to a more ancient way of thinking, which may explain something of the psychological impact that such thinking can have. The impact of metaphorical or double-aspect concepts may not depend at all on being able to explain them in abstract, analytical terms. That is a very different psychological skill. It seems likely that in evolutionary terms as in personal development, the ability to explain metaphors comes much later than the ability to respond intuitively to their impact.

Cognitive Style

Some areas of human cognition are closer to religious thinking than others, and religious and personal knowing may be quite similar to religion, both people's knowledge of themselves and their empathic intuitive knowledge of other people. Since Michael Polanyi (1958), interest has grown in religious knowing as personal knowing. What psychology can add to this is careful empirical investigation of how personal knowing works (Watts and Williams, 1988, chap. 5). This goes back to the point made in Chapter 5 about brain processes that people's sense of relationship to God does not make use of novel or distinctive neural structures but is based on the same kind of processes that allow us to form relationships with other people.

For example, in both personal knowing and religious knowing, there seems to be an important distinction between experiential and propositional knowledge. Psychotherapists have often commented on the distinction between intellectual and personal insight. People may reach essentially correct insights at an early stage of therapy, but with no great benefit. At a later stage, these insights may change in character and become more personal and experiential, and it is then that they contribute to personal change.

In the domain of religious beliefs, a somewhat similar distinction can be drawn between private and public beliefs, in the sense that people can distinguish between adherence to religious orthodoxy and their personal religious beliefs. This can be pursued in relation to people's concepts of God by asking them separately about what they understand to be correct religious belief and what is true for them in their own experience (Zahl et al., 2013). It is an empirical approach to the distinction made in colloquial terms between head and heart in religion (Watts and Dumbreck, 2013).

People probably differ in the extent to which they rely on analytic or intuitive modes of cognition, which provides a helpful way of exploring the link between religion and cognitive style. Gervais and Norenzayan (2012) have recently made a start on such research and have developed questions that can be answered in different ways, and where the answers indicate whether people were tackling the question analytically or intuitively. That gives a general indication of whether people are analytical or intuitive thinkers. All people can be either analytical or intuitive thinkers to some extent. Which people use on a particular occasion will be the result of many subtle factors, including recent experience or "priming."

The interesting fact is that people who showed themselves to be analytical thinkers in the questions that Gervais and Norenzayan used in their research were less likely to be religious. Indeed, on the basis of interventions designed to shift people in an analytical direction, they suggest that analytical thinking tends to weaken religious belief. That is an intriguing finding and one that invites further research.

It should not be assumed that people who mainly use intuitive thinking have no capacity for analytical thinking. It is unlikely that we are dealing here with traits that manifest themselves across all situations. It is also important to emphasize that there will be benefits in using intuitive thinking. Neither mode of cognition will be best in all circumstances; they both have their strengths and weaknesses. The challenge for people is to use the one most appropriate in any particular situation, and religion is an activity that may call for intuitive rather than analytical thinking. People who rely on intuitive thinking will probably be good at a range of things, including emotional empathy.

Cognitive Simplicity vs. Complexity

Another way into these issues is to ask whether people adopt a style of cognitive simplicity or complexity in thinking about religion. Again, I want to be careful not to assume that people who have one style of thinking will apply it in an invariant way across different situations. The key question for present purposes is what cognitive style people use in religious thinking. There are reasons to think that people may tend to adopt a style of greater cognitive simplicity in thinking about religion than about other things.

The notion of cognitive simplicity/complexity has quite a long history in psychology and has been assessed in various ways. Recent research by Sara Savage and her colleagues (Savage, 2013) on complexity in religious cognition has made use of a method of assessing it developed by Peter Suedfeld in political psychology, known as "integrative complexity" (IC) (e.g., Suedfeld et al., 2003). It avoids the assumption that cognitive complexity is a trait that shows itself equally across different situations and looks at how complexity manifests itself in material people write about a particular topic. IC has various levels. At the lowest level, people show evidence of black-and-white thinking. Viewpoints are polarized: one is right and others are wrong. With increasing IC, a recognition begins that other perspectives might have some validity and, as IC increases even further, people show evidence of an ability to synthesize different points of view.

Savage has applied this approach to Islamic radicalization (Savage, 2013). Scoring speeches of Osama bin Laden over the period leading up to 9/11 showed that his IC decreased as the date got closer (Savage and Liht, 2009). Savage has also developed a program designed to raise IC in young Muslims who might be vulnerable to radicalization and found evidence of increasing IC on at least some measures. Part of the skill of this approach is that the program is presented not as trying to bring about changes in what people think, but in the cognitive style with which they hold their views.

Attitudes to religious doubt may be one useful touchstone of cognitive complexity in the religious domain. Religious doubt is often a source of distress (see Hood et al., 2009, pp. 129–31). However, I suggest that will only be the case in traditions that see doubt as reprehensible. Other religious traditions see doubt as a potentially valuable adjunct to faith. Negative attitudes to doubt are likely to be associated with low cognitive complexity about religion, whereas a positive view of doubt requires high complexity about religion. Paul Pruyser in *Between Belief and Unbelief* (Pruyser, 1974) has reflected from the perspective of object relations psychology on the space for spiritual exploration that doubt opens up.

Idealization

An approach to religious thinking from a psychoanalytic perspective, using the concept of "idealization," has reached conclusions somewhat similar to those reached in terms of cognitive complexity. The psycho-analytic tradition from which this work comes involves a different style of cognitive psychology. However, useful work has been done in recent decades on translating psychoanalytic cognitive psychology into the framework of more mainstream cognitive psychology (e.g., Erdelyi, 1985). That has not yet been done on religious thinking specifically, though I see no reason why it could not be. So, for those who care deeply about the empirical verifiability of psychological theory, I also see no reason in principle why these theoretical contributions from psychoana-lysis could not be translated into empirically testable form.

Idealization is probably one of the most distinctive features of religious thinking; nothing else lends itself to idealization as much as religion. It is perhaps also idealization that can give religious thinking its particular potency. However, it is a dangerous fuel that can easily ignite, with destructive consequences.

Idealization is linked to a psychological process of "splitting," in which a sharp contrast is drawn between some people or ideas that are entirely good and others that are entirely bad. This is another way of formulating the black-and-white thinking that is a feature of integrative complexity. James W. Jones (2002) has emphasized the narcissistic basis of idealiza-tion, in which the person concerned places him- or herself within an idealized inner group, which is contrasted with a denigrated outer group. It is easy to see how that can lead to a terrorist crusade against those who have been denigrated. Often these groups are defined in ways that involve sociopolitical identity as well as religious identity, though in many of the world's religions those are closely intertwined.

William Meissner (1995) applies somewhat similar ideas to millenar-ianism, in which a sharp contrast is drawn between the present world order and the one that is imminently predicted. The coming new order is idealized, and the present one is denigrated. Again, an inner group of people understand and are preparing for the new order, and an outer group will be swept away when it arrives. Meissner particularly emphasizes the role of paranoid processes in the formation of this mind-set, and indeed he suggests that such processes are often involved in religious cultic processes.

The extraordinary motivational power of this kind of religious mind-set is seen in both Christian and Islamic fundamentalism. The challenging question posed by Jones is whether there can be religion without idealization. He suggests that there can, and that it will probably involve apophaticism, that is, learning the inadequacy of all human ideas about the divine, and detaching oneself from them. That is no doubt a possible way forward. One key question is whether it will have the transformative power associated with simple forms of idealization.

Summary

- The most general religious belief – belief in God – occurs more frequently than more specific beliefs, even belief in a personal God. Religious beliefs have a cognitive basis, and how they arise can be investigated psychologically. That is distinct from the philosophical question of whether they are rationally justified.

- A distinctive pattern of religious attributions emerges most clearly when examining attributions of real-life events. Positive outcomes are attributed to religion much more often than negative ones, though such attributions can be to a religious community or religious practice as well as to God. Religious attributions often coexist with naturalistic ones.

- Religious thinking often involves an intuitive, personal mode of knowing, and evidence is emerging that a shift to analytical thinking can undermine religious belief. People can think about religious matters in either a simple or complex cognitive style, though low levels of integrative complexity in religion can be associated with fundamentalism. Religious thinking also involves a degree of idealization; that partly explains the psychological power of religion, though idealization can have maladaptive consequences.

8

Spirituality

An interesting recent development in the psychology of religion is that it has broadened to include the study of spirituality, and considerable conceptual work has been done in this area (e.g., Oman, 2013). There have often been complaints (more from theologians than psychologists) that the concept of "spirituality" is hopelessly vague. The lack of precision indeed presents problems, though that is not to say that the concept cannot be clarified. The general cultural movement in many countries to interest in spirituality rather than in religion is one that cannot be ignored by the psychology of religion.

One obvious problem is that there is little agreement about what the term "spirituality" refers to. That is not just a matter of academics reaching agreement among themselves; a broader cultural problem concerns reaching agreement among the general population. Spirituality within a religious tradition means something rather different from spirituality outside religion. There are clearly common elements, but also differences. Even if a common definition is reached, such as "search for the sacred or the transcendent," people may mean such different things by those terms that it only moves the problem on to another level.

Another question that can be raised about spirituality outside religion is whether it has enough institutional structure to constitute a sustainable tradition. Key questions, raised by Philip Sheldrake (2013), are whether there is a tradition that goes beyond the founding generation, whether it is gathering core texts and practices, and whether there can be transmission of a nonreligious tradition of spirituality from place to place. Some strands of nonreligious spirituality may meet those criteria, but most do not. When the New Age movement began, it tended to have clear structures, albeit in relatively small and isolated groups. With the passage of time, there are fewer such structures, and nonreligious spirituality seems to have been incorporated into the general culture in a way that is less organized and less identifiable (Heelas, 2003).

Another problem is that "spiritual" is not used as a term of self-identification as much as is "religious." People generally know whether or not they regard themselves as religious. However, they do not, to the same extent, know whether or not to classify themselves as spiritual. Cross-cultural differences may also exist here. The term "spiritual" may have more resonance in a religious culture such as the United States than it does in secular European cultures. That may be connected with how people enter the domain of "spiritual but not religious." At least as a self-confessed identification, it may be more of a transitional place for people as they move away from religion than it is a category for people who are moving toward spirituality from being nonreligious.

Yet another unsatisfactory feature of the discussion about spirituality and religion as it is currently framed is that "religion" is often a shorthand for Christianity. A discussion about the relationship between spirituality and Buddhism would proceed rather differently, especially if it focused on the earlier, less religious forms of Buddhism. In as far as people who prioritize spirituality are against religion, they are usually more against Christianity than Buddhism, because Christianity is perceived as placing less emphasis on spiritual practice than Buddhism. That is probably a fair comment on institutional Christianity, despite the richness of the Christian tradition of spirituality.

So far, work on broadening the psychology of religion to include spirituality has been largely conceptual. I suggest that the next phase needs to be more empirical. Religion and spirituality can be treated as two independent dimensions (or categories). People can be one or the other, or both, or neither. It is misleading, of course, to set up religion and spirituality as alternatives, because many religious people are also spiritual. There is a category of people who are religious *and* spiritual, as well as people who are "spiritual but not religious." There are also people who are "religious but not spiritual," engaging in a kind of cultural Christianity, or civic religion. However, with the erosion of religious participation since the Second World War, that kind of cultural Christianity is becoming less common. People who regard themselves as more spiritual than religious may not object to religion, provided it gives priority to spirituality. That is different from those who see themselves as spiritual but opposed to religion.

It will be illuminating to know more about the differences between these various groups: religious and spiritual, religious but not spiritual, spiritual but not religious, neither religious nor spiritual, rather than treating people who are religious and/or spiritual as a single category ("R/S" people). Taken together, they constitute such a heterogeneous group that it seems a poor research strategy to lump them all together. The category of religious people was already rather too heterogeneous, but to include spiritual people as well seems to make the problem even worse.

We also need a multidimensional view of spirituality, as we do of religion. The categories of experience, practice, and belief that are useful with religion may be useful here too. As we saw in Chapter 5, there can be spiritual *experiences* that are not interpreted in a religious framework, such as powerful experiences of unity or love. It is not uncommon for atheists and agnostics to have such experiences. Spiritual *practices* such as meditation or mindfulness are widely followed in contemporary society, both by those who regard themselves as religious and by those who do not. Also, nonreligious groups and structures promote spiritual practices, such as meditation classes.

Though spiritual *beliefs* are less clear-cut than religious ones, there can be a spiritual worldview that emphasizes that the world is not merely material but reflects some transcendent meaning and purpose. People can engage in a kind of meaning making that is broadly spiritual but not explicitly religious. Belief in the afterlife may be a good indication of spiritual beliefs. I am inclined to suggest that to be counted as spiritual, people should be identifiable as such in most, if not all, of these various ways.

Meditation

The body of empirical research on meditation has been substantial, the older work focusing mainly on Transcendent Meditation or yoga, and the more recent work on mindfulness. A number of fairly clear results emerge from this work about physiological changes and clinical benefit. For a good review, see Walsh and Shapiro (2006). The evidence for the clinical benefits of meditation is also quite good (Seeman et al., 2003). These include effects on blood pressure, stress management, anxiety and depression, and abuse of drugs and alcohol. Interest has also been increasing in the use of mindfulness in conjunction with cognitive-behavior therapy in the treatment of depression, with very positive results (Williams and

Kabat-Zinn, 2013). However, there are significant divergences about how strong the evidence is for positive effects of meditation, with some taking a positive view (Hanson, 2009) and others remaining more skeptical (Flanagan, 2011).

One significant issue in evaluating the clinical benefits of meditation is how far it can be abstracted from its religious origins. It was an interesting feature of Transcendental Meditation that it claimed that it could deliver benefits without any changes in lifestyle other than the daily practice of meditation. Mindfulness has not gone that far and aims to produce pervasive changes in attitude and cognitive style, including compassion, but it has separated itself sufficiently from its religious origins to be endorsed as a therapy in the UK National Health Service.

Most forms of meditation produce lower levels of autonomic arousal, with reduced heart rate. That is comparable to what might be produced in states of deep relaxation and suggests that the benefits of meditation might be due to the component of deep relaxation. The effects of meditation on cortical arousal are more variable. There seems to be a difference between experienced and novice meditators. Novice meditators mainly show the large alpha waves that would be expected in relaxation. Experienced meditators may show a different pattern, with theta waves and other signs of activation. Meditation may produce an unusual dissociation between arousal systems, with low autonomic arousal but heightened cortical arousal.

Perhaps the most interesting questions about meditation are concerned with what people are actually doing in their mental processes in meditation, and how that delivers the range of benefits that it does. A style of focused attention results in fewer distractions being experienced, though most traditions of meditation warn against trying too hard to achieve tight control over thought processes. Mindfulness makes an important distinction between attention to sensory features of experience, which become more careful and focused than usual, and the evaluative thought processes that are often intertwined with sensory experience, and which people learn to eschew. It is not hard to see how learning to suspend evaluative judgments could make a useful contribution to the treatment of depression.

It will be useful here to make use again of Interacting Cognitive Subsystems, which has already been used by John Teasdale (Teasdale et al., 1995) to offer an account of mindfulness. Whereas cognitive multitasking is the norm, mindfulness aims for a cognitive state in which only one thing is happening at a time. The normal engagement of the central meaning systems with more peripheral subsystems seems to be suspended in meditation.

A rebalancing of activity between the two central subsystems – the more linear and articulate "propositional" subsystem and the more intuitive and holistic "implicational" subsystem – also occurs. Specifically, mindfulness seems to reduce activity in the propositional subsystem, in a way that creates an opportunity for the implicational subsystem to "do its own thing." The propositional subsystem may be either largely shut down or enmeshed with the implicational system in a way that is subservient to it. It is possible that there are considerable personal and restorative benefits for people in spending time, as they do in meditation, liberated from both the normal cognitive multitasking and the heavy demands of propositional thinking.

Meaning, the Transcendent, and the Afterlife

The most general, and perhaps the most important, aspect of religious thinking relates to the ability of religion to give meaning to life. Humans have a strong instinct to adopt a framework of meaning that gives value, purpose, and significance to life, and to relate individual events to that framework (Baumeister, 1991). It is one of the core functions of ideologies to give meaning to life. Religion is not the only ideology that can do that, but it is arguable that it has done so especially well.

Crystal Park (2010) makes a helpful distinction between global meaning and meaning making. Religions provide global meaning by offering a meta-narrative that relates human existence to the unfolding purposes of God, on a grand and sweeping scale. What may seem trivial human events find their place in this overarching narrative framework. Within that framework, everything finds its purpose and significance.

This narrative framework is linked to a set of values. Religious movements are diverse on this, as on almost everything else, and one can probably find an exception to every generalization. However, the vast majority of religions have emphasized love and compassion, peace and reconciliation, and justice and fairness. I would not want to claim that humans can only find moral values within a religious framework. However, religions do convey near-consensual moral values and give them a transcendent authority.

Religious global meanings are exceptionally broad and integrative. As Saroglou (2014) notes, they characteristically bring together truth, beauty, and goodness. From an analytical point of view, there is no reason why these should be connected, but religion postulates that they are, and that they all come from the same transcendent source. Religious global meaning also provides a source of motivation. People feel called on to do things because of their significance in relation to global meaning.

Meaning making is the process of relating individual events to the religious framework of global meaning. Many religious practices, especially personal prayer, seem to be an exercise in doing this. Prayer at the end of the day characteristically involves reviewing the day's events and relating them to a religious meaning framework. Regret over mishaps, gratitude for satisfactions, concerns and needs for other people and oneself are all brought into the felt presence of God and are related to the religious narrative and values.

In the course of this, events that would otherwise have lacked significance find meaning. The religious narrative framework gives significance to events that would have lacked significance, and events that had a nonreligious significance find a new one through a process of reframing. Equally, events that were initially interpreted in a nonreligious way are reinterpreted within the religious framework. All events are related to core religious values. The result is a single meaning framework that gives significance to all events in a coherent and integrative way. Within religious meaning making, everything coheres.

One important aspect of the patterns of thought associated with spirituality is the language that is used for the transcendent. The traditional language of most Christian churches and of most personal prayer is a personal language modeled on how people talk to other humans. In that sense, it is anthropomorphic. In contrast, the language of people who see themselves as more spiritual than religious is often a more impersonal, abstract language about spiritual forces and energies. It would be good to have better survey data about this than is so far available. The tendency will still be to fall back on more anthropomorphic language under stress of the kind that the military often experience, and it is interesting that there seem to be few atheists among the military (Beit-Hallahmi and Argyle, 1997, p. 196). However, the main data on that goes back to the Second World War, and it may be less true now.

I suspect that there is quite a rapid cultural movement toward a preference, under most circumstances, for the more abstract language for the transcendent, and that this creates a gulf between churches and an increasing number of the population who see themselves as more spiritual than religious. The problem is more cultural than theological, as it is a core feature of traditional language to recognize the inadequacy of any language for God, including the anthropomorphic language that a rapidly growing proportion of people seem to find unconvincing.

A distinction can be made between "other-worldly" and "this-worldly" beliefs. Religions have beliefs of both kinds, though the relative emphasis given to them may vary from one religious group to another. Spirituality has a stronger focus on "this-worldly" beliefs. To put it another way, a distinction can be made between two kinds of transcendence, vertical and horizontal. Religion is concerned with both, though again the relative emphasis varies; spirituality is more concerned with horizontal transcendence. However, there may be particular spiritual beliefs, or at least beliefs that are characteristic of people taking a spiritual worldview. This has so far not been well investigated so, not for the first time, we are having to piece things together from a limited research base.

A good place to start is with belief in an afterlife (see Hood et al., 2009, pp. 185–86). The percentage of people who believe in the afterlife is remarkably high, and in the United States is 79 percent. Belief in the afterlife in most European countries is lower, but it is increasing in both the United States and Europe. It is also increasing across various religious groups, including Jews (who have traditionally had less strong belief in the afterlife than Christians) and Catholics. It is notable that some people believe in the afterlife but not in God. That seems parallel to people being more spiritual than religious, and there is probably an overlap between the two groups. Belief in the afterlife is especially strong among people who have high scores on measures of transliminality and other associated personality traits (Thalbourne, 1998).

Belief in an afterlife also seems likely to be correlated with belief in angels, which is probably also increasing, bucking the general trend for religious beliefs to be declining. It may also be correlated with belief in ghosts, evil spirits, and a broad range of parapsychological phenomena. There is a potentially rich interface between the psychology of religion and parapsychology that is only beginning to be explored. It seems reasonable on the basis of current evidence to assume that traits such as transliminality and schizotypy predispose beliefs in afterlife, angels, ghosts, and so on.

Belief in disembodied spirits seems to come naturally to humans, as the cognitive science of religion has suggested (Barrett, 2013). The form such beliefs take is no doubt shaped by culture. One way of conceptualizing this is in terms of "intuitive dualism." The basic idea is that how we think about bodies and minds has different evolutionary origins, so it is natural for such thoughts to be dissociated and for us to think that one can exist without the other.

Spiritual beliefs in angels, spirits, and the afterlife have so far received less investigation than other aspects of spirituality such as the effects of meditation. It seems likely that such spiritual beliefs will show a very different pattern of occurrence from more traditional religious beliefs. There currently seems to be more interest in them outside religious circles than within. Indeed, while spiritual beliefs are increasingly common in general society, mainline religion and academic theology sometimes seem almost embarrassed that they also are a traditional part of Christian belief.

Spiritual Issues in Therapy

One of the attractions of spirituality is that it can find a broader acceptance in nonreligious institutions than can religion. It is easier for secular institutions to make provision for spirituality than for religion. The program of research on workplace spirituality in which Peter C. Hill has played a key role is one example of this (Hill and Dik, 2012). Another interesting place where a focus on spirituality has been developing is in counseling and therapy, where considering spiritual issues, broadly conceived, has been a recent trend. The tendency among psychotherapists used to be to regard religious tendencies as pathological, but the new focus on spirituality has helped overcome that.

Significant developments have occurred in integrating a spiritual focus into therapy (e.g., Pargament, 2007). As Pargament sees it, there are good reasons for incorporating a spiritual perspective into therapy. Sometimes, as Freud recognized, attempts to find religious solutions to psychological problems can become part of the problem and can entrench the problem to which they were intended to be the solution. That calls for sensitive handling. More positively, spirituality can be part of the solution. Clients are often evidently groping for spiritual solutions to their problems and try to articulate that in a language that is more spiritual than psychological. Therapists need to hear such language and be equipped to respond to it. Spiritual aspects of therapeutic work need to be integrated with other aspects of therapy and be handled with skill and sensitivity.

Pargament conceptualizes the spiritual work in therapy in terms of an engagement with a "sacred ring" that extends beyond core concepts of God, or however the core is formulated. The ring includes a sense of meaning and purpose, and of sacred qualities such as transcendence, boundlessness, and ultimacy being manifest in everyday life. The sacred can be sensed, for example, in the self, in other people, in relationships, in particular tasks, and in special times and places. One of the tasks of therapy is to discern what represents the sacred for each particular client. Pargament suggests that whatever is sacred elicits certain spiritual emotions from the client, especially a sense of awe and wonder. The sacred then becomes a resource for the person and an organizing force in his or her ongoing personal journey.

If the therapist is using a spiritually integrated approach, those things will be touched on in the initial session. The therapist will also be vigilant for signs of spiritual struggle, including struggles with God, struggles with themselves, and struggles with church and with other people. They will also look for evidence of spiritual resources that they have tried to use in coping with problems. Pargament identifies five relevant pathways, concerned with knowing (e.g., Bible study), acting (e.g., how people try to behave), relating (staying in regular contact with people who represent spiritual resources), experience (including spiritual practices such as prayer), and religious ways of coping.

Later on an explicit spiritual assessment is undertaken, which will include sacred destinations and goals, sacred pathways that people follow to reach those goals, and people's perception of how efficacious the spiritual has been for them in their life's journey. The therapy itself will draw on a range of spiritual resources, including those that have been identified in the spiritual assessment. It will also address issues about people's spiritual destinations and pathways, especially where they seem maladaptive or unrealistic in some way. It will also look at how well the person's spiritual pathways fit their spiritual goals and, if need be, help bring them into better alignment.

Pargament sets out a broad framework for spiritually integrated therapy that will be applicable to a wide range of clients and which is not confined to pastoral care in religious institutions. Sometimes specific resources derived from spiritual traditions, such as mindfulness, will have a key role in therapy with certain specific problems. Though mindfulness is derived from a spiritual tradition, it has been developed in a way that gives it wider acceptability.

Positive Psychology

The recent development of positive psychology is in many ways quite closely related to the psychology of spirituality. There is indeed a degree of overlap between the two, though there are also differences of emphasis. Positive psychology was initiated by Martin Seligman in his highly influential address to the American Psychological Associated (Seligman, 1999). Though presented as a new development in psychology, it is related to what had previously been called positive mental health. Nevertheless, in its new guise, the field has commanded new energy and resources, and it does now, as intended, provide a good counterweight to abnormal psychology.

Positive psychology is largely concerned with character strengths and virtues. Peterson and Seligman (2004) set out six core virtues or character strengths with which positive psychology is concerned: wisdom, courage, humanity, justice, transcendence, and temperance. It is a plausible list, though there could obviously be debate about exactly what to include. A psychology of such strengths and virtues is, in large measure, a psychology of spirituality. These are strengths and virtues that have long been the concern of religion, but they have now become the focus of wider concern, beyond the confines of religion. The point that needs to be made here, from the perspective of the psychology of religion, is that these strengths and virtues are conceptualized and pursued in somewhat different ways, depending on whether or not that is done in a religious context.

Positive psychology tends to assume that it is self-evident what goals people will want to work toward; they are in effect the goals of positive mental health. Religion sees more room for discussion about goals and is more concerned with moral goals for which there is transcendent authority, with what some would call "sacred strivings." Also, though religion has no problem about embracing positive goals, it tends to want to work toward them with a broader and more balanced view of human nature. In particular, it does not close its eyes to the darker side of personality that, unless it is addressed, may subvert progress toward those positive goals.

There are also differences of emphasis at the level of specific virtues or objectives. In Chapter 3, we looked at some of the differences between psychology and religion in the way forgiveness is approached, though both would agree on its value. As another example here, we can take their somewhat different approaches to hope and optimism (Watts, 2002, pp. 138–41).

A conceptual distinction can be made between hope and optimism (though the word "hope" is often used broadly to refer to either). Optimism is concerned with predictions for the future; it expects the future to be good and assumes that there are rational grounds for believing that. Hope, in contrast, can arise in a wider range of circumstances, including those in which the present situation is so bleak that there is no rational basis for expecting things to improve. It is more a matter of disposition and attitude than of rational expectations about the future. Indeed, hope comes into its own in situations where there is no basis for optimism.

A good deal of interest in hope and hopelessness has arisen in positive psychology. However, in terms of this distinction, I suggest that what is being measured (and fostered) in positive psychology is more optimism than hope. Religion and spirituality have generally been concerned with hope in the broader sense and see hope more as a virtue to be cultivated than as a matter of rationally justified expectation. Though positive psychology has been concerned with the human benefits of hope in the sense of optimism, I suggest that hope in the broader spiritual sense may actually have more far-reaching benefits. Hope in this broader sense would be a good research topic for the emerging psychology of spirituality.

Spirituality and the Churches

The years since the Second World War have seen a remarkable change in the religious landscape in countries such as the United States and the UK (Davie, 2015). There has been marked decline in the membership of the mainline denominations, but an equally dramatic revival in conservative, evangelical, and Pentecostal religion. Nuances could be entered around that summary statement, but the broad outlines are beyond dispute. What conclusions can religious leaders draw?

One conclusion would be that evangelical Christianity is the only kind of Christianity likely to flourish in current society, whether that is attributed to human factors such as confident belief and strong fellowship or to theological factors such as belief in scripture and the power of the Holy Spirit. This raises the question of what future is there for organized religion, especially for non-evangelical forms of Christianity? Perhaps the most important challenge for Christian ministry arises from the distinction between internal and external aspects of religion. There are good grounds for expecting strong survival of internal religion and spirituality, whether that is inside or outside organized churches.

It may be helpful to summarize some of the key points supporting this prediction. A general belief in God is still held quite widely in our society, among those who would not assent to more specific religious beliefs, or even to a "personal God." A growing body of people in our society regard themselves as more spiritual than religious. Powerful life-changing religious experiences occur surprisingly frequently (in about a third of the population), including those who have no specific religious affiliation, and they are more closely tied to whether people think the spiritual side of life is important than they are to religious orthodoxy. Internal and spiritual aspects of religion seem to have a different basis from external religious participation, with internal religion being more rooted in personality and genetic inheritance, and external religion being more a matter of social and cultural influence.

This poses a challenge for religious leaders who stand in the declining, liberal mainline denominations. Is there a way that such churches can connect more effectively with people who are instinctively in tune with spiritual values and practices? Could churches reinvent themselves in a way that would meet the spiritual needs of such people? There is, of course, a paradox in developing a religious movement to serve the needs of people for whom public religious affiliation is the least attractive aspect of religion. It is hard to be sure how successful such a movement might be, but it would be a rational response to the evidence about internal religion continuing beyond present culturally based forms of religious affiliation.

Summary

- The psychology of religion has recently broadened to include the psychology of spirituality, though conceptual issues still need to be resolved about what is meant by that. Spirituality is used as a concept of self-identification less than religion. The growing numbers of people who are more spiritual than religious often do not connect well with mainline churches.
- Though meditation derives from religious traditions, it is now widely used by nonreligious people. It has considerable practical benefits, for example, in treating people who are depressed. It also has significant cognitive and neuropsychological effects.
- Religion is valuable for its contribution to meaning making, and it provides global meanings and values that are unusually broad and integrative. Religion provides a broad narrative framework to which personal events can be related. Belief in the afterlife is growing, though other religious beliefs are declining.
- Interest has been growing in focusing on spiritual issues in therapy, which, broadly conceived, includes a focus on sacred qualities such as

transcendence, boundlessness, and ultimacy as they are manifest in everyday life.

- Interest in the study of character and virtues within the framework of positive psychology has grown recently. Though there is much overlap with the psychology of spirituality, a critique of positive psychology can also be mounted from a religious perspective.

9

Developmental Aspects

Religious development has always been an important part of the psychology of religion. Two quite separate topics need to be covered. One is to examine the development of religion itself, through childhood and into the life-span, and to see what generalizations can be reached about that. The other is to examine how more general aspects of psychosocial development in children influence religion, both in childhood itself, but also what lifelong influences it has on adult religiousness. We will examine these two rather different topics in turn.

So, first we will consider how religion itself develops. One approach to religious development has made use of stage development theories. I will examine that first in children, and then see how it extends to adults. It is probably fair to say that it is no longer an approach that is at the cutting edge of work on religious development, but it raises interesting issues that are worth examining.

It cannot be assumed in advance that it will be possible to make many generalizations about religious "development" at all. Certainly people's religiousness changes over time; that is not in dispute. However, if we are to reach any generalizations about what can properly be called religious development, those changes in religiousness will need to follow a fairly standard pattern. That is an empirical matter; it may or may not be so. In fact, I will suggest that we can reach such generalizations about the development of religion, but only for one very specific aspect of religion (intellectual understanding of religion), and only in childhood, not in adulthood.

Stages of Religious Development in Children

The most researched aspect of children's religion is the development of intellectual understanding. This seems to follow the general scheme that Jean Piaget established for most forms of intellectual development. One of the earliest applications to the religious area was Ronald Goldman's research on the interpretation of Bible stories (Goldman, 1968). The phases that children's understanding of this material go through are roughly:

Age: 5–9	Intuitive (e.g., God as superhuman)
Age: 9–12	Concrete (e.g., God as supernatural)
Age: 13+	Abstract and conceptual thinking

Other aspects of religious understanding, such as views about prayer, seem to show a similar pattern. This pattern of development in religious understanding is well replicated and seems to be near universal (see Hood et al., 2009).

For example, the story of the parting of the Red Sea might be interpreted by young children in terms of God physically making the waters separate. Slightly older children would see God as achieving that through supernatural means. The oldest children might come up with alternative explanations, such as that God suggested to the Israelites to make use of a naturally occurring parting of the waters. There is a similar pattern in the interpretation of petitionary prayer. The youngest children might see it as a magical way of getting a tangible result. At the next stage, God's response to prayer might be seen as mediated more through people's minds and hearts. The oldest children would put more emphasis on altruistic prayer, and on the effects of praying on the person who prays. Similar results have been obtained by numerous researchers, differing in detail, but all showing movements from concrete and magical to more abstract and symbolic.

The fact that children's intellectual development in religion follows a predictable pattern makes it possible to use the short cut of studying children of different ages, rather than following the same children through the span of their childhood. The word "development" is bandied about rather too freely, but it seems to me that in this context we are justified in using it. We have a predictable pattern of development followed by all children with normal cognitive functioning. We do not find some maverick children going from abstract to concrete thinking. They all take the same developmental path, at roughly the same age. It is like infants going through their milestones.

However, research of this kind has significant limitations. We need to remember that it is only concerned with children's understanding of religion. It does not look at how they learn, or at their spiritual experience. Note also that the responses given at the so-called abstract stage are quite diverse. Some "explain away" religious stories, though not all do so. For example, it is very different to say that the Burning Bush in the book of Exodus was a flame of goodness that God put there than to say that the sun shining in a particular direction made it look like flames. Younger children would be unlikely to say either, but these two responses illustrate the diversity of the religious interpretations of older children.

Though children achieve a capacity to think in more abstract and symbolic ways, they do not lose their previous capacity to think more concretely or literally. One way of framing the religious development that takes place in children would be to say that they are capable of relating to religious material in a wider range of ways. We also need to be wary of the implicit assumption that abstract is better. Different approaches may each have their time and place.

Note that the research we have been discussing focuses on how well children can explain their religious thinking; younger children may understand more than they can explain. This kind of research seems to start from an adult understanding of religion and then evaluates children's understanding in relation to it. Children's religion may just be different from adults, but not necessarily inferior. Also, the apparent poverty of children's religious understanding may be largely the result of the adult way in which children are assessed.

We also need to be careful about inferences concerning religious education from this research. Goldman formulated a concept of "readiness for religion." Essentially he suggested that it was premature to try to teach children about religion until they could demonstrate the capacity to understand it. The weakness with this argument is that children may have an intuitive understanding much earlier than they are able to articulate the kind of abstract understanding that an adult would have. So, it may be that young children can understand religion in their own way, but they just understand it differently from how adults do. The solution seems to be to allow children to explain their spirituality in their own terms, not to test them against adult standards.

Stages of Faith Development in Adults

James Fowler's approach to faith development is the most discussed developmental approach to adult religion (Fowler, 1981). He postulates seven stages (0–6):

0. Primal Faith	Prelinguistic trust
1. Intuitive-Projective	Fantasy, images, story, action
2. Mythic-Literal	Able to think about faith, but still concrete
3. Synthetic	Reflective, but still conformist
4. Inductive-Reflective	Moving beyond reliance on authority
5. Conjunctive Faith	Focus on deep aspects of self, paradox, etc.
6. Universalizing	Transcending faith traditions

This is an interesting scheme, but it is open to many criticisms. Data on the sequence of stages was obtained by interviewing adults about their faith history and asking them for a retrospective account of it. What people said about their earlier stages of faith development would have been subject to normal limitations of memory, but it may also have been distorted by the fact that they were no longer at the earlier stages they were trying to describe. That could have led them to either minimize or exaggerate the change that had taken place.

This developmental sequence seems to be trying to cover all aspects of faith. However, it is largely concerned with certain specific ones. First, the focus is on cognitive development (stages 1–3). Next, the focus is on relational aspects of development, concerned with authority and independence (stages 3–5). Finally, the focus is on a kind of spiritual maturity (stages 4–6). It is not clear why these three very different aspects of development are linked in a single, linear scheme, with some stages serving as linking stages between different aspects of development.

Fowler's empirical evidence for progression from one stage to the next is actually not compelling. It is not clear that there is any invariant sequence, comparable to that which is found for children's intellectual understanding of religion, which always runs from concrete to abstract. Fowler's scheme seems to owe as much to his theological assumptions as to actual evidence. This is especially true of the final stage, for which there were no actual examples from the people he studied.

Fowler's research also works with a general definition of faith, as a center of value, with loyalty to images and realities of power, and to a shared master story. That could potentially apply in a wide range of situations and does not seem to be specifically religious. In practice, Fowler mainly studied American Christians. It may have broad applicability to many kinds of faith, but that was not really tested in the research.

My main point here is not so much that the research was done badly. It is more that the project of trying to extend a framework of stages of religious development through the life-span was probably misconceived. It seems unlikely that changes in adult faith follow an orderly, predictable sequence in the way that children's intellectual understanding does. For example, some adults are drawn toward firm religious authority; others want to move away from it. There simply does not seem to be a pattern of people "developing" from one to the other. This has led Heinz Streib to suggest that Fowler's so-called stages should rather be seen as styles (Streib, 2001).

Cognitive Science of Religion

A newer wave of research on the development of religious cognition in children has been guided by the cognitive science of religion (CSR). We encountered that in Chapter 3 in the context of evolution, but I am more enthusiastic about its developmental applications.

One of the core ideas of CSR is that religion is natural; it is summed up in the title of Pascal Boyer's influential book *The Naturalness of Religious Ideas* (Boyer, 1994). Many CSR theorists would assume that religious beliefs are mistaken, an assumption that serves to make it even more puzzling that they occur so pervasively. Suggesting that they are cognitively "natural" provides one approach to that conundrum. Of course, if religion is found to be natural, it does not show it to be mistaken. The naturalness of religion could equally be taken as the basis for a natural theology, and consistent with what would be expected on religious assumptions. Here, as always, psychological research data seems to be compatible with either belief or nonbelief.

If you want evidence to support the assumption that religion is cognitively natural, you can look in various places; one of them is religious development. There should be evidence that religious ideas and assumptions come naturally to children. That does indeed seem to be the case, and the evidence is well presented by Justin Barrett (2012). An important experiment in this research is the "false belief test." For example, a rock may be put into a box, though most people apart from the child do not know that. You ask the child what a certain person would expect to find in the box. The child says the person would expect to find a rock, even if the person concerned would have no way of knowing that.

It seems that you have to reach age four before you can attribute false beliefs to someone, that is, say that he or she would expect to find something other than what was actually there. Before that age, it seems that children assume that everyone is omnipotent (like God). After age four, they consider what a particular person has had the opportunity to learn. The distinction between God (who knows everything) and humans (who do not know everything) seems to arise only at four. Before that, it seems natural to attribute omnipotence to everyone.

Theistic beliefs seem to come naturally to children. For example, children naturally assume that things are there for a purpose, such as to give pleasure or to be beautiful. They naturally assume that things are there because some being or agent decided that they should be, rather than that they arose through impersonal processes. When they start to distinguish between God and humans, they assume that God and not a human person is behind the universe. It also seems to come naturally to children to assume that people have a soul that survives physical death.

This is an important line of research, still being developed. However, the broad conclusion seems secure, that theistic thinking comes naturally to children. There is no evidence of an earlier period of nontheistic thinking from which theism is an extrapolation. Rather, the concept of human minds with their limited mental capacities seems derivative from this earlier theism. It is not so much that young children think about God anthropomorphically, as that they start by thinking about people theistically. The unlimited knowledge and power of God seem to be a more basic concept than the limited knowledge and power of humans.

Spiritual Experience in Children

The research we have looked at so far all has a strong cognitive emphasis. It has focused on religious thinking. However, there is also a growing body of research on religious experience in children, to which we will now turn. It seems that children not only think like theists, they also have a rich life of spiritual experience. Young children usually show no clear distinction between spiritual and religious experiences.

The practical challenge with this research is to find a way to explore children's spiritual experience. If you ask about it in the way you would ask an adult, you may not get much response, not because they have no spiritual experience, but because they cannot easily handle abstract, adult-type questions about it. You therefore need to find a more indirect approach. David Hay and Rebecca Nye (2006) encouraged children to talk, giving the conversation a gentle steer toward spiritually relevant experiences such as those involving wonder and beauty. They asked relatively few questions, and their questions stayed close to what the children were saying. Using that approach, they found evidence of rich spiritual experience in many children. This kind of approach shows that young children can have a rich spirituality, even when it is not yet very well articulated.

Kalevi Tamminen (1994), using a more quantitative approach, reached similar conclusions. He found that 80 percent of 7-year-olds, and 60 percent of 11-year-olds, reported experiences of God's closeness. Such experiences were often triggered by moments of personal unhappiness. There was a trend over time for such experiences to become less common, or at least to be less frequently reported. Also, by adolescence, such experiences tended to be interpreted more naturalistically.

It is interesting that the development of children's ability to think in abstract and propositional terms about religion seems to go in parallel with a decline in religious experience. Goldman's research, which documents the development of adult-type intellectual understanding of religion in children by age 13, seems to be about the development of propositional religion. However, as Tamminen's research shows, the development of propositional thinking seems to be accompanied by a decline in intuitive religious experience.

It is not that religion as a whole is either developing or declining, but there does seem to be a change in the natural profile of religiousness. Various factors probably contribute to that, some cognitive, some social. In terms of the cognitive architecture, it seems that the capacity for propositional thought develops later than the capacity to think intuitively. In terms of Interacting Cognitive Subsystems, the implicational subsystem develops before the propositional subsystem.

The theistic thinking and spiritual experience that come naturally to children seem to arise from a period when the capacity for intuitive thought has not become overlaid with the later capacity for propositional thought. Propositional thought, when it comes on stream, seems to be less naturally theistic and spiritual, and more often seems to be based on naturalistic assumptions. So, as children develop cognitively, and rely more on propositional thought and less on intuitive thought, they become less naturally religious. No doubt social factors come into play as well, as children find their place in a social world beyond the home, and find that it is largely one that makes nonreligious assumptions.

Influences on the Religiousness of Children

Turning from the task of describing how the religion of children changes and perhaps develops, let us look at factors that influence how religious they are and what form that religiousness takes (see Hood et al., 2009, for a good review). The religion of children is much influenced by that of their parents, though that applies to some aspects of religion more than others. Denomination is influenced the most, religious attendance is somewhat influenced, while belief and commitment are least influenced by parents. An increasing body of evidence shows that the extent of parental influence on the religion of their children depends on the closeness of the relationship between them. The influence is greatest for children who have strong relationships with their parents. The influence of parents is also enhanced when they are themselves leading religious lives in a full sense, not just attending church or other religious requirements rather nominally.

School can also be a significant influence, though research findings are less clear-cut. School seems only to have a significant impact when a substantial amount of time is devoted to religion. The effects of school and home can interact, and long-term influence on religiousness is greatest when both are exerting influence in the same direction. However, a strongly religious school can sometimes make the most difference with children from nonreligious homes. Peer influence probably becomes increasingly significant as children grow up but has not yet been so well researched.

Religion as Attachment

We will now consider what has been one of the most fruitful developments in the psychology of religion in recent years, which has looked at people's relationship with God as a kind of attachment relationship, examining how the attachment relationships that children have with their parents can influence their approach to religion throughout their lives. The psychology of attachment is much indebted to the work of John Bowlby, and it has been applied to religion, primarily by Lee Kirkpatrick and Pehr Granqvist (e.g., Kirkpatrick, 2005; Granqvist and Kirkpatrick, 2008; Granqvist, 2010).

Children have a natural tendency to form an attachment relationship with their primary caregivers. Research shows that about two-thirds of children form a secure attachment relationship. A secure attachment serves two key functions. It provides a secure base from which to explore and a safe haven to which they can return in times of stress. Children with a secure attachment relationship assume that their caregivers are both willing and able to look after them in times of difficulty and, at such times, they resist being separated from the person to whom they are attached.

It is clear that God meets many of the criteria for an attachment object, though in an unusual way. It is assumed that attachment figures would want to look after people in times of need, and would be able to do so. Any religious person would assume that of God. As with human attachment objects, people perceive God as stronger and wiser than themselves, providing them with a secure base. People turn to God in times of distress; in that sense, God functions as a safe haven. In all those ways, God seems to function as an attachment object.

However, the fact that God is not directly observable makes God an anomalous attachment object. People stay close to a human attachment object in times of stress, but they cannot go to God at such times because God is not in any particular place. Going to a church or place of worship is not exactly an equivalent. Neither is prayer, because there is often ambiguity about whether God is felt to be actually present in prayer. God often seems to be absent when people pray to God, as is well documented in the "dark night of the soul" described by St. John of the Cross (May, 2004). So, at best we can probably say that there is an analogy between how people relate to God and how they relate to a human attachment figure.

Regardless of how like a human attachment figure God is thought to be, it is an empirical fact that people's relationships to God are predictable from their human attachment relationships. Two main hypotheses have been advanced about the connection between people's attachment history and their relationship to God, the correspondence hypothesis and the compensation hypothesis. We will consider each in turn.

The assessment of attachment style is not a straightforward matter and usually involves retrospective interviewing, which, as we noted in connection with Fowler's work on faith development, is potentially problematic. However, two things are better about this attachment research. One is that the most-used protocol, the Adult Attachment Interview (AAI), has been carefully developed and used extensively. The other is that there is convergent evidence from other non-interview methods.

The correspondence hypothesis states that people's attachment history will influence their attachment to God, and particularly that people with experience of secure human attachments will experience their relationship with God as stable and supportive. People who have been sensitively cared for as children are more likely to be religious as adults. However, a significant caveat has emerged: it seems that it only applies where parents themselves display a high level of religiosity. The implications of that caveat call for further exploration.

Evidence from experimental studies (Granqvist, 2010) adds something important to the usual self-report techniques used in the psychology of religion. The procedure involved activating attachment needs by subliminal presentation of short sentences such as "God has abandoned me" or "Mommy is gone." Compared to other more neutral sentences, primes that activated attachment needs led to an increase in self-reported desire to be close to God.

The other main hypothesis in attachment research is the compensation hypothesis. If a secure human attachment is not available, and if children experience distress, they can turn to a substitute attachment figure such as God. Insecure attachments can take various forms: the child might show a lack of trust, resulting in avoidant attachments; or he or she might show anxiety about whether the attachment person will be reliable and become ambivalent; or the child may become resistant to attachment. These different patterns are often grouped together as insecure attachments.

One of the strongest pieces of evidence in support of the compensation hypothesis is that those who experience sudden religious conversions often have a record of insecure attachments. People with insecure attachments are also likely to turn to God after a romantic relationship has broken down. On the theory, such turning to God is especially likely to happen at times of distress and may not be stable or lifelong. There is also not much evidence so far that insecure human attachments carry over to insecure attachments to God.

It will be noted that both the correspondence and compensation hypotheses describe paths by which people reach attachment to God. So, whatever people's attachment background, it may appear consistent with the theory for people to turn to God. There is some validity in the complaint that the theory can handle almost any data. However, steps can be taken to guard against it and, to some extent, have already been taken. It helps to pay attention to the particular forms of attachment to God that are predicted and the particular circumstances under which they can be expected. It might also be helpful to explore the roots of non-attachment to God from the perspective of attachment theory.

More work needs to be done on the relationship between attachment and religion, but the work in this area discussed here represents one of more significant advances in the psychology of religion in recent years. It has established that the kinds of relationships that children have with parents or caregivers often have lasting implications for their approach to religion.

The Transition to Adulthood

We turn now from childhood to adolescence and early adulthood. For a good and detailed review, see Hood et al. (2009, chaps. 5 and 6). It is difficult to generalize about religion in this stage of life because things vary so much from one culture to another, and indeed from one decade to the next. Most of the available data relates to the United States, and research findings may not generalize to other cultures.

The changes in religiousness that occur in the college years seem more pronounced than those that take place in the high school years. Even there, changes in religiousness when young people go to college are less dramatic than was once supposed, and there is a good deal of continuity with pre-college years. There does seem to be a slight reduction in religious adherence during the college years, though that develops gradually rather than being a sudden and decisive change. However, even that generalization needs to be qualified in several ways. There seems to be a widening of the gulf between more religious people (many of whom get even more religious) and less religious people (who are likely to become even less religious), supporting the polarization theory put forward by Ozorak (1989). Though religiousness in college years declines to some extent, no reduction occurs in the extent to which people are focused on spiritual issues. In fact, the college years seem to be a very spiritual period, though a shift from external to internal aspects of religion takes place.

Parents remain much the most important influence on religiousness in the college years, as they are for children. It is interesting, and perhaps surprising, that parental influence continues to be so strong, even when children have left home and gone to college. Friends and education itself exert some influence on religiousness, but they are not as significant as the continuing influence of parents. Not surprisingly, young adults who are close to their parents are more likely to be influenced by them in their religiousness.

The college years are actually a period of relative stability in religiousness. However, the years after college are period of rapid change, with a 43 percent drop in church engagement of American Christians between teens and early adulthood (Kinnaman, 2011). Some college graduates still believe themselves to be Christian; others do not. Still others feel stuck in a clash between culture and church. We do not have secure predictors of who will de-convert, but rebellion against parents does not seem to be a strong factor. Interest is growing in the formation of identity in the young adult years, and it seems likely that religiousness is often intertwined with that.

As adulthood continues, there is a good deal of religious switching. The Pew Forum on Religion and Public Life of 2008 found that 24 percent of Americans had shifted from the faith in which they had been reared. That rose to 44 percent if switching between Protestant denominations was included. More conservative churches, whether Catholic or Protestant, hold their membership better than the liberal mainline churches. However, significant numbers of people leave evangelical churches, offsetting the numbers who join them, and interest has been growing in the phenomenon of "post-evangelicals."

Many of those who join churches have previously been church members; they are "de-churched" rather than "un-churched." Similarly, most conversions are of people who have a religious background. Many religious groups like to believe that conversions are once-and-for-all, decisive changes, but many conversions are short lived, and some people convert repeatedly. When people return to religion after a period away, it is often to a more conservative form. Underlying all this switching in, out, and within religion, there is the underlying trend after the Second World War, even in the United States, for fewer people to be religious. That trend is much further advanced in Europe than in the United States. It is especially marked in Protestant Northern Europe, though there currently also seems to be quite rapid decline in religious attendance in the Catholic countries of Europe.

Later Life

Older adults (those over 65) are more likely to be religious (Hood et al. 2009, chap. 7), something that is reflected in both religious attendance and private prayer. That is partly a cohort effect, reflecting the fact that older adults were brought up in a more religious era. However, it also seems to be a genuine age effect, in that it remains the case in one cohort after another that people are quite likely to return to religion in later life. Various factors contribute to this. One key factor is that, after retirement, people obviously have more time for religion.

Spiritual issues in old age also have to do with finding meaning and purpose. Older people are more likely to cite loss of relationships than loss of work as leaving them without a sense of purpose. The two probably interact, with loss of both creating more significant problems than loss of either one. There has recently been a burgeoning of interest in spirituality in old age, but also disquiet among a number of researchers about how this tends to be measured (McFadden, 2013). Many approaches to spirituality in older people take spirituality out of a religious context. Given that older people are the most religious group in society, it is doubtful whether that is appropriate and may reflect the preconceptions about spirituality of younger researchers. There is also a good deal of reflection in the literature about the spiritual wisdom that develops in old age, though that may have more to do with romanticization of old age than with established fact.

Religion in its traditional form may actually be helpful to older people in developing a spiritual response to the issues they face. One of the key problems of older people is loneliness, and religious communities can do something to offset that. Religion can also provide people with ways of coping with the health problems of old age (see Chapter 11 for more on religious coping). Older people face problems of physical illness and limited physical capacities. Those are rather different from the problems of loss that occur in people who have recently retired. As we will see in the next chapter, religion generally helps people cope with problems of physical health, and there is no reason to think that is not also true of older people.

Finally, old age brings the prospect of death, and religion has particular resources, particularly belief in the afterlife, to help people cope with that. In general, religion does seem to help adjustment in older people (Hood et al., 2009, chap. 7). Belief in the afterlife, far from being eroded by trends to secularization, actually seems to be increasing (see Chapter 10). Indeed, it is an index of spirituality that may have a different causal basis from many other indices of religion. Coping with impending death may be a point where religion and spirituality have rather different contributions. Nonreligious forms of spirituality usually do not foster belief in an afterlife in the same way as religion does. Though older people are quite likely to believe in an afterlife, it is not clear from the research that fear of death is much affected by that. There may not be much connection between intellectual and emotional aspects of attitudes to death.

Summary

- The cognitive understanding of religion in children is the only change in religiousness that can properly be seen in terms of stages of development; it moves predictably, from concrete to abstract. Other aspects of religious change, including faith development in adults, are too unpredictable to be viewed as a series of stages.
- Focusing too much on the limited intellectual understanding of religion in children obscures their rich spiritual experience. However, with advancing age, fewer older children report spiritual experiences.
- The cognitive science of religion has opened up a promising new line of work on religious development, focusing particularly on young children. Research shows that children only start to develop a distinction between human and supernatural cognitive powers around age four and, prior to that, assume that humans have supernatural powers.
- Children are more likely to be religious if their parents are, especially if the children have close relationships with parents. The religiousness of college students continues to be influenced mainly by parents, but it is a period in which the trend is to become more spiritual than religious.
- People's relationship to God can be seen as a kind of attachment relationship. The way in which adults relate to God is predictable from the kind of attachment relationships they had with their parents.
- Later life is a period of increasing religiousness, and the focus is often on traditional religion rather than spirituality. Religion is associated with good adjustment among the elderly and can contribute to coping with the challenges of later life.

10

Varieties and Types

Religious people differ greatly from one another, so much so that you really cannot put them all in the same category. One of the main differences between the sociology and psychology of religion is how practitioners respond to this issue. Sociologists want to focus on religious culture, which means focusing on what is common to the people of that culture. Psychologists, in contrast, are fascinated by how people differ and want to get down to detail about what they call "individual differences."

Exactly how best to do that, in connection with religion, is not straightforward. You can claim that every person is unique. That leads to case studies of particular religious individuals. That approach can yield much interesting material, but it is hard to move from case studies to generalizations of any kind. We need to find a middle way between assuming that all religious people are the same and of regarding each one as unique. That requires some kind of classification.

Individual differences in religion pose two main questions. One focuses on how religious people differ from nonreligious people. The problem with that question is that religious people differ so much among themselves that it is hard to find clear differences between religious and nonreligious people. The other question focuses on how religious people differ between themselves and seeks to explain those differences psychologically. I suggest that it is helpful to subdivide religious people in some relevant way before comparing them with the nonreligious, else the diversity of religious people confuses the comparison.

In this chapter, I will consider two main ways into these issues. One is to start with demographic variables or general personality variables, and see how religion maps onto them. For example, we can consider how men and women differ. The alternative approach is to survey the many ways in which religious people differ from one another, and to propose some types or dimensions that will be theoretically fruitful in distinguishing among them.

Gender

One of the most interesting differences in religiousness is that between men and women. The basic fact is fairly clear – more women than men attend church in countries such as the United States and the UK, where the psychology of religion has mainly flourished. The best recent overview of research on this topic is that of Leslie Francis and Gemma Penny (2014). On the face of things, a strong and secure research finding is that women are more religious than men. However, we first need to check whether the basic phenomenon is as secure as it appears.

The majority of evidence relates just to church attendance, and it needs to be asked whether women are more religious than men in other aspects of religiousness, such as religious experience, belief, and private religious practices. In fact, it seems that they are and that, when these other aspects of religiosity are examined, gender differences turn out to be even more pronounced than for church attendance (Sullins, 2006).

We also need to consider whether women are more religious than men across faiths and cultures. In fact, this is not invariably the case, which is a cause for concern. There is probably no other topic on which the psychology of religion has been more misled by its selective focus on Christianity in the United States and other related cultures. In Judaism and Islam, men are found to be more religious (Francis and Penny, 2014, p. 328), or at least more involved in public religion. Further, whether or not women are found to be more religious than men seems to depend on the kind of culture studied, and to be found mainly in relatively secular societies (Sullins, 2006).

Why should gender differences be dependent on culture in this way? It might be argued that in non-secular cultures, and in many religions other than Christianity, strong norms about religiosity to some extent override gender-based predispositions. One might there-fore argue that gender predispositions are best observed in secular cultures where religiosity is optional. That is a reassuring view of culture differences, but it may be too easy, and the lack of cultural generalizability deserves more attention than it has so far received from psychologists.

Another view of cultural variations in gender biases in religion is that they are, to some extent, self-perpetuating. Recruits to religion may have a tendency to reflect the prevailing gender balance of existing religious people in that culture. Men may also have a tendency to be more attracted to religion in cultures where the sexes are separated in religious participation, something that tends not to be the case in more secular cultures. Such possibilities all deserve careful consideration.

Leaving this issue of cultural generalizability aside, let us focus down on the undoubted fact that, within Christianity in the United States and related cultures, women are more religious than men. Why should that be?

Much work in this area stems from Sandra Bem's theory of sex roles, and the inventory she developed to measure them (Bem, 1981). She proposed that masculinity and femininity are separate dimensions that are independent of each other, rather than being alternatives. She also proposed that men and women differ significantly in their sex roles. Building on this, Thompson (1991) argued that it should be the sex roles that people have, rather than whether they are men or women, that influences religiosity. The evidence in support of this theory has been quite strong (e.g., Francis and Penny, 2014, p. 326).

Another approach has been to look for general dimensions of personality on which there are gender differences, and which in turn relate to religiosity. One line of work of this kind has been made use of Eysenck's three-dimensional model of personality, extroversion-introversion, neuroticism, and psychoticism (Francis, 2009). Of these three dimensions, psychoticism seems to be most closely related to religiosity, with religious people having lower psychoticism scores. (Psychoticism may not be the best name for this scale; it has turned out to measure psychopathy as much as psychoticism.) As men generally obtain higher psychoticism scores than women, that may contribute to the greater religiousness of women. A complication here, as Francis notes, is that religious people tend to be gender atypical; men training for ordained ministry are unusually high in femininity, and women training for ministry are unusually high in masculinity, as these terms are conventionally understood (Francis and Penny, 2014).

Yet another mediating construct that has been invoked is risk aversion (Miller and Hoffman, 1995). The proposal is that women are more averse to risk than men, and that predisposes them to religion. The debates about this theory have been quite complex (Sullins, 2006; Francis and Penny, 2014). One weakness of risk aversion theory in this context is that it has focused solely on the risk of eternal damnation. Avoiding that risk will be a powerful motivator only for those who believe in eternal damnation, and that is not everybody. Indeed, in predominantly secular societies it is probably a diminishing proportion of the population. Of course, risk assessment theory could be broadened to take account of other risks, and religion may then have a broader role in protecting people from risk.

Though the correlation between sex and gender role, or between sex and risk aversion, is not exact, the assumption is that women will tend to be more feminine (and risk averse) than men. To explain that, people have often invoked the assumption that there are gender differences in upbringing, and that the more feminine sex roles that develop in females are more conducive to religion than those that develop in most men. Indications are that the upbringing of girls tends to place more weight on values and attributes that connect well with religion.

Nevertheless, it should not be too readily assumed that upbringing is the only relevant factor. The tendency has often been to neglect the possible role of biological factors, though it has been argued that gender differences in risk aversion may have a biological basis (see Miller and Stark, 2002). Current developments in epigenetics are eroding the sharp distinction that used to be drawn between nature and nurture, as discussed in Chapter 3.

An alternative to focusing on upbringing is to look at the social roles that adult men and women have in society. There are more men than women in the workplace. Data from the World Bank released in 2014 indicates that in the United States the ratio of female to male labor force participation was 82 percent; in many other countries, the ratio is lower. It might be the different social roles of men and women that explain their differences in religiosity, rather than their different upbringings. That might work in various ways. People who are not employed may have more time and opportunity for religion than those employed, or they might have more need for the support or coping resources that religion provides. It may also be that the values associated with home-based roles are more closely aligned with religion than employment values.

Evidence relating employment to religiosity is inconsistent, and the relationship is likely to be complex. For example, unemployment may have different implications depending on whether it has been chosen or is involuntary, though it would require research with quite large numbers of people to sort all that out. The matter is worth pursuing, as it seems unlikely that employment status is irrelevant to public religiousness.

It is also important to take account of cultural changes. The cultures in which the relationships between gender and religion have been most studied are becoming more secular. Extrapolating from that trend, we might expect gender differences in religion to become more pronounced. However, there are factors moving in the opposite direction. Differences in upbringing between boys and girls are probably less pronounced now than when Bem first proposed her sex role theory. Social expectations of men and women are also becoming more egalitarian. In fact, one of the puzzles in this area is that gender differences in religion, at least in the cultures where they have been most studied, apparently remain so strong despite the erosion of gender-related norms. If that continues, it is bound to make explanations based on gender norms less persuasive.

Social Class and Denomination

Social class is another demographic variable that is connected to religion (see Beit-Hallahmi and Argyle, 1997, chap. 8; Christiano et al., 2015). The general trend is for religion to be positively correlated with social and economic status and educational level. As with gender, it is an important question whether that just applies to observable religious attendance or whether it applies to other aspects of religion, such as powerful spiritual experiences. It seems that it does apply to experience too (e.g., Hay, 1982); most aspects of religion are positively associated with social class and educational level. However, the picture is complicated by the fact that different sections of society show different forms of religious participation. For example, liberal Protestantism shows a different and positive relationship with social class from Pentecostalism, which is stronger in more disadvantaged sections of society. The same may be true of practices such as glossolalia, exorcism, and serpent handling. The fact that patterns of religious practice differ between sections of society makes it difficult to compare overall levels of religiosity.

It should be noted, as with gender, that all this is likely to depend on cultural circumstances, which may well also change over time. Each denomination tends to have a membership that is drawn from a particular socioeconomic age band. In recent decades, membership has declined in mainline denominations, such as American Episcopalians, who have come traditionally from the upper end of the socioeconomic range. On the other hand, there is growth in denominations such as the Pentecostal churches that have recruited toward the lower end of the social class range. If that continues, it will lead to significant changes in the way religion relates to social class.

Less interest has been shown in comparing the forms of religiousness found in different denominations than one might have expected, but it could be interesting psychologically. The problem is that some denominations are quite diverse in their members and do not represent a single approach to religiousness. Also, some of the important categories such as evangelicals cut across denominations. Nevertheless, members of a particular denomination form a more coherent group than religious (or Christian) people in general.

Personality and Values

One of the most widely used approaches to personality in modern psychology is the "Big Five" model that provides measure of neuroticism, extraversion, openness to experience, conscientiousness, and agreeableness. Some of these dimensions may be useful in distinguishing religious from nonreligious people, whereas others may be useful in distinguishing one kind of religious person from another.

Of these five dimensions, religion is most closely related to conscientiousness and agreeableness (Koenig et al., 2012). However, from the point of view of distinguishing different kinds of religious people, openness to experience is the most interesting dimension. Though the relationships are not strong, the trend is for openness to experience to be positively correlated with spirituality, but negatively correlated with fundamentalist religion (Saroglou, 2002). The distinction between spiritual and conservative forms of religion is important, as they are likely to differ in so many ways. If openness to experience proves a good way into that distinction, it could be quite important in the psychology of religion. It may also be that neuroticism and extraversion can distinguish among religious people, even though they do not distinguish religious from nonreligious people.

Religion may actually be more strongly related to values than to personality. The study of values is a recent development in the psychology of religion and seems promising. Most research on values and religion has drawn on the value theory of Shalom Schwartz (Schwartz and Huismans, 1995), which distinguishes ten basic values: achievement, benevolence, conformity, hedonism, power, security, self-direction, stimulation, tradition, and universalism. These are organized around two basic dimensions: self-enhancement vs. self-transcendence, and openness to change vs. conservatism. The results from a series of studies, using different measures and different religious samples, seem fairly clear (see Roccas and Elster, 2014). Religious people place high value on tradition and, to a lesser extent, on benevolence and conformity. In contrast, they place low value on hedonism and, to a lesser extent, on stimulation and self-direction.

So far, research on religion and values has not been used to distinguish between different kinds of religious people, but it could be. For example, in the research so far, religious people seem to be low on two values related to openness to change: stimulation and self-direction. However, from the work on openness to change referred to earlier, it seems that some religious people, if only a minority, place high value on openness to change and lower value on tradition and conformity. Though it is not surprising that religious people place high value on benevolence and low value on hedonism, they may differ in how far those declared values affect their actual behavior, as we will see later in this chapter.

Types of Religiousness

We now turn from this approach, based on mapping religion onto existing variables and dimension, to a more theoretical approach to religious variation. Religious people differ from one another in so many ways that a variety of subdivisions are possible. That raises the question of what would be a really good way of subdividing or classifying them. In brief, I suggest that a theoretically fruitful way of classifying religious people takes an apparently simple way in which religious people differ from one another and shows that it maps onto so many other differences that it can be seen as a really fundamental difference. The aim is that the people assigned to a particular type should be fairly similar to one another, and you try to achieve that without resorting to too many subtypes. You also try to avoid having too many people who do not really fit into any type at all.

We have already encountered some examples of religious typologies. People convert to religion in different ways, and conversion type maps onto many other things apart from religiosity. We now know sudden conversions tend to come earlier in life, to be more emotional, to be linked to conservative theology, to have a strong emphasis on release from sin and guilt, to arise from a sense of deprivation, and to have an element of passivity. People with sudden conversions have a number of other non-religious characteristics too, including being more conservative in their social attitudes and on political issues. The distinction between sudden and gradual conversion types has stood the test of time.

Another distinction that was important to William James is that between the healthy-minded and sick-soul religious types. A similar distinction has reappeared in the work on attachment and religion that we looked at in the previous chapter. People who turn to God to compensate for insecure attachments roughly correspond to James's sick souls, whereas those who transfer a stable attachment style from parents to God are equivalent to healthy-minded religious people.

Another typology that might well be fruitful would be to categorize people according to their predominant type of prayer, whether that is meditative, ritualistic, petitionary, or colloquial (Poloma and Gallup, 1991). I suspect that those categories would be useful markers for wide-ranging differences in forms of religion. Those who share a predominant prayer type will probably have a lot else in common.

Religious Orientation: Intrinsic, Extrinsic, and Quest

One of the most important classifications of religious people to have been proposed is Gordon Allport's distinction between intrinsic and extrinsic religious types (Allport and Ross, 1967). Intrinsics are people whose religion is the dominant motive in their lives, whereas extrinsics are people who are involved in religion because it serves other purposes for them, social purposes for example A similar distinction has been made between committed and consensual religious people.

One hallmark of a theoretically fruitful distinction between religious types is that differences in approach to religion are associated with other nonreligious differences. Allport's distinction was developed to explore the fact that religious people appeared to be socially and racially prejudiced. With more careful research, that proved to be true of extrinsic but not intrinsic types. One very striking finding from the first wave of research on religious orientation was that on measures of social prejudice. Intrinsic and extrinsic religious people differed from the nonreligious population in opposite directions, with extrinsics having more social prejudice than nonreligious people, while intrinsics had less.

However, a problem with this religious orientation research is that the concept of "intrinsic" religion seems to be ambiguous. Daniel Batson suggested a third "quest" type (Batson et al., 1993). Adding a third category of people whose approach to religion is one of spiritual seeking can have consequences for what is meant by intrinsic religion. Compared with quest religion, intrinsics emerge as people who have a dogmatic approach to religion. That is probably somewhat different from what Allport originally intended.

Another correlate of religious orientation that has been explored is "prosocial," or altruistic, helping behavior. Initially it appeared that following the pattern of research on prejudice, intrinsics were more pro-social than extrinsics. However, as Batson and colleagues noted, that only seems to hold up when self-report measures are used. Intrinsic religious people believe themselves to be more pro-social, but there is scant evidence of that in their actual behavior. Batson has claimed that quest religious people are pro-social in their actual behavior; there is indeed some evidence for that, though it is not entirely consistent.

The extent of religious pro-sociality has limits. Rose and Exline (2012) note that it does not occur if prompt retaliation is anticipated as a result of pro-social behavior. There also seem to be limits to the kinds of people to whom pro-social behavior is shown, and it may not extend to people for whom there is religiously based disapproval.

Another interesting feature of recent research in this area is the dissociation between racial prejudice and antigay prejudice (Rose and Exline, 2012). It seems that intrinsic religious people show homophobic prejudice but not racial prejudice, whereas extrinsic religious people show racial but not homophobic prejudice. Quest religious people show neither. The attitudes of intrinsic religious people seem to be most plausibly explained in terms of current church attitudes that condemn racial prejudice but are often intolerant of homosexuality. There is nothing new in finding racial prejudice in extrinsics, but it is interesting that a matching prejudice against homosexuality does not exist.

Opinions are divided about how fruitful the distinction between extrinsic, intrinsic, and quest types has been. Some believe that the conceptual and measurement issues, especially surrounding the difference between intrinsic and quest types, have become complex and intractable. On the other hand, it is impressive that religious orientation has continued to yield interesting research findings over such a long period of time, and also that intrinsic and extrinsic religious people differ so markedly, and on a good range of nonreligious variables. It underlines the importance of not treating religious people as though they were a single heterogeneous category. The distinction between these three types, despite its problems, is the best taxonomy we have so far in the psychology of religion. If it could be replaced by a better approach that had fewer problems, that would be an advance. However, in my view, it would be a retrograde step to revert to treating religious people as a single homogeneous category.

Conservative vs. Liberal

An important distinction among religious people is that between conservatives and liberals. Conservatism spans religious and nonreligious domains, and people who are conservative in religion are generally conservative in their sociopolitical attitudes and values as well. Exciting advances are currently being made in the study of conservatism in political psychology, and it is puzzling that the implications for the psychology of religion are not being pursued more actively. Conclusions about differences between conservatives and liberals in politics are likely to be paralleled by differences between conservatives and liberals in religion.

In examining the genetic basis of religion, I suggested that conservatism in religion might have a significant genetic basis. Conservatism extends beyond religion, but it is massively influential within it. Indeed, given the current preponderance of conservative religion, the danger is that conservatism will swamp any studies of religion that do not explicitly make distinctions between conservative and liberal ways of being religious and give the misleading impression that all religion is conservative.

One potentially fruitful approach to conservatism is in terms of what moral systems or foundations people work with. Jonathan Haidt (2012) has proposed six moral foundations: care/harm for others, fairness/cheating, justice or proportionality, liberty/oppression, loyalty/betrayal, authority/subversion, and sanctity/degradation. It seems that conservatives and liberals differ in the moral foundations they rely on. For example, in an analysis of sermons, it was found that Unitarian preachers focused selectively on care and fairness key words, whereas Baptist preachers focused more on loyalty, authority, and sanctity (Haidt, 2012, p. 188). More generally, Haidt claims that conservatives draw on the full range of moral foundations, whereas liberals focus selectively on just a few of them. This represents an interesting fresh approach to how religious people differ.

John Hibbing and colleagues (Hibbing at al., 2014) reviewed interesting recent work on cognitive and physiological differences between conservatives and liberals. He summarizes the evidence for concluding that conservatism has a genetic basis and documents the broad range of ways in which conservatives differ from liberals, even including preferences for foods. However, it is becoming clear that the key difference is that conservatives are more vigilant for (and react more strongly to) negative stimuli than to positive ones, whereas liberals do not show that bias. It seems that conservatives are vigilant for threat and danger in a way that liberals are not.

The range of methodologies that have been used to document the basic finding of vigilance for threat is impressive, with a rich range of cognitive and physiological measures. It gives me some pleasure that among them is a method that I developed in the 1980s when working on phobic anxiety, the emotional Stroop test. It had long been known that if color words are printed in assorted colors, people find it hard to ignore the actual word and name the color it is printed in. I thought the same might apply with emotionally salient or threat words and found that people with a phobia of spiders were slow to name the colors in which spider-related words were printed. That has now been applied to positive and negative words, and research has found that conservatives are slower to name colors for negative than for positive words. Liberals, in contrast, show no difference in color naming for the two sets of words (see Hibbing et al., 2014).

Differential vigilance for threat and danger seems likely to be a key mediating path between genes and conservatism. It is entirely plausible that some people have a genetic predisposition to be vigilant for threat; it is not difficult to see how that might have evolved. However, there could be advantages in having a society that contained some people who were more vigilant for threat and others who were not. That is what we appear to have. Conservative attitudes, values, and preferences are probably an out-working of that vigilance for threat in our current political context. An important conceptual point here is that conservatism is at least as much about *how* people think as about *what* they think; it is about process as well as content. This recent work on political conservatism points to a parallel body of research that could be carried out on religious conservatism that would be focused more on process rather than content, though also exploring the implications of one for the other.

There may also be interesting links to explore with cognitive complexity. As we noted in Chapter 7, a potentially important distinction among religious people can be made between those with low or high cognitive complexity. It makes a big difference to religion whether or not people can move beyond black-and-white thinking and integrate different perspectives; such differences deserve fuller investigation. A correlation may well exist between conservative religious views and cognitive complexity, but I suggest that there is no necessary connection between process and content. It is possible to be cognitively complex about a conservative position and to be cognitively simple about a liberal one.

Though in general there is a correlation between religious and sociopolitical conservatism (Scobie, 1975), differences also exist. They may show different patterns of correlations with variables such as age, sex, intelligence, and social class. They may also show different types of social prejudice. In view of the dissociation between racial and homophobic prejudice found with intrinsic and extrinsic types, it would not be surprising if religious conservatives showed more homosexual prejudice, and sociopolitical conservatives showed more racial prejudice. Despite the possibility of such differences, it seems likely that similar psychological processes will underlie conservatism in both domains.

Conservatism is a key factor in current religion, with a strong biological and cognitive basis. In Chapter 3, I also suggested that spirituality and the tendency to be open to an unusually broad range of conscious experience may also have a biological basis, and it has also tended to be rather neglected in current psychology of religion. Both of these are distinct from culturally religious people, whose religion is mainly shaped more by culture, environment, and sense of social identity. The threefold distinction between conservative religion, spiritual-experiential religion, and cultural religion may actually be quite similar to the much investigated categories of intrinsic, quest, and extrinsic, but it provides a fresh way of conceptualizing them.

Dimensions of Religiousness

Though working with types is clear and simple and, for that reason, quite attractive, psychologists have generally preferred to work with continuous dimensions. Any personality concept can be formulated in either way. For example, when Jung introduced introversion-extroversion into psychology, he conceptualized it as two basic types. Subsequent research, particularly associated with Hans Eysenck, has conceptualized it as a continuous dimension, measurable by a questionnaire.

Continuous dimensions are preferred for two main reasons. One is that they provide more specific, fine-grained information about each individual if he or she is assigned a place on a continuous dimension than just to say that person is one type or the other. The other more fundamental reason is that if you work with continuous dimensions, you usually find that the majority of people fall in the middle of the dimension. If so, it is a distortion of reality to try to classify everyone as one type or the other. Most psychological variables turn out to follow what statisticians call a "normal" distribution. It is a property of such distributions that, roughly speaking, two-thirds of people fall in the central third of the dimension, and only a third of people fall in the two outlying sections of it. Of course, it may be more informative to compare people at one extreme or the other of a continuous dimension. However, scoring people on a continuous dimension helps identify who the extreme cases actually are.

The standard methodology is to use psychological questionnaires to measure continuous dimensions. A set of questions is assembled that all seem to be getting at roughly the same thing, and the scores for each are added together to provide an overall score. Two main things should be asked of any psychological questionnaire: whether it is concerned with religion or anything else, one is about reliability, the other is about validity.

The various scores that are added together to give an overall score should be from questions that in practice tend to be answered in the same way. That is an empirical matter that can be checked, and it is what justifies adding them together as measures of the same trait. A good questionnaire will have been shown to have high "internal homogeneity," which is an index of how well the questions hang together in the way they are answered. It shows that the questionnaire measures whatever it purports to measure in a way that is sufficiently reliable to be useful.

The other requirement of a good questionnaire is that there should be some independent evidence that the questionnaire really does measure what it purports to measure. Ideally, evidence of such validity should go beyond the face validity of what the questions appear to be measuring. For example, you might hope to find evidence that a self-report questionnaire measure of religious practices correlates well with measures coming from some independent, objective measure of those practices.

Though questionnaires have played an important role in the psychology of religion, the field should not be overdependent on this single methodology. Ideally, a convergence of evidence should always be sought from at least two methodologies. Questionnaires can be validated against a variety of other measures, including interviews, direct observation of behavior, biological measures (such as measures of autonomic nervous system activity, or measures of electric rhythms in the brain, as discussed in connection with studies of meditation), or experimental methods (such as the studies of subliminal priming mentioned in connection with research on attachment).

A wide range of questionnaire measures have been developed for the assessment of religion. An excellent overview of these measures has been provided by Peter C. Hill (2013). Various short measures give a general index of religiosity. That can be justified by the fact that in the general population, different facets of religion tend to be correlated with one another. However, under various circumstances different aspects of religiousness can become dissociated from one another. That would be particularly likely to be true among people who had impairments of one kind or another.

The extent to which a general factor of religiousness is found, reflected in high correlations between measures of various specific facets of religion, depends largely on the nature of the population studied. If you look at a population varied in its overall religiousness, you will find evidence of a strong general religious factor (just as if you look at measures of cognitive ability in a population varied in general intelligence, you will find support for a strong factor of general intelligence). However, if you look at how measures of religiousness correlate with each other in a population where most people are reasonably religious, you will find much stronger evidence for distinct facets of religiousness and less support for an overall general factor.

In view of that, it may be more useful to employ multi-scale questionnaires that provide an indication of how religious people are on several aspects of religion. For example, the five-dimensional model of religiosity developed by Glock and Stark (1965) led to the Dimensions of Religious Commitment Scale (Glock and Stark, 1966), which gives people a score on each of the following dimensions:

- ritualistic dimension (i.e., religious practices)
- ideological adherence (i.e., adherence to religious beliefs)
- experiential dimension (i.e., religious feelings and experiences)
- intellectual dimension (i.e., knowledge about religion)
- consequential dimension (i.e., the effects of religion on a person's life).

Perhaps the most important distinction among aspects of religiousness is between external aspects of religion such as affiliation and attendance and internal aspects such as prayer and personal conviction. Often those aspects will be aligned, but sometimes they will become dissociated. External religious affiliation and attendance have a different significance depending on whether or not they are aligned with internal aspects.

Conclusion

It is one of the most serious disappointments about the psychology of religion that, despite the manifest diversity of religious people, it has so far failed to find any entirely satisfactory taxonomy. Research that looks at religious people as a single group runs the risk of not finding anything very much, because there is too much noise in the data, arising from unexamined religious diversity. It also runs the risk of misrepresenting religion and presenting findings about one way of being religious as though that were true of all religious people. Finding a better taxonomy of religious people, and using it more consistently, is the main thing the field currently needs.

Summary

- Women are often more religious than men, on various measures of religion. However, that is not an invariant pattern across all cultures. There are various explanatory factors, including the effect of upbringing on sex roles and the different positions of men and women in society.
- On personality measures, religious people are found to be conscientious and agreeable. Fundamentalist religious people have low openness to experience, whereas those who emphasize spirituality score highly on it. Religious people place high value on tradition and low value on hedonism.
- The most widely investigated typology of religious people divides them into intrinsic, extrinsic, and quest types. Despite various conceptual and measurement problems, these types have been found to differ on a wide range of variables.
- More research should be undertaken on differences between conservative and liberal religious types, who differ in many ways that extend beyond religion. Evidence shows that political conservatives are more orientated toward threat, and that may also be true of religious conservatives.
- Methodologically, there is value in investigating differences between religious people in terms of continuous dimensions rather than a classification into types. Religious people differ so much among themselves that they should not be treated as a single homogeneous group.

Health and Adjustment

Evidence is growing that religion tends to be good for health and adjustment. I will discuss the evidence for that in relation to physical health, mental health, and moral functioning. However, many complexities surround this relationship. There are particular complexities, as we will see, in the relationship between religion and mental health.

One recurrent issue is about the concept of "religion." As we have seen in other contexts, religion is not a unitary construct. Different aspects of religion may have different associations with health and adjustment. It makes a difference what aspect of religion is measured. A parallel issue concerns sampling. Religious people are diverse, and what relationship is found between religion and other variables will depend on what range of religious people are sampled. For example, conservative religious people may give different results than more liberal ones.

Health and adjustment are difficult to measure too, and important distinctions need to be taken into account. Moral attitudes may give different results than moral behavior. Self-report measures of mental health may give different results than more objective, clinical assessments. Positive measures of good health may give results that are different from, and not merely the inverse of, those for pathology. Religion may have a different relationship with the risk of onset of a health problem than what it has with health outcomes among those who already suffer from the problem.

Yet another problem is that many research studies simply demonstrate that religion is associated with health and adjustment. They often seem to provide reasonable grounds inferring that religion has causal effects, but that is usually an assumption rather than something that has actually been demonstrated. There are, logically, at least two other possibilities. One is that religiousness is affected by health or adjustment; that is, people with certain kinds of problems (such as abuse of drugs and alcohol) may be less likely to be religious simply because of those problems. The other possibility is that the association between religion and health arises because both are related to some third variable. That is difficult to rule out definitively. However, candidates for that third variable, such as socioeconomic class, can be proposed and measured, and then statistical procedures can be used for checking whether the relationship between religion and health/adjustment still holds up when relationships with the third variable are allowed for.

No research study will be perfect from every point of view, though some are better than others; the better the methodological quality of a study, the more reliance can be placed upon it. It also helps to have replication of results from one study to another. If the same relationship is found in a variety of studies, despite differences of detail, that is much more compelling than a finding from just one study.

Religion and Morality

In considering the impact of religion on morality, we need to distinguish different aspects of morality. The research literature has mainly distinguished moral attitudes and moral behavior, but other components could be distinguished too.

A strong association between religion and moral attitudes has been found in numerous studies. Hood et al. (2009, p. 383) give a list. Religious people are more opposed to abortion, AIDS education, divorce, pornography, contraception, premarital sexuality, homosexuality, feminism, nudity in advertising, suicide, euthanasia, amniocentesis (prenatal diagnosis of chromosomal abnormalities), heavy metal and rock music, and women going topless on beaches. In contrast, religious people are more likely to support marriage, capital punishment, vengeance, traditional sex roles, conservative political parties, severe criminal sentences, and censorship of sex and violence in the media.

It is an impressively long list, and there are no doubt more such correlates of religion for which we do not yet have direct evidence. However, it does raise questions again about the diversity of religious people. In some ways, these correlates of religion are only what some people might expect. However, it is surely clear that not all religious people hold these conservative moral attitudes. The diversity of religious attitudes to the touchstone issue of homosexuality is well known. In fact, some religious people might be more liberal than nonreligious people on many of these things. Once again, it is necessary to look for appropriate ways of distinguishing different kinds of religious people so that their diversity does not get drowned in the preponderance of religious conservatism.

The situation is even more complex for moral behavior. Let us postpone altruistic behavior and look first at whether religious people actually refrain from the kind of immoral behavior of which they mostly disapprove (see Hood et al., 2009, chap. 12, for a good review). Religious people show less abuse of drugs and alcohol, though the relevant research (Koenig et al., 2012) has largely used self-report measures, and the association does not seem to be found in all cultures. Religious people are also less likely to engage in premarital sexual activity, though evidence shows diversity in religious attitudes, with extrinsic religious people being more permissive. There is also less crime and delinquency among religious people (Koenig et al., 2012), though some behaviors such as domestic abuse are actually more common in very patriarchal religious families.

Despite the complexities, the basic finding that there is less immoral behavior among religious people is fairly clear. What is not at all clear, however, is what causal relationship underlies this. One can see ways in which religion might act to curb immorality, partly through prohibitions and moral teaching, partly perhaps through steering people toward a lifestyle that meets needs that would otherwise have been met through immoral activities. However, it seems clear that causal effects can work in the opposite direction. People who are delinquent, or who are abusing drugs and alcohol, might well feel that they would not fit in or be welcome in a religious community. It seems likely that causal relationships in both directions play a role, but it is hard at this point to be sure about their relative importance.

A weakness in a great many studies is that they have relied on self-report measures, and results may look different when behavioral measures are used. That has emerged particularly from studies of cheating. It is helpful to note at the outset that no strong trait of honesty spans different situations. The large-scale observational studies of cheating behavior in children carried out by Hartshorne and May in the 1920s (see Mischel, 1968) showed little correlation between cheating at home and school; they also found little correlation between cheating and religion and, as Mischel reports, subsequent research using behavioral measures has largely confirmed that. Lie scores on questionnaires have also not provided any consistent evidence of greater honesty in religious people, though studies have been quite discrepant from one another.

It may be puzzling why cheating is less strongly associated with religion than the other aspects of morality we have looked at so far. One approach to this that may be helpful is Jonathan Haidt's moral foundations theory (Haidt, 2012). The moral issues we have considered so far, on which religious people differ substantially from nonreligious people, look as though they mostly belong to the Sanctity/Degradation system that focuses on purity and disgust. It may well be that religious people, or at least conservative religious people, feel most strongly about such issues. On Haidt's theory, a separate system deals with Justice/Fairness issues, including honesty and cheating, and there may be less difference between religious and nonreligious people on that.

Last, we turn to altruistic and helping behavior or "pro-sociality." That involves yet another aspect of morality. In terms of Haidt's theory, it relates to the Care/Harm system. The best recent review of research on religion and pro-sociality is by Jesse Lee Preston and colleagues (Preston et al., 2014).

The research has been relatively sophisticated in that it has used different measures of helping and has explored the difference between self-report measures and behavioral observation. It has also looked at different types of religious people. In particular, following a hypothesis proposed by Daniel Batson (Batson et al., 1993), it has explored the difference between people with "intrinsic" and "quest" religious motivations.

The majority of studies (e.g., Batson et al., 1993) have shown a commitment to helping behavior in intrinsic religious people, but with two significant caveats. One is that the commitment to helping, evident in self-report measures, is not always matched by observable evidence of helping behavior. The other is that helping behavior tends only to be shown to people who share their moral values and of whom they do not disapprove. In intrinsic religious people, the Sanctity/Degradation moral system seems to trump the Care/Harm system. These caveats do not seem to apply in the same way to quest religious people, who are more likely to show actual helping behavior, and to be less selective in who they show it to. The distinction between intrinsic and quest types indicates the variability of religious people as far as helping is concerned, though it may not be the ideal marker of differences among religious people in helping behavior.

Physical Health

A growing volume of research evidence supports a relationship between religion and physical health. (We will deal with mental health separately in the next section.) The most thorough recent review is the monumental *Handbook of Religion and Health* by Harold Koenig and colleagues (Koenig et al., 2012). It will be necessary to look at a sample of different health issues separately. However, in most cases, the position is that the majority of studies, though by no means all, support a positive relationship between religion and health. They also show that religious people tend to live longer. However, despite these clear trends, the research evidence is somewhat patchy. Another general problem is that we have little firm knowledge of what the causal mechanisms are. There are various plausible possibilities, but little that is actually established. One important distinction that needs to be made is between the role of religion in protecting against the development of particular health problems and its role in securing a good outcome among those who develop health problems. Religion can probably make a positive contribution at both points, but the causal pathway may well be quite different.

Religion and spirituality can affect physical health in various ways, and Koenig and colleagues (2012) distinguish three main ones: behavioral, psychological, and social. There is evidence to support all three.

For most major diseases, lifestyle factors significantly impinge on the risk of developing the disease. Health is often adversely affected by diet, smoking, and drinking. Equally, health can be improved by exercise and better compliance with health advice. Evidence shows that religiousness is associated with healthier lifestyles in all these respects. That is presumably one of the key pathways by which religion improves health, and it presumably explains the good health of Mormons and Seventh-Day Adventists (Koenig et al., 2012). However, the causal links may not be all one way; it may also be the case that healthy people are more drawn to religion.

Religion is also associated with a number of psychological factors, which in turn are likely to be related to good health. In this connection, Koenig and colleagues (2012) list forgiveness, altruism, gratefulness, positive emotions, well-being, quality of life, hope and optimism, meaning and purpose, self-esteem, and personal control. In addition to these effects of religion on positive mental health, there is a tendency, as we will see in the next section, for religion to be associated with the absence of mental illness. Religion is also associated with effective coping styles, something we will also consider later in this chapter. Those can play a part in helping people handle stresses that could otherwise lead to health problems. They can also play a significant role in helping people cope with whatever illness they develop, leading to better health outcomes.

Finally, religion is associated with social factors that can contribute to good health. Social support is especially important. One possible pathway is that social support might lead to better positive mental health, which in turn would lead to better physical health. Also, among those who developed health problems, good social support would probably help them cope with their illness, leading to better outcomes. People differ in what kind of social support they find most helpful. For some people, a significant social network is helpful; for others, a single close confidant is the most useful thing. Evidence shows an association between social support and religion (Koenig et al., 2012), though some religious communities may only provide relatively superficial social support. Religion tends to be associated with greater marital stability, which may be good for social support, though marriage can itself be a source of stress.

To turn to details, religion tends to be associated with lower blood pressure, though, as is often the case, the research evidence is not consistent. Religion could well have an impact on several of the well-established risk factors associated with high blood pressure. Religious people tend to have less cardiac disease, and again that is likely to be mediated by the link between religion and cardiac risk factors such as exercise. It also seems that religion can contribute positively to better outcomes among those with heart disease. That is probably mediated, at least partly, by spiritual practices such as meditation.

Religion also seems to be associated with lower risk of cancer, which is entirely plausible. Various emotional factors are known to be associated with the risk of cancer, which are also associated with endocrine and immune systems, which in turn are related to the risk of cancer (Boivin and Webb, 2011). Religious frameworks of meaning and spiritual practices could well influence these emotional and immunological factors, providing a clear causal pathway by which religion could influence the risk of cancer. Among those who develop cancer, religion can be a good coping resource. Good emotional coping with cancer is associated with immune functioning, which in turn affects the course of cancer. So, again, it is not hard to see how religion could have a favorable impact on the course of cancer.

Pain is an interesting psychosomatic phenomenon that is intertwined with religious belief and spiritual practice (Coakley and Shelmay, 2007). It is well known that the amount of pain people experience is only partly dependent on their level of tissue damage; it is also much influenced by processes in the central nervous system that affect how much pain is actually experienced. At least two processes seem to be involved to which religion could be relevant. Pain seems to be influenced by processes of interpretation, to which religious beliefs are clearly relevant, through the meaning making function of religion. Pain is also influenced by spiritual practices such as mindfulness that teach the skill of being aware of physical sensations without reacting to them with distress.

Mental Health

The research literature on religion and mental health is large, but it is also complex and inconclusive (e.g., Batson et al., 1993; Hood et al., 2009; Koenig at al., 2012). Though it seems that religion generally tends to be good for mental health, that depends on a range of factors.

The relation between religion and mental health depends on what kind of religion you are looking at. As with social prejudice and pro-sociality, the distinction between intrinsic, extrinsic, and quest types of religious-ness may be important. The distinction between religious experience, practice, and belief may also be useful, but has not been much studied in this connection. The relationship that is found between mental health and religion depends on what kind of measures of mental health you use. One distinction is between positive and negative measures of mental health. However, it looks as though an even more relevant distinction is that between objective measures (e.g., diagnosed mental illness, observable abuse of drugs and alcohol) and self-report measures (whether of emotional problems or good psychological adjustment). Different aspects of mental health have different relationships with religion. For example, depression seems to be more closely associated with religion than anxiety.

There is once again the problem of the causal interpretation of correla-tional data. It cannot be assumed that correlations are always to be explained solely in terms of the effects of religion on mental health. Religion may result in better mental health, but the association could equally well be due to mental health affecting religious participation (e.g., people with alcohol problems may stay away from church), or be the result of a third variable, such as socioeconomic class.

Religion can sometimes be associated with *poor* mental health. That creates the intriguing problem of why religion is sometimes helpful and sometimes unhelpful as far as mental health is concerned. Certain forms of religion may be a symptom of poor mental health or may affect mental health adversely. Sometimes both positive and negative relationships between religion and mental health are intertwined and superimposed on each other.

To get deeper into the complexity of the relationship between religion and mental health, we will consider different aspects of mental health studies separately. Religion has its strongest relationship with self-report measures of positive mental health and a sense of well-being (Koenig et al., 2012). It used to be thought that satisfaction with life was mainly related to people's economic situation, though it is now clear that their *relative* economic situation is more important than *absolute* wealth. Also, psychological variables such as hope, purpose, and meaning are important for well-being, and religion feeds directly into those. Though there is a clear relationship between religion and well-being, one caveat is that research in this area depends largely on self-report measures. Another is that the relationship between religion and well-being probably depends to some extent on the kind of religion under consideration, and Batson and colleagues (1993) suggest that it does not work so well for extrinsic forms of religiousness.

Turning to depression, the predominant trend is for religion to be associated with lower rates of depression. That includes some prospective studies in which religion was found to reduce the risk of becoming depressed (Koenig et al., 2012). The most plausible explanation is that religion protects against depression or helps people cope with it. The puzzle is that this relationship is not found more consistently. Koenig offers several possible explanations. For example, genetic factors might tend to produce a positive association between religion and depression. Also, it is noteworthy that several studies that have found more depression in religious people have been carried out in secular cultures in which people are less likely to turn to religion to help them cope. In any culture, the lethargy associated with depression may deter people from religious engagement. That may indeed be one of the vicious circles that keep people locked into depression.

Some forms of religion may be unhelpful in this context. For example, nominal religious adherence and church attendance, without any active spiritual life or religious modes of coping, may be no help. Other forms of religion may foster guilt or low self-esteem that tends to lead to more depression. Indeed, different factors lead religion to be associated with either less or more depression. In many circumstances, the former predominate, but not in all.

One would expect anxiety to relate to religion in the same way as depression, and there is a trend in that direction, though it is a little less consistent than for depression. Research on information processing and emotional disorders has found that depression has a wider range of cognitive effects than anxiety. Williams et al. (1997, chap.11) suggest that the main effects of anxiety are on perception and attention, whereas depression has more effect on conceptual encoding and self-concepts, which in turn shows itself in memory biases. In terms of that distinction, it is plausible that religion has more effect on depression than anxiety because self-encoding is intertwined with religious belief and thinking.

It would be a mistake to lump all anxiety disorders together, as it is likely that different anxiety disorders will have different relationships to religion, though no exhaustive review of the relevant research has tried to sort that out. It seems likely that religious coping will be more effective with general anxiety conditions than with specific ones such as phobias. Also, some anxiety disorders may become intertwined with excessive religiosity, leading to a positive association between religion and anxiety. That seems most likely to be the case in obsessive-compulsive disorder (Abramowitz et al., 2004).

Though the trend is for religion to be inversely related to emotional disorders such as depression and anxiety, the situation is different for psychotic disorders such as schizophrenia (Koenig et al., 2012). In fact, religious beliefs and practices seem to be quite common in schizophrenia. Some psychotic symptoms are actually rather similar to normal religious beliefs. That sometimes creates a problem in distinguishing normal religious belief from psychotic delusions. It seems that the distinction can often be made better by someone who is part of the relevant culture than by someone outside it. Some people with psychotic disorders turn to religion to cope, though others seem to avoid religion because it leads them toward areas where they can easily fall into delusion.

Religion could affect mental health positively in several ways (see Hood et al., 2009, chap. 13). Religious teaching and social pressure may help control certain forms of mental illness behavior, such as abuse of drugs and alcohol. Church membership can provide a supportive community, and social support is often critical in coping with stress. It may also shelter people from some of the normal stresses of life, though that would only apply to people whose life was based around the church. Religious practices such as prayer can be therapeutic and help people cope with stress. Similarly, religious beliefs can provide a framework of meaning that helps people handle difficult experiences.

The beneficial effects of religion fall into two main categories, social and cognitive, and usually both come into play. In key empirical studies, the helpful role of religion seems to have been mediated in complex ways. For example, George Brown, in his study of depression in the Hebrides islands, found that religious women were less likely to become depressed and concluded that was mediated through social support, better self-esteem, and a sense of spiritual support (Brown and Harris, 1978). Daniel McIntosh and colleagues found that religious parents coped better with infant death and concluded that it was mediated though social support, cognitive processes, and the ability to find meaning (McIntosh et al., 1993).

Religion can become intertwined with poor mental health in a bidirectional way. As Hood and colleagues (2009) note, it can be an expression of mental disorder, and it can also be a threat to mental health. Here again, it is important to distinguish different forms of religion, as each can become pathological in its own way. Conservative religion can become rigid and intolerant in ways that contribute to poor mental health. New Age religion is associated with unstable attachment relationships (Farias and Granqvist, 2007). Ritualistic religion can become intertwined with obsessionality. Religious teaching and practices concerning sin can both appeal to and exacerbate problems with guilt. Some religious communities can foster abusive leadership styles and excessively submissive attitudes in participants.

Perhaps the key issue is whether, if people become religious, they engage with a form of religion that exacerbates their potential psychopathology or whether their religion introduces balance and helps liberate them from their potential psychopathology. At worst, religion can become part of a vicious circle that maintains psychopathology. At best, it can limit and counteract pathological tendencies.

Religious Coping

At several points in this chapter, we have referred to religious coping and, in this final section, we will explore that more fully. It is an area of the psychology of religion in which significant advances have been made in recent years, and in which the research of Kenneth Pargament has played a key role (Pargament, 1997).

Religious coping can be understood within the general framework of the psychology of coping, and Pargament has made particular use of the approach to coping formulated by Richard Lazarus and Susan Folkman (1984), which makes a distinction between primary and secondary coping. Primary coping affects how an event is understood, and what personal significance it is perceived as having, for good or ill. Secondary appraisal concerns the extent to which people believe themselves to have access to the resources needed to meet whatever challenge an event presents, whether those resources are their own or are available from others.

Several religious approaches to coping make different assumptions about control. These are analogous to the distinction made in Chapter 7 between internal or external attributions, or some hybrid between the two. At one extreme is a deferring style of religious coping that leaves everything to God. At the other is a style-directed style of coping that emphasizes the role of the individual religious person in coping with stress. Between these two is what Pargament calls collaborative coping, in which God and the person work together. No one coping style is best for all people in all circumstances. Also, the different coping styles can sometimes be used in conjunction with one another. Nevertheless, research shows that the collaborative style generally works best. It is related to lower anxiety and better self-esteem and is most helpful in coping with serious mental illness (see Nelson, 2009, pp. 322–26).

A distinction also needs to be drawn between positive and negative religious coping. Positive coping is orientated to problem solving and draws on religious resources. In contrast, negative religious coping tends to focus on blame, either on God or the religious community. There is no surprise in the fact that negative religious coping is not generally helpful. However, it is surprising that the evidence of an association between positive religious coping and mental health is not stronger. Indeed, mental health tends to be more strongly related to general measures of religiousness than to measures of religious coping. Koenig et al. (2012) discuss some of the possible reasons for this disappointing state of affairs. One possibility is that mental health may be most strongly related to religious coping in more religious cultures, whereas, in secular cultures, less use is made of religious coping.

There is also the methodological problem that the severity of the problems people face varies widely, which may lead to a tendency for people with more severe stresses to turn to religious coping more extensively. That could mask the beneficial effects of coping and even lead to a positive association between religious coping and stress. The solution to this would be to look at a group of people, all of whom have experienced severe stress. In line with that, studies of people who have experienced recent stress have generally found strong evidence of an association between religious coping and stress-related growth (e.g., Park and Fenster, 2004). That has been found even in research with college students, and there would probably be even stronger evidence for the contribution of religion to stress-related growth among these who had experienced a really major stress such as bereavement or injury.

It is not surprising that religion should contribute to coping with trauma, as coping with suffering, and even death, is central to much religious teaching. Some religions, such as Christianity, are built around coping with the trauma of the death of a religious leader. Indeed how Jesus' followers coped with his death can itself be seen as an example of stress-related growth (McGrath, 2006).

Summary

- Religion tends to be associated with good health and adjustment, though not invariably so. The research data usually demonstrates a correlation rather than a causal relationship, and various causal interpretations are often possible.
- The majority of religious people hold conservative moral views on a wide range of issues, but that would not be true of all religious people and depends on the sample studied. Religious people tend to believe in behaving altruistically, but may not do so in practice. Religious people exhibit relatively little immoral behavior, though the causal basis of that is not clear.
- Religion tends to be positively associated with good health on a wide range of measures, for example, with lower blood pressure, less cardiac disease, lower risk of cancer, and less pain. There are various factors by which religion could have health benefits, including health-related behaviors, psychological and emotional processing, and social structure and support.

- Religion is also associated with good mental health. It is especially strongly related to positive mental health but is also associated with less depression and anxiety, and less abuse of drugs and alcohol. Religion can also be associated with poor mental health, including schizophrenia. The major challenge is to understand how the impact of religion on mental health can sometimes be helpful and sometimes unhelpful.
- A substantial body of work now shows the contribution religion can make to coping, with a variety of specific findings, such as that a collaborative coping style of religious coping generally usually works best.

Personal Transformation

This chapter will be devoted to the relationship of religion to personal change and transformation. We will look at both how and why people change when they opt in or out of religion and at how ongoing engagement with religion can contribute to personal growth and well-being.

Conversion

Joining and leaving religion provide an interesting opportunity to study the effects of religion on personality and adjustment. It was a major topic in the early years of the psychology of religion in the late nineteenth and early twentieth centuries, though with a rather restricted focus on conversion as it occurred in American Protestant Christianity. There was a particular fascination with the sudden conversions of "born-again" Christians, and St. Paul's experience on the road to Damascus was taken as the paradigm of religious conversion. More recent work on conversion has been done more by sociologists than psychologists, and it has had a particular focus on people joining and leaving new religious movements (see Hood et al., 2009, chap. 8).

Despite the restricted focus of early work on conversion, we have inherited from it some useful conceptualizations. George Coe defined conversion as (i) a transformation of self (ii) that comes about through some definite process, not just maturation; (iii) has radical consequences (iv) in a higher direction; and (v) occurs in a social context (Coe, 1916). That definition would still be widely accepted. Distinctions were made in this early work between once-born and twice-born Christians and between sudden and gradual conversion types, and it was recognized that different conversion types had different correlates.

More recently, Lewis Rambo (1993) developed a stage model of conversion that moves through (i) the personal and social context in which conversion occurs, (ii) a crisis that destabilizes the person's previous religious identity, (iii) the quest through which he or she seeks for alternatives, (iv) an encounter where he or she meets someone who presents an alternative, (v) an interaction with a new religious community, (vi) an act of commitment of joining a new religious community, and (vii) the outcome of finding whether or not it meets his or her needs. It is a welcome feature of this model that it recognizes the complex and interactional nature of conversion. However, it seems to be presenting an ideal-type of conversion that may not be followed in all cases. There are also different ideas about how to explain conversion. For example, it may arise out of social deprivation, it may resolve a sense of personal crisis, or it may be a regression into passivity. However, conversions are again probably too diverse for any single theory to explain them all.

We do not actually know very much about the effects that conversion has on people because we do not have much longitudinal research that tells us what people were like before they were converted. Kate Loewenthal (1995, chap. 4) offers what is probably still the best review. Most of the available data is retrospective, but it seems clear that most converts at least say that they were in some distress prior to conversion. However, that claim needs to be probed at a number of points. One is whether it is corroborated by independent, contemporaneous observations. The data is patchy, but, in at least some cases, there is indeed independent corroboration. We know that other factors apart from relief of distress influence conversions; for example, social networks often influence conversions. However, it seems that an element of distress often comes together with other factors to result in conversion.

One of the most secure and well-replicated findings in this area, using standard methods for looking at childhood attachment patterns, is that sudden religious conversions are more likely to arise in people who had insecure attachments in childhood, whereas gradual conversions are more likely in people who had experienced secure attachments (Granqvist and Kirkpatrick, 2004). That also makes it plausible that sudden conversions tend to arise out of personal distress.

It seems that conversions often produce a honeymoon effect, and that people feel quite good for a period after conversion, better than they did before. Evidence using objective methods of assessment as well as self-report measures supports that (Loewenthal, 1995). Various psychological factors probably contribute to that honeymoon effect (apart from the possible role of God, about which psychology cannot comment). For example, conversion gives meaning and purpose to people's lives and provides them with leadership, pastoral care, and a supportive social network. Cognitive dissonance may also play a role, that is, people will have made sacrifices in the course of conversion and will therefore be predisposed to believe that those sacrifices were worthwhile. The honeymoon period that follows conversion may lead people to exaggerate the distress that they were in before it.

People feel good in the period immediately after conversion, but that feeling may not last. It may give way to a more fluctuating period in which people vary in how positive they feel about conversion. The sense of well-being after conversion may gradually revert to what it was before and may result in people leaving whatever religious movement they joined. In due course, they may convert again and feel the honeymoon benefits another time. Loewenthal (1995) has pointed out that research that focuses on conversion may tend to give it a more decisive place than it really deserves in people's ongoing life story of change and development. This is a point where religious and psychological perspectives on conversion diverge somewhat, with psychologists tending to question whether conversion is as decisive as religious people tend to believe it to be.

Though conversion is, by definition, a religious process, somewhat similar processes of personal change may actually occur in nonreligious contexts. For example, the decision to stop smoking sometimes can seem like a sudden conversion. In health crises, people may decide quickly and firmly that they do not ever want to smoke again. There are some anecdotal indications that sudden conversions to nonsmoking may be unusually effective. It might help us understand religious conversion to put the study of it in the context of research on similar nonreligious processes of personal change.

De-conversion

Leaving religion has, until recently, been studied mainly in relation to people leaving cults, and there has been considerable alarm about the mental health of people who leave cults. Though undoubtedly some people leave cults in a state of distress, that is by no means always the case. There has also been great alarm about the coercive and manipulative methods that cults are thought to use to recruit members, and to hold on to them, and about the harm they are believed to do to members.

The widespread alarm about cults is an interesting social phenomenon in itself. The important point to note here is that relevant empirical research has consistently failed to give much support to these allegations against cults (Galanter, 1989). Cults actually find it hard to recruit and retain members, and they generally do not use coercive methods in trying to do so. On the contrary, they often seem to help their members with personal issues. When people leave cults in a state of distress, that usually reflects problems that have arisen in the process of leaving, rather than delayed effects from having been a cult member.

There has recently been a growth of interest in de-conversion, that is, the processes involved when people leave religious commitment (for a good overview, see Paloutzian et al., 2013). They have identified four key narratives among people who de-convert. For some, this is a step into autonomy, shaking off a form of religious commitment that may have arisen from family influence, and which marks a step toward a more autonomous and reflective mode of spirituality. Second are those who came to religion in midlife, hoping that it would meet personal needs and heal earlier losses, but who reach the disappointing conclusion that religion is not going to help. Third are some for whom de-conversion represents a switch to a new frame of reference, where leaving one religious commitment is often associated with finding a new one. Finally are those who have a lifelong pattern of seeking the right form of religion, in which they have frequently moved in and out of various forms of religious affiliation. Many de-conversions are accompanied by a movement toward more autonomous and integrative forms of faith, as set out in Fowler's theory of faith development. There is also often a movement toward the category of being more spiritual than religious.

It seems that de-conversion is in many ways a mirror image of conversion, and that the range of issues that triggers de-conversion, and the various routes out of religion, parallel those for converts coming into religion. In both cases, there are usually no basic changes in personality traits, but there are changes in their concerns, patterns of meaning making, and strivings.

The Role of Religious Practices

Many religious practices can make a significant contribution to helping people with their personal problems and contribute to personal transformation. It is important for those engaged in religious ministry to take into account that we live in a consumerist society in which people are likely to ask, at least implicitly, what they will get out of joining a church or religious organization. It might seem that the evangelical churches, which have grown so conspicuously in recent decades, contradict that. However, I suggest that such churches may actually have found a very effective way of helping people change and feel better, without always being explicit about that being their objective. Their effectiveness in meeting personal needs and helping people change may actually be one of the main reasons why they are flourishing. Equally, if non-evangelical Christianity is to flourish, it will probably need to be as effective as evangelicalism in delivering personal transformation. There seems to be no good reason, in principle, why that should not be the case.

As we saw in the last chapter, religion potentially provides considerable benefits for coping, adjustment, and health. Religion can sometimes be detrimental, though that happens more rarely; religion can also sometimes just be neutral in its effects. We lack solid information about when religion delivers its potential personal benefits and when it does not. However, it seems likely that if people are to derive personal benefits from religion, one of the things that they need to do is make a regular and significant commitment to prayer or some other forms of personal spiritual practice. Otherwise, the potential benefits of religion are unlikely to be felt. It is one of the strengths of evangelicalism, and perhaps one of the main reasons why it is flourishing, that it very strongly encourages members to engage in serious private prayer.

The evangelical tradition contains numerous prayer manuals, with a core emphasis on listening to what God is saying to people, through Bible reading and prayer. Doing that on a regular basis, for half an hour a day, as recommended in most manuals, seems crucial. Luhrmann (2012) comments in an interesting way on how such prayer practice contributes to personal transformation. It seems to bring about an increase in sensitivity to what God is saying (or, if you want to interpret it in naturalistic terms, an increased sensitivity to a deep level of personal wisdom of which people were not previously aware).

Such encouragement to prayer is often not given as strongly in more liberal churches, with the result that the potential benefits of religion will be experienced less often. I suspect that a range of spiritual practices are potentially beneficial, including some that would fit more readily into liberal religion. For example, meditation is central to internal religion, and currently mindfulness has engendered a huge interest. If a Christian church put something akin to mindfulness in the context of the Christian contemplative tradition and provided effective guidance in it, it might find that it was meeting a large-scale current need and would be offering significant personal transformation to its members.

A psychological understanding of the processes of meaning making and reframing that are involved in some traditional aspects of prayer (as discussed in Chapter 6) could contribute significantly to practical guidance in such prayer. For example, an understanding of the processes of reattribution involved in thanksgiving could enhance the benefits that people derive from it. In contrast, the theology of prayer seems to have rather little to contribute to practical instruction as it tends to focus on the essence of prayer rather than on the practice of it.

Among spiritual practices, spiritual healing is the one that most explicitly aims to deliver personal benefits. It is used increasingly in charismatic Christianity, as well as in secular New Age healing. It is also used in an increasing number of churches in mainline denominations, though often with a puzzling tentativeness, and a reluctance to create any expectation of specific benefit. However you suppose that spiritual healing conveys whatever benefits it has, it seems unlikely to fulfill its potential to bring about change without an explicit, committed expectation that it will do so.

There has been uncertainty in Christian churches over how to connect the revival of spiritual healing that has taken place since the late nineteenth century with the development of psychological methods of counseling and therapy that have developed in the twentieth century. Though we lack good data on this, my impression is that Christian ministers have often used one or the other. I suggest that there is potentially a helpful interplay between psychological methods of therapy and spiritual approaches to personal healing, and that they may be more effective when used in combination than when either is used alone. That is a hypothesis that could be tested in an empirical study.

Pastoral Care in Religious Contexts

Pastoral care in religious contexts, with people who are religiously committed, has the opportunity to engage with the religious aspects of personal problems in an unusually explicit way. It is often helpful to look at pastoral ministry from the dual perspectives of theology and psychology. That is not to "reduce" theology to psychology but to enable religious ministry to be conducted with a greater awareness of the human resonance and significance of what is being said and done within religion.

Interest has been growing recently in how forms of belief can become intertwined with personal problems, and some religious pastoral work focuses on the personal and emotional implications of belief. Issues about the personal significance of religious belief come into practical focus in approaches to counseling and psychotherapy that include a focus on people's image of God. That constitutes a recent and potentially fruitful development in pastoral care (Moriarty and Hoffman, 2007). It makes a distinction between people's God "concept" (their intellectual understanding of God) and their God "image" (their personal, intuitive experience of God).

When people are experiencing personal problems such as depression, their God image is likely to be affected, even if their God concept remains unchanged. Research on attachment and religion considered in Chapter 9 shows that the enduring attachment styles that develop in childhood affect how people relate to God over their lifetimes. In addition, there seem to be transient effects of mood-state on people's God image. So, during periods of depression, God is experienced as less loving and supportive than in happier periods. Evidence is accumulating (e.g., Moriarty, 2013, pp. 204–5) that as emotional distress recedes, people's God image normalizes and God is once again perceived as being supportive.

That seems to happen regardless of whether or not the God image is an explicit focus of the therapy. The key question now is whether it helps the therapeutic process to focus explicitly on the God image. Ways are being developed of exploring people's actual God image, in contrast to their intellectual God concepts. For example, people can be asked to draw themselves and God, or how they feel they and God look when they have done something wrong. If the God image is important to the person concerned, it will be helpful to explore it with them. In doing so, it will be important to maintain a clear focus on how God is actually experienced rather than on how God is understood intellectually.

Work on anger at God provides another way of working with the God image and helping people with spiritual struggles (Exline and Martin, 2005). In Chapter 6 we noted that the cognitive work of self-exploration that occurs in prayer takes place in a felt relational context, and in that it is rather like the self-exploration that takes place in psychotherapy. It is well known that, in therapy, emotional relationship with the therapist can become quite turbulent; it seems that can also be true of the relationship with God. It is at times when people are in greatest emotional distress that they struggle most in their relationship with God.

Anger at God seems to arise for much the same reasons as anger at another human being, and can have much the same consequences as any other anger. Anger is stressful and impinges on people emotionally and physically. However, it can also represent a welcome honesty in a relationship and provide the opportunity for growth. A key factor in whether or not growth occurs is probably whether anger at God coexists with positive feelings toward God, and whether the person concerned has reached a stage of psychological development that enables him or her to work through and integrate such conflicting feelings.

One way of integrating religion with pastoral care is for therapists to pray with their clients, though that is controversial. Clearly, many clients would not want it, and it would not be appropriate in many institutional settings. It also significantly changes the nature of the relationship between the therapist and the client. However, with the right client and at the right stage of pastoral work, including prayer in pastoral counseling can have a significant impact and seems able to make a useful contribution to change. Churches could probably do more to help people with health and adjustment issues if they used spiritual and psychological resources in conjunction with one another and did so confidently and skillfully.

Church Community and Ministers

Though one-to-one pastoral care can be important in religious settings, it can also be helpful for the religious community as a whole to make a contribution to pastoral care. That raises issues about social processes at work in churches (e.g., Watts at al., 2002, chaps. 11–12; Savage and Boyd MacMillan, 2007). Much work has been done on group processes in psychotherapy, and some of that has looked at the specific issues that arise about group processes in religious contexts (e.g., Meissner, 1966). Part of the rationale for sometimes doing therapy in a group setting is that personal issues often involve problems in relationships, and those problems are more readily observed in group settings, making it possible to work on them explicitly.

Some members of a church congregation may be willing to engage in formal group therapy with other members of the congregation. However, it will more often be appropriate to bring limited elements of group work into the religious community as a whole, so that it becomes to some extent a therapeutic community. That requires a culture in which people feel able to be open with each other about personal issues, and in which there is a culture of listening in an attentive and nonjudgmental way to one another, and respecting confidentiality where that is appropriate. Where pastoral care of church members happens in the context of a pastorally sensitive religious community, it diffuses issues about dependency on one particular pastor, who may leave. It replaces that with a healthier dependency on the community, which is more stable, and where dependency is more reciprocal.

It is possible in a church setting to encourage a culture in which there is healthy networking, and people support one another. Many problems can be diffused if people have a sense both of their own needs and of their responsibility to help meet the needs of others. Churches create a space for one-to-one pastoral care, but it is wise for that to be embedded in a pastoral community in which people both give and receive. Again, psychology can help people be more aware of the group and systemic processes involved in that.

Finally, the body of psychological research on Christian ministers themselves and on the social processes at work in churches is growing (e.g., Francis and Jones, 1996; Watts et al., 2002, chap. 13), though it is a surprisingly neglected aspect of the psychology of religion. Being a church minister is, in part, a pastoral role, and it triggers the kind of processes that arise in all caring work. Projections onto church ministers are often emotional and arise more from the issues of church members than from the ministers themselves. Those projections can be either positive or negative, or a mixture of the two. The religious context makes idealization of ministers even more likely than in other caring professions, though that can lead to extreme denigration when ministers are found to fall short of the idealized images that have been projected onto them.

Structural factors also make these issues harder to handle than in other professions. There will inevitably be more unplanned, informal contact between church members and ministers than with other helping professions, making boundaries more difficult to maintain. Also, church ministers often have multiple professional roles in relation to church members including, for example, religious instruction and pastoral care. The role ambiguity that arises from multiple roles makes intense projections harder to handle.

There is, in fact, a more general problem of role ambiguity in the work of church ministers. They have an unusually high degree of autonomy in their work, which is combined with having general and demanding goals.

It is often far from clear how those general goals are to be achieved, and how they translate into specific duties. The expectations on ministers are often beyond what could possibly be met, making a degree of failure almost inevitable, leading to a cycle of guilt and failure.

It may be tempting to deal with that by relying on secular management approaches, but that involves a degree of distancing from the religious identity that brought people into church ministry in the first place. Indeed, one of the key sources of stress for church ministers is the discrepancy between what they find themselves doing and what they felt called to do when they offered themselves for ministry. That discrepancy usually involves doing more administration than they expected, or want to do. Additional problems arise from managing an organization in which many people in the workforce are volunteers. That makes it difficult to get the right balance between being focused on the tasks that need doing and meeting the relational expectations of volunteers.

It is also important to be aware of the psychological pressures at work on church members. They may have joined the church with high expectations, some of which may have been unrealistic. That often creates a vulnerability, which can be exploited by pastors who are not alert to the dangers of doing so. However, it is probably more common for any high hopes, with which people joined a church, to just die a slow death through disappointment. None of these problems is intractable. Key elements in coping with them are to be aware of the nature of the problems and to understand the structural factors that contribute to them. The development of psychological studies of churches, and of the psychological issues that arise in providing Christian ministry, can help in raising awareness.

Finally, there are dangers of church communities becoming too absorbing for their members. Religious faiths usually have a commitment to service of the world in general, and the danger is that people might become so focused on church life that they have no time or energy left to make a reality of that broader social commitment. Personal growth often seems to arise in the context of relationships in which people become dependent, and most schools of therapy recognize the value of that, as well as its dangers. However, it is important, once people have changed, to move on from that dependency. In pastoral care an oscillation is needed whereby people enter, but then leave, dependent relationships (Reed, 1978), whether the dependency is on an individual pastor or on the wider church community.

Summary

- Conversion is a much investigated topic in the psychology of religion, and conversion types (sudden and gradual) differ from each other in various ways. For example, people who have sudden conversions often had insecure attachment relationships in childhood. People often experience distress before conversion and feel better after it, though that does not always last. Research interest in de-conversion is growing.
- Ways are being developed of focusing on specifically religious issues in the course of pastoral care, for example, on people's image of God, which can be intertwined with depression. Anger at God can also be intertwined with personal adjustment issues. Practices such as prayer and spiritual healing seem able to deliver personal benefits, though there is scope for more research on that.
- Churches can offer pastoral care as a community, analogous to that provided by a therapeutic community. Understanding is growing of the pressures on church ministers, who work with high levels of role ambiguity, and often with expectations that are discrepant with their sense of vocation.

13

Scripture and Doctrine

This chapter will focus on how psychology can be used to help understand religious doctrine, especially its personal and human significance. It will focus specifically on Christian doctrine, as an example, though parallel remarks can be made about doctrine in other faith traditions. We will look first at the contribution of psychology to the interpretation of scripture.

Psychology and Scripture

An important religious application of psychology involves using it as a tool for the interpretation of scripture. There has long been considerable interest in the use of the social sciences in biblical interpretation, but more recently there has been growing interest in the use of psychology. Wayne Rollins (1999) provided a helpful overview of such work, and the four volumes of *Psychology and the Bible* edited by Ellens and Rollins (2004) provide a good sample of some of the better work. Rollins and Kille (2007) have edited a helpful anthology.

It is often assumed that psychological exegesis is bad exegesis, as the leading Testament scholar, Gerd Theissen, acknowledges in his impressive psychological study of St. Paul (Theissen, 1987). I submit that that need not be the case; it is not difficult to set out guidelines for avoiding the worst pitfalls of psychological exegesis.

First, psychological exegesis should build on what is known in biblical scholarship generally about the texts being interpreted. If it ignores that, or gets it wrong, it will be unconvincing. Second, it should recognize that psychology is diverse and contains different subdisciplines. Various approaches to psychology may elucidate different aspects of a passage of scripture. Both of those points are well illustrated by Theissen in his work on St. Paul. For each passage of St. Paul that he considers, he first does a text analysis and then a "tradition analysis," giving a survey of issues that have been raised in the interpretation of the passage. Only then does he bring in psychology, and when he does so, he looks at the passage from three psychological perspectives: learning theory, psychodynamic psychology, and cognitive psychology.

Using a variety of psychological perspectives also helps guard against another pitfall with psychological exegesis, which is making overconfident claims. Particular problems arise with claims made on the basis of psychoanalysis, which itself has a somewhat problematic status, as we saw in Chapter 2. It is also important to avoid "reductionism," suggesting that the meaning of a passage of scripture can be reduced entirely to psychology. That is never something that psychology can establish. It can only comment on the psychological significance of a passage; it cannot establish whether or not it has any significance beyond psychology.

Psychology can focus on various different aspects of scripture. Some psychologists have tried to present a psychological portrait of particular characters, such as Ezekiel or Paul. I suggest that we ought to be especially cautious about that approach, mainly because we generally lack a rich enough body of material to carry it through in a dependable way. It is tempting to fill in the gaps in our material with speculations and to place too much confidence in them.

Scriptural material is quite diverse in scope, and different kinds of material lend themselves to different uses of psychology. Narrative material, for example, is very different from more abstract religious teaching. One psychological perspective focuses on what the reader brings to the text. It can look, for example, at how different personality types connect with scripture in different ways. It will help now to consider some particular examples of how psychology can be used in scriptural exegesis.

Many of the classic stories of the Old Testament can be seen as parables of people's spiritual journey through life. For example, Sara Savage looked at the story of Joseph from that point of view (Savage, 2011). Joseph's life seems to have started well in terms of relationships, and we can infer from the story that he was able to form secure attachments. However, he later experienced the trauma of betrayal by his brothers, being thrown into a pit and abandoned, and then rescued to be sold into slavery in Egypt. That provides a helpful parable of the journey into depression and the resources needed to emerge from it. The story also includes Joseph's time in a position of power in Egypt and illustrates the resources needed to cope with the stresses of responsibility. When his brothers visit Egypt, he has the opportunity to forgive, and Joseph is seen wrestling with the demands that forgiveness always makes. The story is so rich that many of the psychological issues that arise in the journey of life can be illustrated in relation to it.

A rather different body of Old Testament material that is interesting from a psychological point of view is the "lament" material in the psalms and elsewhere, in which the writers lament their situation and protest to God about it. It is challenging to find such material in the Bible as it sits uneasily with people's assumptions about how it is appropriate to talk to God. Nevertheless, there is an honesty about it that is refreshing and attractive. Walter Brueggemann (1995) comments on this material from the perspective on object relations theory, as formulated by Winnicott and others. He suggests that in lament the believer, through railing against God, is able to develop the ego resources needed for a mature faith. On that view, lament has a role at a particular psychological stage of faith development, but not a permanent one.

A particularly interesting chapter in the New Testament, from a psychological point of view, is chap. 7 of St. Paul's letter to the Romans (e.g., Rubenstein, 1972; Theissen, 1987). Paul is describing the process of transformation that someone experiences as he or she moves from a religion governed by law to one of relationship with Christ. There is debate about how far this chapter is autobiographical, but that is not a crucial issue. It lends itself to being read through the lens of Freudian psychology, with the concept of the id corresponding to what Paul calls "lower nature," and the superego corresponding to the overstrict requirements of the law. Paul describes how someone can be buffeted between these two forces, which would be the experience of someone with a weak ego. He also describes how that is transformed by a sense of union with Christ, which seems to provide resources to strengthen the ego and bring liberation from the warfare between id and superego.

The gospels are a rich body of material that can be approached psychologically in a variety of ways (Watts, 2007a). These include psychological approaches to the mind and personality of the professional Jesus, the psychological significance of the encounters with Jesus recorded in the gospels, how psychology can understand the cognitive processes of interpretation that take place as people read the gospels, and how different psychological types are likely to respond to the gospel material.

Psychology and Doctrine

Psychology can also be used in understanding the human significance of Christian doctrine and can elucidate the personal significance of religious teaching. This is somewhat analogous to the method of correlation developed by Paul Tillich in his systematic theology. Tillich is probably the most significant theologian of the twentieth century to have made sustained use of psychology in his interpretation of Christian doctrine (see Cooper, 2001).

Of major doctrinal themes, the theology of salvation (or atonement) is probably the one that lends itself best to a psychological approach. Though the main focus is on humanity collectively, it has resonance for the salvation of particular individuals. How any particular person hears and responds to the general doctrine of human salvation will be influenced by his or her personal situation and spiritual journey.

Another reason why the doctrine of the atonement is an interesting test case is that, over the centuries, various theories of the atonement have been proposed, with no consensus about which one is correct. It seems likely that which of these theories resonates most with particular people will depend in part on their psychological outlook. (It will depend on other things too, such as denominational affiliation.)

Developing this idea, Paul Pruyser (1991, chap. 6) suggested how three paradigmatic theories of the atonement might connect with people's predominant emotions and mental structures (as conceived within Freudian theory). Thus, he suggests that ransom theories that emphasize the victory of Christ on the cross will resonate with those whose predominant emotion is anxiety, and who fear the dark impulses of the Freudian id. Similarly, he suggests that satisfaction theories that emphasize Jesus' taking the burden of guilt on himself will resonate with those whose predominant emotion is guilt, and who feel oppressed by the Freudian superego. Third, he suggests that theories that emphasize the benefits of the cross being mediated through Jesus' moral example will resonate with those whose predominant emotion is shame, and who feel the gulf between the ego and ego-ideal.

People will inevitably hear doctrine in a way that resonates with them personally. That carries risks and I am not necessarily advocating it; it can lead to rather selective attention to Christian doctrine and a somewhat selective understanding of it. However, I do suggest that it is inevitable, psychologically, that people will hear doctrine in a way that is influenced by their personal standpoint. Pruyser goes on to reflect on this issue, after setting out his mapping of theories of the atonement onto psychological types.

It is arguable that a broad and balanced understanding of doctrine will help people in their journey toward a mature and balanced personality. If people only hear doctrines that resonate with their current psychological outlook, their religious beliefs may keep them trapped there in a vicious circle. So, people who are personally predisposed to guilt may attend selectively to theologies that emphasize guilt, which would only serve to entrench them further in their sense of guilt. There is, on the other hand, a possibility of balanced religious doctrines contributing constructively to a broadening and balancing of personality.

A danger somewhat analogous to "splitting" occurs in how religious doctrines are understood and presented. Splitting is the tendency, at a primitive stage of psychological development, to see some people as entirely good and others as entirely bad. That is usually followed by a more integrative way of relating to people, in which it is possible to recognize that the same person can be both good and bad. Something similar to splitting seems to happen in Christian doctrine, especially in the way it is presented through the church year.

For example, the cross can be seen as entirely evil (neglecting the victory of the cross), and the resurrection can be presented as entirely joyous (neglecting the fear and tears of Jesus' followers on the day of the resurrection, and the scars of the risen Jesus). In fact, many facets of the Christian story seem to integrate components that are both sad and joyful. The birth narrative sets the joyful birth of Jesus against the background of the hardship of Mary and Joseph, and Herod's slaughter of innocent children. The Last Supper celebrates a remarkable union between Jesus and his disciples, but it takes place on the evening of Jesus' betrayal. The story of Jesus' ascension is both a sad occasion of parting and a celebration of his ascendency.

It is striking how often positive and negative elements are held together in the Christian story. However, things are not always presented in that way. In particular, the dissociation between Good Friday and Easter weakens the capacity of the story as a whole to serve as a paradigm of the transition from sadness to joy. I suggest that an integrative presentation of doctrine that avoids that kind of splitting will enable it to contribute more effectively to a healthy integration of personality.

Jung and the Interpretation of Doctrine

Jungian psychology has a particularly important role to play in the psychological interpretation of doctrine. However, it is worth making a distinction here between the work that Jung himself did on human doctrine and that of other Jungian scholars who developed his ideas. Jung's own approach was often theologically unorthodox, something that led to a breakdown in his fifteen-year theological collaboration with the British Dominican Victor White (see Lammers, 1994). I suggest that a Jungian approach to doctrine does not need to be as unorthodox as that of Jung himself. Probably the most sustained Jungian engagement with the Bible and with Christian teaching from a Jungian point of view was that of Edward Edinger, a Jungian analyst who was based in New York (e.g., Edinger, 1972).

As we saw in Chapter 2, Jung himself saw an equivalence between religious dogmas and the archetypes of the unconscious. A key point is that Jung sees the Self (the whole and complete person we have the potential to become) as the image of God in the psyche. That introduces a parallelism between how the ego relates to the Self in the individual psyche and how humanity collectively has related to God. In that sense, something analogous to the salvation history of humanity is being played out in the psyche of each individual person as he or she goes through life's journey.

How the individual responds to the image of God in the psyche is analogous to how humanity has collectively responded to God's revelation of himself in Christ. There are the same opportunities and pitfalls in each case. The interpretative connection can go both ways. People can place their personal journeys toward individuation in the context of broader salvation history, and they can use that to understand themselves better. They can also use that connection to understand better the personal and human significance of the doctrine of salvation.

In both cases, Jung assumes an original state of psychic wholeness in which ego and Self are not yet differentiated; so the first task is the differentiation of the ego. This differentiation occurs through an act of ego inflation, which is then followed by rejection. There is a parallel in the Genesis 3 myth of the original Garden of Eden, which narrates the inflationary act of Adam and Eve in acquiring knowledge of good and evil, and then being cast out of the garden. Out of that banishment, a relationship is reestablished between God and humanity (cf. Self and ego), leading to a reintegration being accomplished in Christ.

The aspect of Jungian thought that seems to be most richly suggestive from a theological point of view is the relationship between the ego (the center of consciousness) and the Self (the higher, complete person we have the potential to become). As Jung sees things, it is essential for individuation, the personal journey toward wholeness, that there should be a healthy axis between the two. I suggest a parallel between the relationship or axis between ego and Self and the relationship between humanity and God. More specifically, there is a parallel in how the personal journey of individuation unfolds and the Christian story of salvation history, as suggested by Edinger in *Ego and Archetype* (Edinger, 1972).

In Jungian theory, at a point, characteristically in midlife, the Self announces itself to the ego and seeks to establish connection between the two. Similarly, in salvation history, there is a point when God (in Christ) announces Godself to humanity and seeks to draw humanity toward salvation. Jung is firm in his view that there is no wholeness based on the ego alone, without the Self; just as any Christian would believe that there is no salvation from humanity alone, without God. In personal life, the ego-Self axis can go wrong in one of two ways. The ego can feel so crushed that it has no sense of connection with the Self. Alternatively, the ego can become so inflated that it pretends already to be the Self and has no sense of the journey to be undertaken. Similarly, humanity can lose all sense of the possibility of drawing close to God, or it can become so inflated that it has no sense of the need to do so.

With many issues in Christian doctrine, a balance needs to be maintained and extremes avoided. I suggest that the pitfalls are often analogous to an ego that is inflated or crushed, and that a healthy ego-Self axis is analogous to a healthy balance in doctrine. For example, Christology needs to maintain a proper two-natures balance and avoid an over-human or over-divine Jesus. Eschatology needs to maintain the balance of an inaugurated eschatology and avoid the extremes of an eschatology that is either over-imminent or over-distant. I suggest that a rich theological hermeneutic could be developed around the parallel with the ego-Self axis, which could be applied to many Christian doctrines.

Key episodes in the story of Jesus also lend themselves to a Jungian interpretation. For example, Baptism is a key moment in the establishment of the ego-Self, Son-Father axis, and it leads to the differentiation of good and evil in the wilderness. The relationship between Jesus and the Father is drawn especially vividly in John's Gospel (e.g., John. 8. 28–29). Much of Jesus' teaching can also be seen as being about individuation, the personal journey toward wholeness. For example, Edinger interprets the Beatitudes as praise for the humble, non-inflated ego. Particularly interesting is Matthew 16. 24–26, "If anyone would come after me, let him deny himself . . . whoever would save his life will lose it, and whoever loses his life for my sake will find it." (Note here that "life" is a translation of "psyche.")

Jung's approach to doctrine is both intriguing and exasperating. I suggest that it is important that theology and psychology should be clearly distinguished from each other, and for any interpretation of one in the light of the other to be approached cautiously and critically. Jung himself is sometimes too inclined to revise doctrine in the light of psychology. Psychology can perhaps raise questions about the personal impact of doctrines, but it can never, on its own, provide the basis for doctrinal revision.

Other Approaches

Though Jungian psychology offers a particularly rich approach to the interpretation of doctrine, it is by no means the only approach. A helpful approach also comes from a Freudian perspective, illustrated by Pruyer's work on the atonement mentioned earlier. Another notable contributor to the Freudian interpretation of doctrine was the Jesuit psychoanalyst William Meissner. He made significant contributions to general psychoanalytic theory, but also published a series of important theoretical books on psychoanalysis and religion, such as *Life and Faith* (Meissner, 1987).

Meissner's methodology explicitly avoids reducing doctrine to psychology. He takes a complementary perspectives approach, in which theology and psychology answer different but related questions. So, in his interpretation of grace, he adopts a theological position that sees it as arising from relationship with God. He suggests that psychology, in contrast, focuses on how resources from outside the ego allow a person to overcome obstacles in their development that they would otherwise not have the psychological resources to surmount. He elaborates that in some detail, drawing on object relations theory.

A recurrent concern in Meissner's general psychoanalytic theorizing is with paranoid processes, and he applies that to the development of cultic processes, especially the strong boundaries that are often drawn between those inside the community of the saved, and those outside (Meissner, 2000). In fact, religious thinking may be more varied on this point than he fully recognizes. Religious people vary in how sharp a contrast they draw between those inside and outside the community of salvation. Some would take a universalistic position on that issue, rather than the cultic stance on which Meissner focuses. However, the kind of psychoanalytic theorizing he develops would be a useful tool in understanding the psychological significance of that.

Another important figure in the psychoanalytic interpretation of Christian thinking is the radical German Catholic Eugen Drewermann. His influence in the English-speaking world has been limited by the fact that little of his monumental output has so far been translated into English, though Matthias Beier has written a helpful introduction to his work (Beier, 2004). Drewermann is in many ways a post-Holocaust theologian. He is exercised not so much by the traditional theological question of how God could permit such evil as by the more anthropological question of how humans could bring such suffering on one another. He suggest that religious ideas have a significant impact, and that a key factor is having a violent God image that may lead people to do violence to one another. The stories of Adam and Eve and of Cain and Abel (Genesis 3–4) in the Old Testament and the crucifixion in the New Testament have been important in his thinking. He also ponders other human roots of human violence that are influenced by religious thinking, including fear, splitting, and idealization, which he describes as people trying to be better than they need to be, at the price of the suffering of others.

A broad range of psychologies could potentially be used to unpack the human significance of religious doctrine, though therapeutic psychologies seem to serve this purpose best. Another approach that has been used theologically is the person-centered or nondirective approach developed by Carl Rogers. It has been suggested that the therapeutic qualities enunciated by Rogers, warmth, empathy, and genuineness, provide a good theology of love (see Thorne, 2012). Don Browning has used the person-centered approach in elucidating the human significance of the atonement. For a thoughtful assessment of the religious significance of a range of therapeutic psychologies, see Browning and Cooper (2004).

Doctrines of Human Nature

One of the most interesting areas of doctrine from a psychological point of view is obviously the doctrine of the human person, or "theological anthropology." It can play a crucial mediating role in relating contemporary psychology to Christian doctrine and affords a meeting ground where the two can connect.

Issues about splitting occur acutely in connection with the doctrine of human nature. Though issues about body, soul, and spirit raise the most obvious psychological issues, it may actually be the way in which moral issues about human nature are handled that is of greatest psychological significance. Here again is a danger of splitting, with an overdominant emphasis either on the goodness or wickedness of human nature. Properly understood, Christian teaching about human nature always holds these together. The touchstone of human goodness is contained in the doctrine of humans being in the image of God; the sinfulness of humans is represented in the doctrine of fallenness.

Peter Morea (1997) has undertaken a helpful mapping between theological approaches and psychological theories to personality that is somewhat similar to Pruyser's mapping of theories of the atonement. So, for example, there seems a natural connection between the pessimism of Freudian psychology, with its emphasis on the id, and Augustinian theology, with its emphasis on original sin. The parallels that can be found between approaches to doctrine and to psychological theory are intriguing. Given that theology is much the older tradition, it is hard to avoid the conclusion that theological ideas tend to migrate across into secular culture, including psychological theory.

The concept of original sin is an interesting example. On the face of things, there seems to be an analogy with the idea of the id in Freudian theory, the source of dark impulses. An analogy may also be possible with Richard Dawkins's concept of the selfish gene (Dawkins, 1976), even though it was put forward in part to explain the puzzling (from the point of view of natural selection) phenomenon of altruism. It appears to postulate negative moral qualities at the core of our being; it is again a kind of original sin. On the other hand, humanistic psychology seems closer to modern theological approaches that, like Thomas Merton's, are more optimistic about human nature and put the emphasis on self-actualization.

For many religious thinkers, it is not just that a balance needs to be kept between good and bad aspects of human nature; it is that good and evil are always intertwined in humanity, and in creation. Jung puts forward the theologically strange idea that good and evil are intertwined in God too. So, for example, when reflecting in *Answer to Job* (Jung, 1984) on the Epistles of St. John, with their extraordinary celebration of light and love, Jung asks where the author's shadow can be found and makes the suggestion that it is to be found in the terrible, gory material in the book of Revelation (though almost every Biblical scholar would now take the view that the two books are written by different authors).

The human sciences have tended to regard evil as a concept inappropriate to their discourse. However, in recent decades, there have been signs of it being readmitted, something that might be seen as reflecting the shift from modernity to postmodernity. It is also a major step in increasing the compatibility of theology and the human sciences. The topic of evil illustrates a number of key themes in the study of religion. One is about social categories. We have become sensitized to how far each of our concepts is a "social construction," and to some extent contingent. Societies have understood evil in different ways in different historical periods. In this sense, evil is a social construct. However, it is important to beware of sliding from that obvious point to the more contentious conclusion that evil is nothing but a social construct, a view that would sit uneasily with most theologies, and for which there is no justification in the human sciences.

The human sciences provide accounts of how evil conduct arises. Various such accounts have been offered, and one of the best is that in Roy Baumeister's *Evil: Inside Human Cruelty and Violence* (Baumeister, 1997). First, he distinguishes four roots of evil: the desire for material gain, threatened egotism, idealism, and the pursuit of sadistic pleasure. However, these roots of evil are pervasive, and he explains the fact that evil is less common than it might be by saying that a breakdown of inhibitions is also needed. Such breakdown can arise from inadequate upbringing, stress and emotional upset, or deviant culture that legitimizes the loss of self-control.

For present purposes, the details of this account are less important than the question of how such accounts sit alongside religious accounts of evil. One move that may be made here is to say that because we have a human sciences account of evil, we do not need a religious account. A similar point might be made about the human sciences account of conversion, and so on. While a human sciences account may reduce the motivation to put forward a religious account, it certainly does not show that the latter is wrong.

A related move is to say that the account of evil in the human sciences makes the concept of radical (or pure) evil misplaced. Baumeister, for example, objects to a notion of evil that is deemed to be outside a person and to invade them in some way. The human sciences may reduce the motivation to invoke that view of evil, but they do not actually show that it is wrong. In considering the concept of external evil, it is important to distinguish causal factors from culpability. Though people tend to choose between human sciences and religious accounts of evil, they do not need to do so. The two approaches can be regarded as complementary and compatible.

Jung makes a quite different move from most psychologists (see Philp, 1958), which is to argue that the pervasiveness and intensity of human evil requires a corresponding notion of evil at the metaphysical or ontological level. Indeed, he wants to incorporate evil into his concept of God. Strictly, of course, this is not a legitimate inference, but it is nevertheless an understandable move. Jung also represents, in a clear way, the strand of Christian thinking, which has advocated redeeming evil, at the personal level, rather than shunning it.

Summary

- Psychology can contribute to the interpretation of scripture, and examples are given from both the Old and New Testaments. Not all psychological exegesis is dependable, and guidelines are given for doing it well. It should be done critically, building on general biblical criticism, and be aware of the perspectives of different psychological approaches.
- Psychology can also contribute to the interpretation of Christian doctrine. People will probably be drawn to different doctrinal emphases depending on their psychological outlook. Some interpretations of doctrine seem to involve a psychologically primitive process of splitting, whereas it is suggested that it is psychologically helpful to integrate light and dark aspects.
- Jungian psychology has proved a particularly rich resource for interpreting doctrine. A good axis between ego and Self, which is central to individuation, has many doctrinal analogues, eschatology, for example. Several psychoanalytic thinkers in the Freudian tradition have made important contributions to elucidating the psychological significance of doctrine.
- There is a rich interface between psychology and theological doctrines of human nature, though they approach issues in distinct but complementary ways. The nature of evil serves as good example.

14

Human Nature and Personality

In this chapter, we will bring into dialogue the perspectives of psychology and religion on human nature and personality. General issues about human nature need to be considered, such as the relationship between social, biological, and personal life. Other issues include the place of religion itself in human life and whether, for good or ill, humans are essentially religious creatures.

We have already made the point that psychology is really a family of subdisciplines that are often only loosely related. In particular, psychology is both a biological and a social science. Though most psychologists would acknowledge that each has a place within the overall discipline, there is often little contact between them, and little attempt at integration. Where integration is attempted, it sometimes takes the form of greedy reductionism, in which biology tries to explain social life.

The problem arises in part from biological and social psychology being different kinds of sciences, with different methodologies. Both are sciences in the broad, continental sense of being careful, systematic forms of enquiry. However, biological psychology is a natural science in a way that social psychology is not. That relates to the fact that the entities with which biological psychology is concerned, such as DNA or the frontal lobes of the brain, have a tangible reality in a way that, for example, the social processes that lead to religious radicalization do not. There is, of course, a general sense in which all our concepts, even of DNA for example, are social constructions, but in some cases there is more tangible reality to what is being construed than in others.

The psychology of religion now includes both biological and social approaches, though the current emphasis on genetics, evolution, and the brain is a relatively recent addition. For the most part, the psychology of religion has not so far really tried to connect biological and social approaches. One topic where that is raised in an interesting way is religious experience. There is probably a genetic predisposition to some kinds of religious experience, and brain processes are certainly involved. On the other hand, it is in a social context that people learn how to facilitate certain kinds of religious experience through religious practice and learn how to interpret it in a religious framework.

The two-factor theory of religious experience that we discussed in Chapter 5 makes provision for both. The first factor is concerned with relatively immediate experience that is minimally conceptualized, and in which biological processes probably play a significant role. The other is more focused on interpretation and is more dependent on social and cultural context.

There is a recurrent tendency to prioritize biology, though that is sometimes countered by strong forms of social constructionism that want to prioritize the social. I suggest that neither is prior in any general sense, and for all purposes. Explanations arise in a variety of contexts and for different purposes. Biological explanations may be needed in one context, and social in another. To understand anything as complex as religious experience, we need multiple approaches that sit alongside one another. I recommend a systemic approach in which different explanatory discourses illuminate different aspects of whatever is under discussion, and that we envisage a degree of mutual influence between biological and social approaches.

Though psychology does not find it easy to integrate its biological and social wings, it is potentially one of the strengths of psychology that it is both a biological and a social science. Humans are both biological and social creatures and can only be understood by a discipline that takes both into account. That applies to the psychology of religion as much as to any other aspect of psychology.

Embodiment

Psychology and religion have a tendency to take a different view of these issues. Psychology has embraced a variety of approaches, but, in recent decades, academic psychology has increasingly tended to prioritize biological approaches. In some ways, that applies to the psychology of religion less than to some other areas of psychology, partly because most researchers in the psychology of religion have a background in social psychology. At present, evolutionary and neuropsychological approaches to religion do not seem well integrated with the rest of the field.

Religion is often assumed to embrace a dualistic approach, emphasizing an eternal soul that is relatively independent of the body. For scientists who prioritize biological aspects of human nature, such as Francis Crick (1994), religion, with its emphasis on the soul, seems incompatible with the scientific approach of disciplines such as psychology, which Crick sees as essentially physicalist in their approach (i.e., they want to explain everything about people in terms of physical processes).

In fact, things are not necessarily set on that kind of collision course, for various reasons. For one thing, religion has been more diverse in its approach to human nature than is widely appreciated. The Jewish tradition in the Hebrew Bible (Old Testament) takes a unitary view of human nature that has been summarized as an "ensouled body"; it really is not dualistic.

It is more debatable where St. Paul stands on these issues, though on careful study he is not as dualistic as is often supposed. It is true that he sometimes makes a sharp contrast between flesh and spirit, but these are the extreme concepts in a complex and subtle conceptualization of the human person in which at least five facets can be distinguished: flesh, body, heart, soul, and spirit (e.g., Welker, 2014). Flesh is distinguished from the body, the latter being a kind of functional organization that is intertwined with flesh. The distinction between flesh and body is perhaps not unlike that between anatomy and physiology. The Greek term "psyche" is difficult to translate. Welker suggests translating it as "life," though it may indeed be best left untranslated, as what it means in St. Paul is fairly close to what "psyche" means in modern psychology. It generally does not mean an immortal soul. It can be distinguished from "heart," an important concept in St. Paul's anthropology that relates to what modern psychology might call hot or affective cognition. Both psyche and heart are distinct from spirit, the one concept of the five here that may be puzzling from the point of view of the modern psychology; the other concepts are more readily intelligible. It should also be emphasized that St. Paul is not talking here about five components of the human person that are completely separate from one another; he is just making conceptual distinctions between different facets of the human person.

Christian theology over the centuries has not been as consistently dualistic as is often supposed. Aquinas, for example, thinks about the human person in a holistic way. It is true that Christian theology entered a more dualistic period after Descartes, but for the most part it has now left that behind. Philosophy of mind since the middle of the twentieth century has largely abandoned the reification of mind as an entity that is separate from the body. Theology has generally followed philosophy of mind in that, and it has applied the same approach to "soul" that, for the most part, is also not now reified. Rather, it sees the soul as a facet of a person, integrated with the physical, rather than as a separate entity, and an emergent property of it (e.g., Ward, 1998). "Soul" is increasingly seen more as a set of qualities than as a distinct entity, or as a perspective on the person as whole.

Embodied Cognition and Systemic Biology

Important recent developments in biology have steered it away from the greedy reductionism to which people like Crick were committed, developments that bring scientific thinking about the human person closer to the viewpoint of the religious traditions. Biology has recently become much more systemic and contextual (e.g., Noble, 2006) in a way that makes reducing everything to the physical processes seem quaintly old-fashioned. The new systemic biology represents a significant paradigm shift.

Various developments in biology have contributed to this. One is the new movement in genetics, known as "epigenetics," which emphasizes that how genes operate is regulated by environmental conditions. Hardly anything is pure "nature"; almost everything is the result of interaction between "nature" and "nurture." Second, within psychology, the study of cognition has increasingly emphasized that cognition proceeds in a way that reflects our embodiment. The new approach emphasizes the embodied context of cognition, which is interactive and systemic rather than reductionist. Third, interest has been growing in how brain *function* (i.e., the way it is used) can affect brain *structure*, through neural plasticity. Function affects structure as well as structure determines function. Watts (2013b), focusing especially on embodied cognition, has argued that this new systemic biology brings science very close to how human nature has often been conceived in religious traditions and largely dissolves the apparent clash over human nature between psychology and religion.

The new, more systemic scientific approach also has implications for the study of religion. Many religious practices are associated with specific physical postures or movements. For example, people often kneel for prayer. Various specific postures often associated with meditation. Spiritual healing is often accompanied by the laying on of hands.

Glossolalia involves uttering speech sounds. Adult baptism often involves total immersion in water. Participation in the Mass or Eucharist involves eating and drinking. There are intrepid spiritual practices such as handling dangerous serpents. Monks often allow themselves only restricted diet and sleep.

Gilbert and Gilbert (2011) discuss the basic affect regulation systems operating in humans and other related species. The soothing/contentment system is activated by gentle, safe physical contact. The contact used in spiritual healing may well activate this system and have evolutionary antecedents in grooming. Rather different religious practices may be linked to activity, excitement, and seeking of rewards, which are linked to the dopamine system. Charismatic religious practices may also activate that system, and it may be one of the key benefits of engaging in such practices with other people that the system is activated more effectively.

In fact, very few religious practices are not also physical practices; indeed, it is one of the interesting features of religion that it involves cognition that is more obviously embodied than is the case with many other activities. It is highly likely that the way in which people think during such practices is shaped by what they are doing with their bodies. Investigating in detail how that works would constitute a rich and interesting research program. Note that we are looking here at how cognition is influenced by embodiment, rather than at how it is reducible to the physical.

The new contextual biology also recognizes the extent to which people are affected by their social context. Simply being in the presence of another person has quite far-reaching psychological consequences, and that is further affected by how many people there are, what they are doing together, whether physical contact occurs, and so on. Social contact is often linked to physical activity, so the two cannot easily be separated.

Another intriguing question that arises here is what the impact is of solitude, when chosen for religious reasons, such as a monk who spends many hours each day in solitude, or even a hermit. It seems possible that what monks experience in solitude is different from what others might feel. It seems possible that monks and nuns learn to have such a vivid sense of the presence of God that they function as though they were in quiet contact with someone else rather than on their own. In fact, it may be the purpose of extended solitude that it challenges people to develop a vivid sense of the presence of God in order to survive.

Emotions

We will turn to psychological and religious perspectives on what we would now call "emotion." There is a religious tradition of reflection on what would now be called emotions, which predates the current psychology of emotion. Jonathan Edwards is an important voice in what is, in effect, a prescientific psychology of the "affections" (see Dixon, 2006).

Religion has always been much concerned with feelings, with what Charles Wesley memorably called the "warmed heart." That does not imply any contrast between cognition and emotion. A long-standing assumption is that emotions are to be contrasted with cognition, and that they can undermine rationality. However, psychology, as well as philosophy (de Sousa, 1987), has more recently recognized (e.g. Williams et al., 1997) that emotions are closely intertwined with cognition, serve important adaptive functions, and have their own rationality. A hot, affective cognition of the heart operates alongside a cooler, more analytical mode of cognition. The relationship between the affective cognition of the "heart" and the more analytical cognition of the "head" is a promising theme in the psychology of religion (Watts and Dumbreck, 2013).

Emotions seem to connect closely with both cognition and behavior and may play a role in integrating them. In terms of the old distinction between passions and affections, affections play a more integrative role than passions do. It seems likely that religion is closely intertwined with emotional regulation (Watts, 2007b), and that many of the benefits of religion are mediated through its emotional correlates. Certain emotions, such as gratitude, awe, reverence, and hope, play a particularly important role in religion, and which Emmons has called "sacred emotions" (Emmons, 2006). The emotions that are important in religion form relatively stable dispositions and, in that, are similar to moods.

A close analogy, psychologically, between emotions and religion suggests that psychology of religion can learn useful theoretical and methodological concepts from the psychology of emotion. Emotions are complex and multi-faceted, and in that are similar to religion. For example, Klaus Scherer has distinguished five components of emotion, serving different functions (Scherer et al., 2001): (i) cognitive stimulus processing that subserves evaluation of the environment, (ii) neuropsychological processes that subserve system regulation, (iii) motivation and behavior tendencies that subserve preparation for action, (iv) motor expression that subserves communication of intention, and (v) subjective feeling states that allow reflection and monitoring. Most of those have parallels in religion, which also has components of cognition, feeling, and behavior.

Emotions are somewhat heterogeneous, and many theorists have distinguished between simple and complex emotions. That distinction can be made in different ways (Oatley et al., 2006), but the one that I favor is to see simple emotions as arising with an immediacy that is almost reflex-like (disgust seems to be one of the most immediate emotions in that sense), and secondary emotions as involving a much greater degree of cognitive elaboration, and connecting in a rich way with people's self-concept. Religion is, for the most part, a deeply reflective activity that arises from people's self-concept and in turn refines and elaborates it. Understood in that way, secondary emotions will be especially important in religion (Watts, 2016).

It seems that many religious practices contribute to emotional regulation (Watts, 2007b). That is true of reflective practices such as prayer and highly focused practices such as meditation. Other more active religious practices such as glossolalia may well serve to bring about an uplift in mood. Indeed, it is perhaps not too much to see religion as something that, in various ways, delivers powerful emotional regulation. It has been argued that many of the benefits of religion on health may be mediated by its effect on emotions (Park and Slattery, 2012).

An interesting recent line of research has focused on affect valuation theory (Tsai et al., 2013), which makes the potentially important distinction between ideal affect and actual affect. The general point that emerges from this line of research is that culture affects ideal affect more than actual affect. Culture here includes religion, which affects what emotions people would wish to have more than what emotions they actually experience.

In some ways, that is not surprising, though two caveats are needed. One is that there are considerable differences between religions in what pattern of emotion they lead people to aspire to. Also, in any one tradition contains differences from one historical person to another. Religious traditions are not static in this regard (Corrigan, 2004). The other point is that, though religions may have their most immediate effect on what emotions people aspire to, they would also hope eventually to influence what emotions people actually experience. However, that would probably only be found in people who had a long-standing and serious religious commitment, including a transformative pattern of religious practice.

The effects of religion and culture on emotion are best illustrated in relation to specific emotions. Anger provides a good example (see Watts, 2007b). How to handle anger for the best is a long-standing cultural issue and an oscillation can be discerned between periods that have required strict control and other periods that have seen anger as allowable, provided it is appropriately channeled. Implicit codes can be found that allow anger to some people but not others, or in service of some objectives but not others.

Religions differ on this. For example, Islam is theologically more supportive of at least some expressions of anger than is Buddhism (Stratton, 1923). One issue that needs to be faced by religious traditions that favor strict control of anger is whether the strategies used are actually effective, or whether they might be counterproductive and have harmful consequences. An important distinction needs to be made between approaches that affect the extent to which people even feel anger and those that focus instead just on whether people express the anger that they are experiencing.

Another emotion of religious interest is shame (Watts, 2001b). It has often been recognized that there is an oscillation between guilt and shame cultures, and it is generally thought that we are currently living in a shame-orientated culture. There is no clear agreement about how to draw the distinction between shame and guilt, but guilt has generally been seen as a response to observable behavior, whereas shame is a response to a more pervasive sense of being an unworthy person. Another strand in the distinction is that being shamed arises from failings that are publicly exposed, whereas guilt can be a more private self-evaluation. In general, religion has tended to focus more on guilt, through the practice of confession and forgiveness, than on shame. It is perhaps a challenge to religions in contemporary culture to find ways of addressing issues of shame more directly.

Though most emotion theorists make a distinction between positive and negative emotions, they may not be mirror images. In terms of the distinction made in older religious discourse between passions and affections, there are clearly negative passions such as rage, but it is less clear that there are passions with a positive emotional tone. Positive emotions normally seem to be milder and to be affections. The range of negative emotions seems to be wider than that of positive emotions. Indeed, some theorists think that the only basic positive emotion is joy, which can be elaborated in different ways in different contexts.

The distinction between positive and negative emotions seems to be based on whether they are associated with pleasure or distress. From a religious point of view, that is not the most important issue. More important is whether or not particular emotions have a constructive moral and religious impact. Looking at emotions in terms of that criterion leads to a different classification. Indeed, emotions such as anger, guilt, and shame are usually negative experiences but, from a religious point of view, may have a constructive impact.

Plurality, Integration, and Narrative

Psychological interest in the plurality of the sense of self has recently increased. We have already noted that there is a great deal of situational specificity in how people behave; it is simply not the case that people manifest the same personality traits in all situations. It is widely recognized, as society gets more complicated and people have a wider range of social interactions, that the tendency for people to behave differently in different situations gets more acute and can lead to a loss of a core sense of self-identity that can be a source of distress.

It is interesting that psychology and religion seem to have different approaches to this issue (Turner, 2008; van Huyssteen and Wiebe, 2011), and that psychology is more comfortable than religion (or at least Christianity) with a plural self. Christian assumptions about the unity of personality probably arise from the concept of the soul, which can be seen as the core of personality. A widespread, though by no means universal, idea is that the soul is God-given. That naturally leads to the view that it is healthy for a person's life to be based around the soul that is at the core of his or her being, and that any fragmentation of self represents a departure from the unity that should properly exist around the God-given soul.

Psychology tends to start, more pragmatically, from the reality that people experience a degree of fragmentation. It generally sees no need to adopt a theoretical view, whether in terms of soul or anything else, that overlays that experiential reality. Starting from there, whatever sense of the unity of self is experienced seems a hard-won achievement, resulting from overcoming the natural fragmentation that arises from living in a wide range of different contexts. It seems to be a human instinct to work at constructing a sense of self that, if not singular, can integrate disparate elements.

Some psychologists have rejected a unitary sense of self as illusion, a view that is probably influenced by the very different religious approach to these matters taken by many within the Buddhist tradition (Varela et al., 1991). I suggest that extremes here are unconvincing and are best avoided. To insist on a unitary self as a given reality sits uneasily with the human experience of diversity and fragmentation. On the other hand, to reject any notion of a coherent self sits too uneasily with the effort that most people invest in working toward a degree of integration, even if that work remains incomplete. The middle way here seems to be to operate, not with a unitary sense of self, but with an integrative view of self that acknowledges diversity but also envisages some degree of integration. Though much of the Christian tradition has adopted a view of the self as unitary and given, other views can be found. Existentialist theologians such as Kierkegaard have a stronger sense of the self as something that is "becoming," rather than something unitary and given (see Morea, 1997).

Léon Turner (2008) makes the helpful suggestion that the process of constructing an integrative sense of self is one that makes use of narrative processes. It seems to be part of the ordinary stuff of life to develop some kind of self-narrative, though people vary in how explicitly they do that. Psychotherapy provides an opportunity for doing it in a highly structured way. It has long been an important part of religious life and is often conceptualized in terms of vocation and the purpose that God is thought to have in mind for the individual. Religious people often reflect on how their self-development has been shaped by God, in ways they may not have been aware of at the time. It was a religious purpose that led Augustine to write his *Confessions*, one of the first autobiographies of any kind. A growing psychology of narrative processes can now be applied to the psychology of religion (e.g., Nelson, 2009, pp. 294–301), and there has also been much recent interest in narrative theology.

Homo Religiosus?

It has often been suggested that humans are a uniquely religious species, that we are "homo religiosus." Another version, in the title of a book, is that we are "the believing primate" (Schloss and Murray, 2009). There is something in this, but I suggest that neither of these phrases gets it quite in focus. Numerous things are more characteristic of humans than any other species. Religiosity may be one of them, but it needs a stronger argument before you can claim that it is *the* defining feature of humans.

Religion is certainly ubiquitous among humanity, though not universal. It is estimated that 85 percent of contemporary humanity is religious. However, clear evidence shows cultural variability in religion. In Europe, the percentage of people who are religious is much lower than in the rest of the world. Europe may well be the exception (Davie, 2002) but the fact that there is such an exception at all significantly weakens the statistical case for assuming humanity to be naturally religious. Also, as we have seen, some genetic predispositions and neuropsychological capacities are *relevant* to religion, but in neither case is "religion" quite the right term for what they influence. There are genes relevant to aspects of religion, but probably no gene for religion itself. Equally, there are brain mechanisms relevant to religion, but no God spot, or spot for religion in the brain.

A stronger case can probably be made for saying that humans are "spiritual" creatures than for saying they are "religious" creatures. That can sound vague unless we put some flesh on it, but the psychology of religion may help do that. One of the most promising of such theories is the work of Robert Emmons on the "sacred strivings" that religion encourages in humans (Emmons, 1999). He proposes that humans have a tendency to strive for goals that they regard as sacred, goals that exemplify moral values such as compassion. Religion shapes and transmits those sacred goals, and it gives them transcendent authority. Such goals then play a coordinating role in people's system of values. It is probably the most promising theory of what is involved in humans being spiritual.

However, this theory has problems, though perhaps not insuperable ones. For one thing, not all religions, Buddhism for example, encourage sacred strivings. Of the Four Noble Truths, the third is the truth of the goal, which is non-striving. Buddhism encourages people to renounce all striving, seeing it as based on illusion. It seems that Buddhism can only be made to fit a theory of the role of religion in encouraging striving if you embrace the paradox that Buddhism makes non-striving the goal for which people are encouraged to strive. Alternatively, if strivings are broadened to include goals for what kind of person to *be*, as well as what goals can be achieved by *doing*, then Buddhism can be seen as placing all its emphasis on the former, whereas other religions such as Christianity can be seen as encouraging people to work for goals such as peace and justice.

Lee Kirkpatrick (2013) has questioned, from an evolutionary point of view, theories that see religion and spirituality in terms of a limited number of superordinate spiritual goals. He suggests that an evolutionary perspective would lead you to expect a wide range of more specific human goals, not a small number of superordinate goals. However, theories of the key function of spirituality do not need to claim that they provide an exhaustive account of human motivation, just that they are identifying elements in motivation that are distinctively human.

Just as some humans are not religious, some do not seem to be spiritual in the sense of having spiritual strivings. The Generation Y clubbers studied by Sara Savage are one example (Savage et al., 2006). They seemed to be focused entirely on the goal of personal happiness, and to lack any moral or transcendent goals. So, if we are to propose that humans are a spiritual species in the sense of having sacred strivings, it will once again have to be cast in the form of saying that humans have a capacity or propensity to have spiritual strivings, not that all humans do actually have them. However, there is no problem, from either a religious or psychological point of view, in framing the idea of humans as a spiritual species in those terms.

Yet another issue here is just how different humans are from other higher primates. That is a question that gets intertwined with religious belief, with religious people often wanting to maximize the distinctiveness of humans and nonreligious people wanting to minimize them. I suggest that neither extreme is really defensible. On the one hand, it is hard to find any distinctive feature of humans for which antecedents cannot be found in other species. On the other hand, many features of humans are much more developed in us than in any other species. Language, for example, is not unique to humans, but it is distinctively human.

On balance, it does seem reasonable to claim that spirituality, in the sense of meaning making, self-transcendence, and so on, is a distinctive feature of humans. Scientifically, it may not be the root cause of everything that is distinctive about humans. However, from a theological point of view, it is a feature of human distinctiveness that is of central significance.

Summary

- Psychology is both a biological and a social science and aspires to integrate those perspectives. It is suggested that a theology of human nature needs to do the same. Science often makes physicalist assumptions. The religious perspective, in contrast, wants to avoid reductionism, though it is less dualistic than is often supposed. Various philosophical approaches have been suggested to reconcile the two, but recent scientific work on embodied cognition promises to provide the most effective reconciliation.

- Emotions play a central regulative role in human life and are also of religious interest. Religion can contribute to emotional regulation and would often want to distinguish between different forms of emotions such as anger and guilt.

- Psychology has increasingly recognized that people present themselves in different ways in different circumstances, though they can work toward personal integration. Christianity has generally taken a stronger view than psychology of the essential unity of personality, though recognizing that it can fragment.

- It is doubtful whether humans can be said to be a religious animal, though they may be a spiritual one in the sense of being drawn to overarching meanings and transcendent values.

15

Summing-Up

In this final brief chapter, I will draw together three themes that have recurred through the book.

The Complexity of Religion

The first is about the complexity and multidimensionality of religion. In some ways, this is already widely recognized. Almost every leading researcher in the field would endorse the value of using multidimensional measures. What I think is largely lacking and currently needed is a theoretical perspective that leads to differential predictions about various facets of religion. We need a theoretical basis for predicting when dissociations between facets of religion are going to occur and what the consequences of those dissociations will be.

There are currently rather mixed feelings in the field about the categories of intrinsic, extrinsic, and quest religious motivations. However, despite the conceptual and methodological complexities that work on those categories has run into, it has at least provided a coherent approach to research on different types of religiousness. We badly need other comparable research programs.

I suggest that the distinction between internal and external religion may provide that. External religion is mere religious affiliation and activity. Internal religion is concerned with private experience and heart-felt inner commitment and is close to spirituality. External religion can exist on its own or in conjunction with internal religion. To put forward some specific hypotheses, I suggest that (i) internal religion has a stronger biological basis, whereas external religion is largely a cultural phenomenon; (ii) internal religion makes more of a contribution to personal change and adjustment than external religion; and (iii) internal religion will be less affected than external religion by any future trends toward secularization.

I also suggest that the psychology of religion should pay more careful and critical attention than it has so far to the phenomenon of conservatism, and how that relates to religion. Conservatism seems to have a relationship to religion that is in some ways parallel to that between spirituality and religion. Another important reason for attending to the impact of conservatism in religion arises from its current dominance. Unless researchers adopt a deliberate strategy of distinguishing conservative from more liberal forms of religion, they may find that they are actually just studying conservative religion when they believe they are studying religion more generally. It seems that liberal religion is currently going underinvestigated because it is swamped by conservative religion.

Conservatism is a broad sociopolitical-religious phenomenon that extends beyond the confines of religion itself, but it impacts religion and sometimes almost seems to take it over. It is puzzling that psychologists of religion have shown so little interest in the parallel body of research on political conservatism, whereas cognitive neuroscience is making advances in understanding how the conservative mind/brain works. Both spirituality and conservatism extend beyond the confines of religion but have a significant impact on it. I suggest that both spirituality and conservatism have a stronger biological basis than many other aspects of religion.

Two-Factor/Two-System Theories

I have also emphasized at several points the importance of two-factor theories. Several related points can be made here. One is the value of distinguishing different aspects of religion – those that depend heavily on a religious interpretative framework and those that are relatively independent of it. I suggest that some such distinction is important in understanding different aspects of religious experience. I do not imagine that it can be applied in an absolute way, as I do not imagine that any experience stands entirely outside any interpretative framework. However, I do believe that humans are capable of applying their interpretative frameworks relatively lightly, and that some religious practices help them do that.

There is a related distinction between different cognitive systems, such as the one made in Interacting Cognitive Subsystems between the more intuitive "implicational" system and the more articulate "propositional" system (though similar distinctions can be made within other theoretical frameworks). That distinction is important for understanding religion in several ways.

From an evolutionary point of view, I suggest that humans are unique in having two such cognitive systems, which enables them to develop a range of capacities, including the capacity for religion. The two cognitive systems have different degrees of prominence in various forms of religion. For example, the propositional system has less role in the religion of children who have not yet fully developed their capacity for abstract thought. Also various forms of meditational practice seem designed to minimize the role of the propositional system. Protestant Christianity has been much more word based. However, even where words play a crucial role in religion, they are often used in an evocative, poetic way rather than in a more straightforward referential way.

It seems likely that the brain is used in somewhat different ways in religion than in many other human activities, though art and music may be parallel in some ways. This is not a proposal that a God spot exists in the brain. What I am suggesting here is that the complex, mutually interacting systems that exist within the brain are deployed and configured in religion in ways that differ from how they are deployed in much everyday life. Indeed, it may be precisely that fact that gives religion much of its appeal. For example, the nondominant right brain may be more important in religion than in many other things. However, I have been careful not to suggest that the dominant left brain cannot do religion, just that it does it in different ways, some of which can distort the religious process toward fundamentalism.

Religion as Both Phenomenon and Perspective

In this book, I have also wanted to keep religion in play in two ways. Religion is, of course, in part a phenomenon to be studied by psychology. Following the practice of empirical science, psychology generally conducts that study in as objective and disinterested a way as it can. Much can be said for that objective approach. However, there are other useful methodologies. Some psychological research on religion is close to anthropology in the methods it uses, and it relies on deep immersion in a religious community or tradition to understand what is going on. Such methods can be valuable too, and there is value in bringing what comes out of different methods into dialogue with one another.

Religious traditions have their own perspective on religious experience, practice, and belief, and I have tried to bring that into play too. My general position is that psychological research does not (and cannot) rule the religious perspective in or out in a definitive way. However, it may nuance it and suggest how it could be reframed more convincingly, and I think there can be a useful dialogue between the perspectives of religious participants and psychologists.

I have also tried to broaden the aspects of religion to which psychology can contribute a useful perspective. That includes aspects of pastoral ministry. Psychology can help understand the processes at work there, just as therapeutic psychology does for more secular forms of therapy. Psychology is in both cases playing a double role. It is both guiding the pastoral and therapeutic process but also standing back and studying what is going on.

I have also brought psychology to bear in interpreting the human significance of scripture and doctrine. Psychology, I have claimed, is a methodological hybrid, part natural science and part interpretive science, and both can play a role in a broadly conceived psychology of religion. When psychology plays the role of interpretative science, it needs, to some extent, to get inside the perspective of the religious person and to see things from his or her point of view. It is a methodology that cannot be pursued with the same kind of detachment as when it is studying religion with the methodology of a natural science.

Summary

- Three recurrent themes are emphasized: (i) the complexity of religion and the possibility of its different components becoming dissociated, (ii) the complementary roles of experience and interpretation, and (iii) the value of treating religion as a perspective as well as a phenomenon to be studied.

Further Reading

Suggestions for further reading on particular subjects are scattered through the text and it would be redundant to repeat them here. However, it will be helpful to give advice about general books on the psychology of religion.

For mid-level books, it is necessary to go to two older books, which are still worthwhile:

Beit-Hallahmi, B. and M. Argyle. (1997) *The Psychology of Religious Behavior, Belief and Experience*. London: Routledge.

There are also two larger texts published more recently:

Hood, R. W. Jr., P. C. Hill, and B. S. Spilka. (2007) *The Psychology of Religion: An Empirical Approach*, Fourth Edition. New York: Guilford Press.
Nelson, J. M. (2009) *Psychology, Religion and Spirituality*. New York: Springer.

The first of these focuses specifically on empirical research and covers that complex territory remarkably well. The second covers a broader territory, including more on psychological theory and from different faith traditions. Both are invaluable resources for those who want to go into detail.

There has recently been a plethora of handbooks and edited books on the psychology of religion. That inevitably means a less unified approach, but with chapters written by experts on particular topics:

Miller, L. (2012) *Oxford Handbook of the Psychology of Religion and Spirituality*. New York: Oxford University Press.
Paloutzian, R. F. (1996) *Invitation to the Psychology of Religion*. Second Edition. Boston: Pearson.
Paloutzian, R. F. and C. L. Park. (2013) *Handbook of Psychology of Religion and Spirituality*. Second Edition. New York: Guilford Press.
Pargament, K. I. (2013) *APA Handbook of Psychology, Religion and Spirituality*. *Volume 1: Context, Theory, and Research. Volume 2: An Applied Psychology of Religion and Spirituality*. Washington DC: American Psychological Association.

Saroglou, V. (2014) *Religion, Personality and Social Behavior*. New York: Oxford University Press.

Miller has the strongest emphasis on spirituality rather than religion. Paloutzian and Park present an excellent one-volume summary of the field. Pargament's two-volume handbook is the most thorough and extensive. Saroglou has a particular focus on how the study of religion contributes to personality and social psychology, which gives his book a particular coherence.

References

Abramovitz, J. S., B. J. Deacon, C. M. Woods, and D. F. Tolin. (2004) "Association between protestant religiosity and obsessive–compulsive symptoms and cognitions." *Depression and Anxiety* 20 (2), 70–76.

Allport, G. W. and J. M. Ross. (1967) "Personal religious orientation and prejudice." *Journal of Personality and Social Psychology* 5 (4), 432–43.

Asch, S. E. (1958) "The metaphor: A psychological enquiry." In *Person Perception and Interpersonal Behavior*. R. Tagiuri and L. Petrullo (eds.), 86–94. Stanford: Stanford University Press.

Ayer, A. J. (1988) "What I saw when I was dead." *The Sunday Telegraph*. 28 August 1988.

Bakan, D. (1958) *Sigmund Freud and the Jewish Mystical Tradition*. Princeton, NJ: D van Nostrand.

Barbour, I. G. (1974) *Myths, Models, and Paradigms: A Comparative Study in Science and Religion*. New York: HarperCollins.

Barfield, O. (1972) *What Coleridge Thought*. London: Oxford University Press.

Barfield, O. (1973 [1928]) *Poetic Diction: A Study in Meaning*. Third Edition. Middletown, CT: Wesleyan University Press.

Barnard, P. J., D. J. Duke, R. W. Byrne, and I. Davidson. (2007) "Differentiation in cognitive and emotional meanings: An evolutionary analysis." *Cognition and Emotion* 21 (6), 115–83.

Barrett, J. L. (2004) *Why Would Anyone Believe in God?* Lanham, MD: Altamira Press.

Barrett, J. L. (2012) *Born Believers: The Science of Children's Religious Belief*. New York: Free Press.

Barrett, J. L. (2013) "The cognitive science of religion." In *Handbook of the Psychology of Religion and Spirituality*. Second Edition. R. P. Paloutzian and C. L. Park (eds.), 234–55. New York: Guilford Press.

Batson, C. D., P. Schoenrade, and L. Ventis. (1993) *Religion and the Individual*. New York: Oxford University Press.

Baumeister, R. F. (1991) *Meanings of Life*. New York: Guilford Press.

Baumeister, R. F. (1997) *Evil: Inside Human Cruelty and Violence*. San Francisco: W. H. Freeman & Co.

Beauregard, L. (2012) "Neuro-imaging and spiritual practice." In *The Oxford Handbook of the Psychology of Religion and Spirituality*. L. J. Miller (ed.), 500–13. New York: Oxford University Press.

Beier, M. (2004) *A Violent God-Image: An Introduction to the Work of Eugen Drewermann*. New York, London: Continuum.

Beit-Hallahmi, B. and M. Argyle. (1997) *The Psychology of Religious Behavior, Belief and Experience*. London: Routledge.

Bellar, R. N. (2011) *Religion in Human Evolution: From the Paleolithic to the Axial Age*. Cambridge, MA: Harvard University Press.

Bem, S. L. (1981) "Gender schema theory: A cognitive account of sex typing." *Psychological Review* 88 (4), 354–64.

Boivin, M. J. and B. Webb. (2011) "Modeling the biomedical role of spirituality through breast cancer research." In *Spiritual Healing: Scientific and Religious Perspectives*. F. Watts (ed.), 128–39. Cambridge: Cambridge University Press.

Bourne, D. and F. Watts. (2011) "Conceptualizations of spiritual healing: Christian and secular." In *Spiritual Healing: Scientific and Religious Perspectives*. F. Watts (ed.), 77–89. Cambridge: Cambridge University Press.

Boyer, P. (1994) *The Naturalness of Religious Ideas*. Berkeley: University of California Press.

Boyer, P. (2001) *Religion Explained: The Human Instincts That Fashion Gods, Spirits and Ancestors*. London: Vintage Books.

Bradshaw, M. and C. G. Ellison. (2008) "Do genetic factors influence religious life? Findings from a behavior genetic analysis of twin siblings." *Journal for the Scientific Study of Religion* 47 (4), 529–44.

Brown, G. W. and T. O. Harris. (1978) *Social Origins of Depression: A Study of Psychiatric Disorder in Women*. London: Tavistock.

Browning, D. S. and T. D. Cooper. (2004) *Religious Thought and the Modern Psychologies*. Minneapolis: Fortress Press.

Brueggemann, W. (1995) "The costly loss of lament." In *The Psalms: The Life of Faith*. P. D. Miller (ed.), 98–11. Minneapolis: Fortress Press.

Bucci, W. (1997) *Psychoanalysis and Cognitive Science: A Multiple Code Theory*. New York: Guilford Press.

Bulbulia, J., R. Sosis, E. Harris, R. Genet, and K. Wyman. (2008) *The Evolution of Religion: Studies, Theories and Critiques*. Santa Margarita: Collins Foundation Press.

Burrell, D. B. (1974) *Exercises in Religious Understanding*. South Bend: University of Notre Dame.

Christiano, K. J., W. H. Swatos Jr. and P. Kivisto. (2015) *Sociology of Religion: Contemporary Developments*. Third Edition. Lanham: Rowman and Littlefield.

Clarke, I. (2010) *Psychosis and Spirituality: Consolidating the New Paradigm*. Second Edition. New York: Wiley.

Clarke, J. J. (1992) *In Search of Jung: Historical and Philosophical Enquiries*. London: Routledge.

Coakley, S. and K. K. Shelmay. (2007) *Pain and Its Transformations*. Cambridge, MA: Harvard University Press.

Coe, G. A. (1916) *The Psychology of Religion*. Chicago: University of Chicago Press.

Coles, A. (2008) God, theologian and the humble neurologist. Brain 131 (7), 131–37.

Cooper, T. D. (2001) *Paul Tillich and Psychology: Historic and Contemporary Explorations in Theology, Psychotherapy and Ethics*. Macon, GA: Mercer University Press.

Corrigan, J. (2004) *Religion and Emotion: Approaches and Interpretations*. New York: Oxford University Press.

Crick, F. (1994) *The Astonishing Hypothesis: The Scientific Search for the Soul*. London: Simon & Schuster.

d'Aquili, E. G. and A. B. Newberg. (1999) *The Mystical Mind: The Biology of Religious Experience*. Minneapolis: Fortress Press.

Davie, G. (2002) *Europe: The Exceptional Case: Parameters of Faith in the Modern World*. London: Darton, Longman & Todd.

Davie, G. (2015) *Religion in Britain since 1945: A Persistent Paradox. Second revised edition*. Oxford: Wiley-Blackwell.

Dawkins, R. (1976) *The Selfish Gene*. New York: Oxford University Press.

Dawkins, R. (2006) *The God Delusion*. Boston: Houghton Mifflin.

Deikman, A. J. (1990) "De-automatization and the mystic experience." In *Altered States of Consciousness*. Third Edition. C. Tart (ed.), 34–57. San Francisco: HarperSanFrancisco.

De Sousa, R. (1987) *The Rationality of Emotion*. Cambridge, MA: MIT Press.

Dixon, T. (2006) *From Passions to Emotions: The Creation of a Secular Psychological Category*. Cambridge: Cambridge University Press.

Donald, M. (1991) *Origins of Mind: Three Stages in the Evolution of Culture and Cognition*. Cambridge MA: Harvard University Press.

D'Onofrio, B. M., J. E. Lindon, L. Murrelle, H. H. Maes, and B. Spilka. (1999) "Understanding biological and social influences on religious affiliation, attitudes and behaviors: A behavior genetic perspective." *Journal of Personality* 67 (6), 953–84.

Dunbar, R. (2014) *Human Evolution: A Pelican Introduction*. London: Penguin.

Eaves, L. J., P. K. Hatemi, E. C. Prom-Womley, and L. Murrelle. (2008) "Social and genetic influences on adolescent religious attitudes and practices." *Social Forces* 86 (4), 1621–46.

Edinger, E. (1972) *Ego and Archetype: Individuation and the Religious Function of the Psyche*. New York: Putnam.

Edwards, J. (1959) *A Treatise Concerning Religious Affections*. New Haven: Yale University Press.

Ellens, J. H. and W. G. Rollins. (2004) *Psychology and the Bible: A New Way to Read the Scriptures. Volumes 1–4*. Westport: Praeger Publishers.

Emmons, R. A. (1999) *The Psychology of Ultimate Concerns: Motivation and Spirituality in Personality*. New York: Guilford Press.

Emmons, R. A. (2006) "Sacred emotions." In *Soul, Psyche and Brain: New Directions in the Study of Religion and Brain-Mind Science*. K. Bulkeley (ed.), 93–112. New York: Palgrave Macmillan.

Emmons, R. A. and M. E. McCulloch. (2003) "Counting blessings versus burdens: An experimental investigation of gratitude and subjective well-being in daily life." *Journal of Personality and Social Psychology* 84 (2), 377–89.

Enright, R. D. and R. P. Fitzgibbons. (2000) *Helping Clients Forgive: An Empirical Guide for Resolving Anger and Restoring Hope.* Washington, DC: American Psychological Association.

Epstein, S. (1991) "Cognitive-experiential self theory: An integrative theory of personality." In *The Relational Self: Convergencies in Psychoanalysis and Social Psychology.* R. Curtis (ed.), 111–37. New York: Guilford Press.

Erdelyi, M. (1985) *Psychoanalysis: Freud's Cognitive Psychology.* New York: W. H. Freeman.

Erikson, E. H. (1977) *Toys and Reasons: Stages in the Ritualization of Experience.* New York: W. W. Norton.

Exline, J. J. and A. Martin. (2005) "Anger toward God: a new frontier in forgiveness research." In *Handbook of Forgiveness.* E. L. Worthington (ed.), 73–88. New York: Routledge.

Farias, M. (2013) "The psychology of atheism." In *The Oxford Handbook of Atheism.* S. Bullivant and M. Ruse (eds.), 468–82. New York: Oxford University Press.

Farias, M. and P. Granqvist. (2007) "The psychology of the New Age." In *Handbook of the New Age.* I. D. Kemp (ed.), 123–50. Leiden: Brill.

Feuerbach, L. (2008/1841) *The Essence of Christianity.* New York: Dover Publications.

Fingelkurts, A. A. (2009) "Is our brain hardwired to produce God, or is our brain hardwired to perceive God? A systematic review on the role of the brain in mediating religious experience." *Cognitive Processing* 10 (4), 293–326.

Finkel, D. and M. McGue. 1997. "Sex differences and nonadditivity in heritability of the multidimensional personality questionnaire scales." *Journal of Personality and Social Psychology* 72 (4), 929–38.

Flanagan, O. (2011) *Bodhisattva's Brain: Buddhism Naturalised.* Cambridge MA: MIT Press.

Flew, A. (1978) "Transitional objects and transitional phenomena: Comments and interpretations." In *Between Reality and Fantasy.* S. A. Grolnick, L. Barkin, and W. Muensterberger (eds.), 483–501. London: Jason Aronson.

Forman, R. K. C. (1990) *The Problem of Pure Consciousness: Mysticism and Philosophy.* New York: Oxford University Press.

Fowler, J. (1981) *Stages of Faith: The Psychology of Human Development and the Quest for Meaning.* San Francisco: Harper & Row.

Fox, K. C. R., S Nijeboer, M. L. Dixon, J. L. Floman, S. P. Rumak, P. Sedlemeier, and K. Christoff. (2014) "Is meditation associated with altered brain structure? A systematic review and meta-analysis of morphometric neuroimaging in meditation practitioners." *Neuroscience and Biobehavioral Reviews,* 43 (1) 48–73.

Francis, L. J. (2009) "Comparative empirical research in religion: Conceptual and operational challenges within empirical theology." In *Empirical Theology in Texts and Tables: Qualitative, Quantitative and Comparative Perspectives.* L. J. Francis, M. Robbins and J. Astley (eds.), 127–52. Leiden: Brill.

Francis, L. J. and G. Penny. (2014) "Gender differences in religion." In *Religion, Personality and Social Behavior*. V. Saroglou (ed.), 313–37. New York: Psychology Press.

Frazer, J. G. (1980 [1890]) *The Golden Bough: A Study in Magic and Religion*. Third Edition. London: Macmillan.

Freud, S. (1959 [1907]) *Obsessive Actions and Religious Practices*. Standard Edition, Volume 9. London: Hogarth.

Freud, S. (1961 [1927]) *The Future of an Illusion* (J. Strachey, trans.). New York: Norton.

Freud, S. (1965 [1910]) *Leonardo da Vinci: A Memoire of His Childhood*. New York: W. W. Norton.

Galanter, M. (1999 [1989]) *Cults: Faith, Healing and Coercion*. New York: Oxford University Press.

Gendlin, E. T. (1962) *Experiencing and the Creation of Meaning: A Philosophical and Psychological Approach to the Subjective*. New York: Free Press of Glencoe.

Gervais, W. M. and A. Norenzayan. (2012) "Analytic thinking promotes religious disbelief." *Science* 336 (6080), 493–96.

Gibson, J. J. (1979) *The Ecological Approach to Visual Perception*. Boston: Houghton Mifflin.

Gilbert, P. and H. Gilbert. (2011) "Spiritual healing in the context of the human need for safeness, connectedness and warmth: A biopsychosocial approach." In *Spiritual Healing: Scientific and Religious Perspectives*. F. Watts (ed.), 112–27. Cambridge: Cambridge University Press.

Glock, C. Y. and R. Stark. (1965) *Religion and Society in Tension*. Chicago: Rand McNally.

Glock, C. Y. and R. Stark. (1966) *Christian Beliefs and Anti-Semitism*. New York: Harper & Row.

Goldman, R. (1968) *Religious Thinking from Childhood to Adolescence*. London: Routledge & Kegan Paul.

Goodman, F. D. (1972) *Speaking in Tongues: A Cross-Cultural Study of Glossolalia*. Chicago: University of Chicago Press.

Gould, S. J. (2002). *Rocks of Ages: Science and Religion in the Fullness of Life*. New York: Ballantine Books.

Granqvist, P. (2010) "Religion as attachment: The Godin award lecture." *Archive for the Psychology of Religion* 32 (1), 5–24.

Granqvist. P. and L. A. Kirkpatrick. (2004) "Religious conversion and perceived childhood attachment: A meta-analysis." *The International Journal for the Psychology of Religion* 14 (4), 223–50.

Granqvist, P. and L. A. Kirkpatrick. (2008) "Attachment and religious representations and behavior." In *Handbook of Attachment: Theory, Research and Clinical Applications*. Second Edition. J. Cassidy and P. R. Shaver (eds.), 906–33. New York: Guilford Press

Greeley, A. M. (1974) *Ecstasy: A Way of Knowing*. Englewood Cliffs, NJ: Prentice Hall.

Griffith, E. E., T. English, and V. Mayfield (1980) "Possion, prayer and testimony." *Psychiatry*, 43 (2) 120–28.

Haidt, J. (2012) *The Righteous Mind: Why Good People Are Divided by Politics and Religion*. New York: Pantheon.

Hamer, D. (2004) *The God Gene: How Faith Is Hardwired into Our Genes*. New York: Doubleday.

Hanson. R. (2009) *Buddha's Brain: The Practical Neuroscience of Happiness, Love and Wisdom*. Oakland CA: New Harbinger Publication.

Harré, H. R. and P. F. Secord. (1972) *The Explanation of Social Behavior*. Oxford: Blackwell.

Harris, S., S. A. Sheth, and M. S. Cohen. (2008) "Functional neuro-imaging of belief, disbelief and uncertainty." *Annals of Neurology* 63 (2), 141–47.

Hay, D. (1982) *Exploring Inner Space: Scientists and Religious Experience*. Harmondsworth: Penguin.

Hay, D. and A. Morisey. (1978) "Reports of ecstatic, paranormal, or religious experience in Great Britain and the United States: A comparison of trends." *Journal for the Scientific Study of Religion* 17 (3), 255–68.

Hay, D. and R. Nye. (2006) *The Spirit of the Child*. Revised Edition. London: Jessica Kingsley Publishers.

Heelas, P. (2003) "An ageing new age?" In *Predicting Religion: Christian, Secular and Alternative Futures*. G. Davie, P. Heelas, and L. Woodhead (eds.), 229–47. Farnham: Ashgate Publishers.

Heisig, J. W. (1979) *Imago Dei: A Study of C. G. Jung's Psychology of Religion*. Lewisburg: Bucknell University Press.

Hibbing, J. R., K. B. Smith, and J. R. Alford. (2014) *Predisposed: Liberals, Conservatives, and the Biology of Political Differences*. New York: Routledge.

Hill, P. C. (2013) "Measurement assessment and issues in the psychology of religion." In *Handbook of the Psychology of Religion and Spirituality*. R. F. Paloutzian and C. L. Park (eds.), 48–74. New York: Guilford Press.

Hill, P. C. and B. J. Dik. (2012) *Psychology of Religion and Workplace Spirituality*. Charlotte, NC: Information Age Publishing.

Hillman, J. (1979) "Peaks and vales." In *Puer Papers*. J. Hillman (ed.), 54–74. Dallas: Spring Publications.

Homans, P. (1970) *Theology after Freud: An Interpretive Enquiry*. Indianapolis, IN: Bobbs-Merrill.

Hood, R. W. Jr., P. C. Hill, and B. Spilka. (2009) *The Psychology of Religion: An Empirical Approach*. Fourth Edition. New York: Guilford Press.

Hood, R. W. Jr. and W. P. Williamson. (2008) *Them That Believe: The Power and Meaning of the Christian Serpent-Handling Tradition*. Berkeley: University of California Press.

Huber, S. and O. W. Huber (2010) "Psychology of Religion." In *Studying Global Pentecostalism: Theories and Methods*. A. Anderson, M. Bergunder, A. Droogers and C. van der Laan (eds.), 133–55. Berkeley: University of California Press.

James, W. (2012 [1902]) *The Varieties of Religious Experience: A Study in Human Nature*. New York: Oxford University Press.

Jones, J. W. (2002) *Terror and Transformation*. London: Routledge.

Jones, J. W. (2008) *Religion and Psychology in Transition: Psychoanalysis, Feminism and Theology.* Cambridge MA: Harvard University Press.

Jones, L. G. (1995) *Embodying Forgiveness: A Theological Analysis.* Grand Rapids MI: William B. Eerdmans Publishing.

Jung, C. G. (1938) *Psychology and Religion.* New Haven: Yale University Press.

Jung, C. G. (1977 [1938]) *Psychology and Religion.* New Haven: Yale University Press.

Jung, C. G. (1992 [1953]) Collected Works of C. G. Jung, Vol. 12: Psychology and Alchemy. G. Adler and R. F. C Hull (eds.) Princeton: Princeton University Press.

Jung, C. G. (1984 [1952]) *Answer to Job: Researches into the Relation between Psychology and Religion.* New York: Psychology Press.

Kapogiannis, D., A. K. Barbey, M. Su, G. Zamboni, F. Krueger, and J. Grafman. (2009) "Cognitive and neural foundations of religious belief." *Proceedings of the National Academy of Sciences USA* 106 (12), 4876–81.

Katz, S. T. (1978) *Mysticism and Philosophical Analysis.* London: Sheldon Press.

Kinneman, D. (2011) *You Lost Me: Why Young Christians Are Leaving Church and Rethinking Faith.* Grand Rapids, MI: Baker.

Kinsey, B. (2011) "The psycho-dynamics of spiritual healing and the power of mother kissing it better." In *Spiritual Healing: Scientific and Religious Perspectives.* F. Watts (ed.), 90–111. Cambridge: Cambridge University Press.

Kirkpatrick, L. A. (2005) *Attachment, Evolution, and the Psychology of Religion.* New York: Guilford Press.

Kirkpatrick, L. A. (2013) "Evolutionary psychology as a foundation for the psychology of religion." In *Handbook of the Psychology of Religion and Spirualiaty.* Second Edition. R. F. Paloutzian and C. L. Park (eds.), 118–37. New York: Guilford Press.

Koenig, L. B. and T. J. Bouchard Jr. (2006) "Genetic and environmental influences on the traditional moral values triad – authoritarianism, conservatism and religiousness – as assessed by quantitative behavior genetic methods." In *Where God and Science Meet Volume I: How Brain and Evolutionary Studies Alter Our Understanding of Religion.* P. McNamara (ed.), 31–60. Westport, CT: Praeger.

Koenig, L. B., D. King, and V. B. Larson. (2012) *Handbook of Religion and Health.* Second Edition. New York: Oxford University Press.

Lammers, A. C. (1994) *In God's Shadow: The Collaboration of Victor White and C. G. Jung.* New York: Paulist Press.

Lash, N. (1988) *Easter in Ordinary: Reflections on Human Experience and the Knowledge of God.* London: SCM Press.

Lazarus, R. S. and S. Folkman (1984) *Stress, Appraisal and Coping.* New York: Springer Publishing.

Lee, R. S. (1948) *Freud and Christianity.* Harmondsworth: Penguin.

Loewenthal, K. M. (1995) *Mental Health and Religion.* London: Chapman & Hall.

Loewenthal, K. M. (2000) *The Psychology of Religion: A Short Introduction.* Oxford: Oneworld.

Luhrmann, T. (2012) *When Gods Talk Back: Understanding the American Evangelical Relationship with God*. New York: Vintage Books.

Lupfer, M. B. and E. Layman. (1996) "Invoking naturalistic and religious attributions: A case of applying the availability of heuristic? The representativeness heuristic?" *Social Cognition*, 14 (1), 55–76.

Lutz, A., H. A. Slagter, J. D. Dunne, and R. J. Davidson. (2008) "Attention regulation and monitoring in meditation." *Trends in Cognitive Sciences* 12 (4), 163–69.

Macmurray, J. (1961) *Persons in Relation*. London, Faber and Faber.

Maloney, H. N. and A. A. Lovekin. (1985) *Glossolalia: Behavioral Science Perspectives on Speaking in Tongues*. New York: Oxford University Press.

May, G. G. (2004) *The Dark Night of the Soul: A Psychiatrist Explores the Connection between Darkness and Spiritual Growth*. New York: Harper & Row.

Mayer, J. D., L. J. McCormick, and S. E. Strong (1995) "Mood-congruent memory and natural mood: New evidence." *Personality and Social Psychology Bulletin*, 21 (7) 736–46.

McClenon, J. (2006) "The ritual healing theory: Therapeutic suggestion and the origin of religion." In *Where God and Science Meet: How Brain and Evolutionary Studies Alter Our Understanding of Religion. Volume I: Evolution, Genes and the Religious Brain*. P. McNamara (ed.), 135–58. Westport, CT: Praeger.

McFadden, S. H. (2013) "Old persons, old age, aging and religion." In *Handbook of the Psychology of Religion and Spirituality*. R. F. Paloutzian and C. L. Park (eds.), 198–212. New York: Guilford Press.

McGilchrist, I. (2009) *The Master and His Emissary: The Divided Brain and the Makings of the Western World*. New Haven: Yale University Press.

McGrath, A. E. (2004) *The Twilight of Atheism: The Rise and Fall of Disbelief in the Modern World*. London: Rider.

McGrath, J. C. (2006) "Post-traumatic growth and the origins of early Christianity." *Mental Health, Religion and Culture* 9 (3), 291–306.

McIntosh, D. N., R. C. Silver, and C. B. Wortman. (1993) "Religion's role in adjustment to a negative life event: Coping with the loss of a child." *Journal of Personality and Social Psychology* 65 (4), 812–21.

McNamara, P. and P. M. Butler. (2013) "The neuropsychology of religious experience." In *Handbook of the Psychology of Religion and Spirituality*. Second Edition. R. P. Paloutzian and C. L. Park (eds.), 215–33. New York: Guilford Press.

Meissner, W. W. (1966) *Group Dynamics in the Religious Life*. Notre Dame, IN: University of Notre Dame Press.

Meissner, W. W. (1984) *Psychoanalysis and Religious Experience*. New Haven: Yale University Press.

Meissner, W. W. (1987) *Life and Faith: Psychology Perspectives on Religious Experiences*. Washington, DC: Georgetown University Press.

Meissner, W. W. (1995) *Thy Kingdom Come: Psychoanalytic Perspectives on the Messiah and the Millenium*. Kansas City: Sheed & Ward.

Meissner, W. W. (2000) *The Cultic Origins of Christianity: The Dynamics of Religious Development*. Collegeville, MN: Michael Glazier Inc.

Meng, H. and E. L. Freud. (1963) *Psychoanalysis and Faith: The Letters of Sigmund Freud and Oskar Pfister*. London: Hogarth Press.

Miller, A. S. and J. P. Hoffman. (1995) "Risk and religion: An explanation of gender differences in religiosity." *Journal for the Scientific Study of Religion* 34 (1), 63–75.

Miller, A. S. and R. Stark. (2002) "Gender and religiousness: Can socialization explanations be saved?" *American Journal of Sociology* 107 (6), 1399–423.

Mischel, W. (1968) *Personality and Assessment*. New York: Wiley.

Mithen, S. J. (1996) *The Prehistory of the Mind*. London: Thames & Hudson.

Moore, A. L. (1889) *Science and the Faith: Essays on Apologetic Subjects*. London: Kegan Paul, Trench, Trubner & Co.

Morea, P. C. (1997) *In Search of Personality: Christianity and Modern Psychology*. London: SCM Press.

Moriarty, G. L. (2013) "Head god and heart god: Pastoral work to help clients overcome harmful god images." In *Head and Heart: Perspectives from Religion and Psychology*. F. Watts and G. Dumbreck (eds.), 195–222. Philadelphia: Templeton Press.

Moriarty, G. and L. Hoffman. (2007) *God Image Handbook for Spiritual Counseling and Psychotherapy: Research, Theory and Practice*. Binghampton, NY: Routledge/Haworth.

Nelson, J. M. (2009) *Psychology, Religion and Spirituality*. New York: Springer.

Newberg, A. (2010) *Principles of Neurotheology*. Farnham: Ashgate.

Newberg, A., M. Pordehnad, A. Alavi, and E. G. d'Aquili. (2003) "Cerebral blood flow during meditative prayer: Preliminary findings and methodological issues." *Perceptual and Motor Skills* 97 (2), 625–30.

Noble, D. (2006) *The Music of Life: Biology beyond Genes*. Oxford: Oxford University Press.

Novak, M. A. and S. Coakley. (2013) *Evolution, Games and God: The Principle of Co-operation*. Cambridge, MA: Harvard University Press.

Oatley, K., K. Dacher, and J. M. Jenkins. (2006) *Understanding Emotions*. Second Edition. Malden: Blackwell Publishing.

Olds, L. E. (1992) *Metaphors of Inter-relatedness – Towards a Systems Theory of Psychology*. Albany: State University of New York Press.

Oman. D. (2013) "Defining religion and spirituality." In *Handbook of Psychology of Religion and Spirituality*. Second Edition. R. F. Palouzian and C. L. Park (eds.), 23–47. New York: Guilford Press.

Otto, R. (1950[1917]) *The Idea of the Holy*. Second edition. Oxford, Oxford University Press.

Ozorak, E. W. (1989) "Social and cognitive influences on the development of religious beliefs and commitment in adolescence." *Journal for the Scientific Study of Religion* 28 (4), 448–63.

Paloutzian, R. F. (1996) *Invitation to the Psychology of Religion*. Second Edition. Boston: Pearson.

Paloutzian, R. F., S. Murken, H. Streib, and S. Namini. (2013) "Conversion, deconversion and transformation: A multilevel interdisciplinary view."

In *Handbook of the Psychology of Religion and Spirituality*. Second Edition. R. F. Paloutzian and C. L. Park (eds.), 399–421. New York: Guilford Press.

Pargament, K. I. (1997) *The Psychology of Religion and Coping: Theory, Research, Practice*. New York: Guilford Press.

Pargament, K. I. (2007) *Spiritually Integrated Psychotherapy: Understanding and Addressing the Sacred*. New York: Guilford Press.

Park, C. L. (2010) "Making sense of the meaning literature: An integrative review of meaning making and its effects on adjustment to stressful life events." *Psychological Bulletin* 136 (2), 257–301.

Park, C. L. and J. R. Fenster. (2004) "Stress-related growth: Predictors of occurrence and correlates with psychological adjustment." *Journal of Social and Clinical Psychology* 23 (2), 195–215.

Park, C. L. and J. M. Slattery. (2012) "Spirituality, emotions and mental health." In *The Oxford University Press Handbook of Psychology and Spirituality*. L. Miller (ed.), 379–87. New York: Oxford University Press.

Pattison, E. M. (1968) "Behavioral science research on the nature of glossolalia." *Journal of the American Scientific Affiliation* 20 (3), 73–86.

Persinger, M. A. (1983) "Religious and mystical experiences as artifacts of temporal lobe function: A general hypothesis." *Perceptual and Motor Skills* 57 (3), 1255–62.

Peterson, C. and M. E. P. Seligman. (2004) *Character Strengths and Virtues: A Handbook and Classification*. Washington, DC: American Psychological Association.

Pew Religious Landscape Survey. (2008) Retrieved from http://religions .pewforum.org/pdf/report-religious-landscape-study-full.pdf

Pfister, O. (1993) "The illusion of a future: A friendly disagreement with Prof. Sigmund Freud." *International Journal of Psychoanalysis* 74 (3), 557–79.

Philipchalk, R. and D. Mueller. (2000) "Glossolalia and temperature change in the right and left cerebral hemispheres." *International Journal for the Psychology of Religion* 10 (3), 181–85.

Philp, H. L. (1958) *Jung and the Problem of Evil*. London: Rockliff.

Polanyi, M. (1958) *Personal Knowledge: Towards a Post-Critical Philosophy*. Chicago: University of Chicago Press.

Poloma, M. and G. Gallup. (1991) *Varieties of Prayer: A Survey Report*. Philadelphia: Trinity Press International.

Power, M. (2012) *Adieu to God: Why Psychology Leads to Atheism*. Chichester: John Wiley.

Preston, J. L., E. Salomon, and R. S. Ritter. (2014) "Religious prosociality: Personal, cognitive and social factors." In *Religion, Personality and Social Behavior*. V. Saroglou (ed.), 149–69. New York: Psychology Press.

Proudfoot, W. (1987) *Religious Experience*. Berkeley: University of California Press.

Proudfoot, W. and P. Shaver. (1975) "Attribution theory and the psychology of religion." *Journal for the Scientific Study of Religion* 14 (4), 317–30.

Pruyser, P. (1974) *Between Belief and Unbelief*. New York: Harper.

Pruyser, P. (1991) *Religion in Psychodynamic Perspective: The Contributions of Paul W. Pruyser*. H. N. Maloney and B. Spilka (eds.). New York: Oxford University Press.

Rambo, L. R. (1993) *Understanding Religious Conversion*. New Haven: Yale University Press.

Rappaport, R. A. (1999) *Ritual and Religion in the Making of Humanity*. Cambridge: Cambridge University Press.

Reed, B. D. (1978) *Dynamics of Religion: Process and Movement in Christian Churches*. London: Darton, Longman & Todd.

Rizzuto, A.-M. (1979) *The Birth of the Living God: A Psychoanalytic Study*. Chicago: University of Chicago Press.

Rizzuto, A.-M. (1998) *Why Did Freud Reject God? A Psychodynamic Interpretation*. New Haven: Yale University Press.

Roccas, S. and A. Elster. (2014) "Values and religiosity." In *Religion, Personality and Behavior*." V. Saroglou (ed.), 193–212. New York: Oxford University Press.

Rollins, W. G. (1999) *Soul and Psyche: The Bible in Psychological Perspective*. Minneapolis, MN: Fortress Press.

Rollins, W. G. and D. A. Kille. (2007) *Psychological Insight into the Bible: Texts and Readings*. Grand Rapids, MI: W. B. Eerdmans Publishing.

Rose, E. D. and J. J. Exline. (2012) "Personality, spirituality, and religion." In *Oxford Handbook of the Psychology of Religion and Spirituality*. L. Miller (ed.), 85–103. New York: Oxford University Press.

Rubenstein, R. L. (1972) *My Brother Paul*. New York: Harper & Row.

Samarin, W. J. (1972) *Tongues of Men and Angels*. New York: Macmillan.

Saroglou, V. (2002) "Religion and the five-factors of personality: A meta-analytic view." *Personality and Individual Differences* 32 (1), 15–25.

Saroglou, V. (2014) "Conclusion: Understanding Religion and Irreligion." In *Religion, Personality and Behavior*. V. Saroglou (ed.), 361–91. New York: Psychology Press.

Savage, S. B. (2011) *Joseph: Insights for the Spiritual Journey*. London: SPCK.

Savage, S. B. (2013) "Head and heart in preventing religious radicalization." In *Head and Heart: Perspectives from Religion and Psychology*. F. Watts and G. Dumbreck (eds.), 157–94. Philadelphia: Templeton Press.

Savage, S. B. and E. Boyd-MacMillan. (2007) *The Human Face of Church: A Social Psychology and Pastoral Theology Resource for Pioneer and Traditional Ministry*. London: SCM Press.

Savage, S. B., S. Collins-Mayo, B. Mayo, and G. Cray. (2006) *Making Sense of Generation Y*. London: Church House Publishing.

Savage, S. B. and J. Liht. (2009) "Radical religious speech: How to assemble the ingredients of a binary world view." In *Extreme Speech and Democracy*. J. Weinstein (ed.), 488–507. Oxford: Oxford University Press.

Scherer, K. R., A. Schorr and T. Johnstone. (2001) *Appraisal Processes in Emotion: Theory, Methods, Research*. New York: Oxford University Press.

Schleiermarcher, F. (1958 [1799]) *On Religion: Speeches to Its Cultured Despisers*. J. Oman (ed.) New York: Harper & Brothers.

Schlitz, M. (2011) "Spirituality and health: Assessing the evidence." In *Spiritual Healing: Scientific and Religious Perspectives*. F. Watts (ed.), 141–52. Cambridge: Cambridge University Press.

Schloss, J. and M. Murray. (2009) *The Believing Primate: Scientific, Philosophical, and Theological Reflections on the Origin of Religion*. New York: Oxford University Press.

Schwartz, S. H. and Huismans. (1995) "Value priorities and religiosity in four Western religions." *Social Psychology Quarterly*, 58 (2), 88–107.

Scobie, G. E. (1975) *Psychology of Religion*. London: Batsford.

Seeman, T. E., L. Fagan-Dubin, and M. Seeman. (2003) "Religiosity/spirituality and health: A critical review of the evidence for biological pathways." *American Psychologist* 58 (1), 53–63.

Seligman, M. E. P. (1999) "The president's address." *American Psychologist* 54 (8), 559–62.

Sheldrake, P. (2013) *Spirituality: A Brief History*. Second Edition. Chichester: Wiley-Blackwell.

Sosis, R. and E. R. Bressler. (2003) "Co-operation and commune longevity: A test of the costly signaling theory of religion." *Cross-Cultural Research* 37 (2), 211–39.

Spilka, B. and K. L. Ladd. (2012) *The Psychology of Prayer: A Scientific Approach*. New York: Guilford Press.

Stratton, G. M. (1923) *Anger: Its Moral and Religious Significance*. London: George Allen and Unwin.

Streib, H. (2001) "Faith development theory revisited: The religious styles perspective." *The International Journal for the Psychology of Religion* 11 (3), 143–58.

Suedfeld, P., K. Guttieri and P. E. Tetlock. (2003) "Assessing integrative complexity at a distance: Archival analyses of thinking and decision making". In *The Psychological Assessment of Political Leaders: With Profiles of Saddam Hussein and Bill Clinton*. J. M. Post (ed.), 246–272. Ann Arbor: University of Michigan Press.

Sullins, D. P. (2006) "Gender and religion: Deconstructing universality, constructing complexity." *American Journal of Sociology* 112 (3), 838–80.

Swinburne, R. (1970) *The Concept of a Miracle*. London: Macmillan & Co.

Tamminen, K. (1994) "Religious experiences in childhood and adolescence: A viewpoint of religious development between the ages of 7 and 20." *International Journal for the Psychology of Religion* 4 (2), 61–85.

Teasdale, J. D. and P. J. Barnard. (1993) *Affect, Cognition and Change*. Hove: Lawrence Erlbaum.

Teasdale, J. D., Z. V. Segal, and J. M. G. Williams. (1995) "How does cognitive therapy prevent depressive relapse and why should attentional control (mindfulness) training help?" *Behavior Research and Therapy* 33 (1), 25–39.

Thalbourne, M. A. (1998) "Belief in life after death and its relationship to transliminality-relevant variables." *European Journal of Parapsychology* 14 (1): 16–30.

Thalbourne, M. A. and P. S. Delin. (1999). Transliminality: Its relation to dream life, religiosity and mystical experience. *The International Journal for the Psychology of Religion*, 9 (1): 45–61.

Theissen, G. (1987) *Psychological Aspects of Pauline Theology*. Edinburgh: T. & T. Clark.

Thompson, E. H. Jr. (1991) "Beneath the status characteristic: Gender variations in religiousness." *Journal for the Scientific Study of Religion* 30 (4), 381–94.

Thorne. B. (2012) *Counselling and Spiritual Accompaniment: Bridging Faith and Person-centred Therapy*. Oxford: Wiley-Blackwell.

Tremlin, T. (2006) *Minds and Gods: The Cognitive Foundations of Religion*. New York: Oxford University Press.

Tsai, J. L., B. Koopmann-Holm, M. Miyazaki, and C. Ochs. (2013) "The religious shaping of feeling: Implications of affect valuation theory." In *Handbook of Religion and Spirituality*. Second Edition. R. F. Paloutzian and C. L. Park (eds.), 274–91. New York: Guilford Press.

Turner, L. (2008) *Theology, Psychology and the Plural Self*. Basingstoke: Ashgate.

Ulanov, A. B. and B. Ulanov. (1982) *Primary Speech: A Psychology of Prayer*. Atlanta: John Knox Press.

Van Huyssteen, J. W. and E. P. Wiebe. (2011) *In Search of Self: Interdisciplinary Perspectives on Personhood*. Grand Rapids, MI: Eerdmans.

Varela, F. J., E. Thompson, and E. Rosch. (1991) *The Embodied Mind: Cognitive Science and Human Experience*. Cambridge, MA: MIT Press.

Vergote, A. and A. Tamayo. (1981) *The Parental Figures and the Representation of God*. The Hague: Mouton.

Winnicott, D. W. (1971) *Playing and Reality*. London: Tavistock.

Walsh, R. and S. L. Shapiro. (2006) "The meeting of meditative disciplines and Western psychology: A mutually enriching dialogue." *American Psychologist* 61 (3), 237–39.

Ward, K. (1998) *Religion and Human Nature*. Oxford: Oxford University Press.

Watts, F. (2001a) "Prayer and psychology." In *Perspectives on Prayer*. F. Watts (ed.), 39–52. London: SPCK.

Watts, F. (2001b) "Shame, sin and guilt." In *Forgiveness and Truth*. A. McFadyen and M. Sarot (eds.), 53–69. Edinburgh: T. & T. Clark.

Watts, F. (2002) *Theology and Psychology*. Basingstoke: Ashgate.

Watts, F. (2007a) *Jesus and Psychology*. London: Darton, Longman & Todd.

Watts, F. (2007b) "Emotional regulation and religion." In *Handbook of Emotional Regulation*. J. J. Gross (ed.), 504–20. New York: Guilford Press.

Watts, F. (2011) *Spiritual Healing: Scientific and Religious Perspectives*. Cambridge: Cambridge University Press.

Watts, F. (2013a) "Dual system theories of religious cognition." In *Head and Heart: Perspectives from Religion and Psychology*. F. Watts and G. Dumbreck (eds.), 125–56. Philadelphia: Templeton Press.

Watts, F. (2013b) "Embodied cognition and religion." *Zygon* 48 (3), 745–58.

Watts, F. (2014) "Religion and the emergence of differentiated cognition." In *Evolution, Religion and Cognitive Science: Critical and Constructive Essays*. F. Watts and L. Turner (eds.), 109–31. Oxford: Oxford University Press.

Watts, F. (2016) "Self-conscious emotions, religion and theology". In *Issues in Science and Theology: Do Emotions Shape the World?* D. Evers, M. Fuller, A. Runehov and K. W. Saether (eds.) Cham: Springer International Publishing.

Watts, F. and G. Dumbreck. (2013) *Head and Heart: Perspectives from Religion and Psychology*. Philadelphia: Templeton Press.

Watts, F. and L. Gulliford. (2004) *Forgiveness in Context: Theology and Psychology in Creative Dialogue*. London: T. & T. Clark.

Watts, F., R. Nye, and S. B. Savage. (2002) *Psychology for Christian Ministry*. London: Routledge.

Watts, F. and L. Turner. (2014) *Evolution, Religion and Cognitive Science: Critical and Constructive Essays*. Oxford: Oxford University Press.

Watts, F. and M. Williams. (1988) *The Psychology of Religious Knowing*. Cambridge: Cambridge University Press.

Welker, M. (2014) *The Depth of the Human Person: A Multidisciplinary Approach*. Grand Rapids, MI: Eerdmans.

Whitehouse, H. (2000) *Arguments and Icons: Divergent Modes of Religiosity*. Oxford: Oxford University Press.

Wildman, W. J. and L. A. Brothers. (1999) "A neuro-psychological semiotic model of religious experiences." In *Neurosciences and the Person: Scientific Perspectives on Divine Action*. R. J. Russell, N. Murphy, T. C. Meyering, and M. A. Arbib (eds.), 348–416. Vatican City State: Vatican Observatory and Berkeley: Center for Theology and Natural Sciences.

Williams, J. M. G. and J. Kabat-Zinn. (2013) *Mindfulness: Diverse Perspectives on Its Meaning, Origins and Applications*. London: Routledge.

Williams, J. M. G., F. N. Watts, C. MacLeod, and A. Mathews. (1997 [1988]) *Psychology and Emotional Disorders*. Second Edition. New York: Wiley.

Williams, R. J. and F. Watts. (2014) "Attributions in a spiritual healing context: An archival analysis of a 1920s healing movement." *Journal for the Scientific Study of Religion*, 53(1): 90–108.

Wilson, D. S. (2002) *In Darwin's Cathedral: Evolution, Religion and the Nature of Society*. Chicago: University of Chicago Press.

Winnicott, D. W. (1971) *Playing and Reality*. London: Tavistock.

Worthington, E. L. (2006) *Forgiveness and Reconciliation*. New York: Routledge.

Zahl, B. P., C. A. Sharp, and N. J. Gibson. (2013) "Empirical measures of the religious heart." In *Head and Heart: Perspectives from Religion and Psychology*. F. Watts and G. Dumbreck (eds.), 97–124. Philadelphia: Templeton Press.

Index